Microsoft® Office 97

GLENCOE VISUAL SERIES

maranGraphics™

GLENCOE
McGraw-Hill

New York, New York   Columbus, Ohio   Woodland Hills, California   Peoria, Illinois

Microsoft® Office 97

Glencoe/McGraw-Hill

A Division of The **McGraw·Hill** *Companies*

Office 97 / maranGraphics. – Student ed.
            p. cm.– (Glencoe visual series)
        Includes index.
        ISBN 0-02-803963-7
1. Microsoft Office.   2. Business–Computer programs.
I. MaranGraphics Development Group.   II. Series.
HF5548.4.M525033   1998
005.369–dc21   97-7648
                                                           CIP

Printed in the United States of America.

Send all inquiries to:

Glencoe/McGraw-Hill
936 Eastwind Drive
Westerville, OH 43081
ISBN 0-02-803963-7

        6 7 8 9   003   02 01 00 99

The animated characters
are the copyright of
maranGraphics, Inc.

WORD

INTRODUCTION

4 EDIT A DOCUMENT

5 FORMAT TEXT

6 FORMAT PAGES

7 WORKING WITH TABLES

EXCEL

5 FORMAT A WORKSHEET

6 PRINT A WORKSHEET

7 USING MULTIPLE WORKSHEETS

8 WORKING WITH CHARTS

POWERPOINT

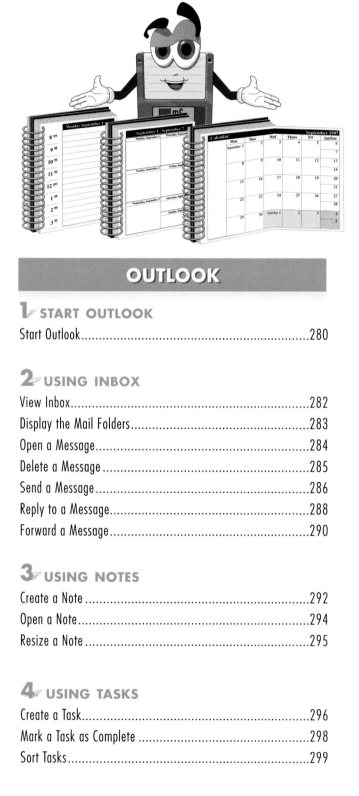

OUTLOOK

OFFICE AND THE INTERNET

PREFACE

GETTING TO KNOW THE GLENCOE VISUAL SERIES

Welcome! You are using the Glencoe Visual Series to embark on a hands-on tour of Office 97–one of the most popular software suites on the market. Whether you use Office for school, business, or personal use, and whether you're a newcomer to computers or an experienced "techie" who uses various applications with ease, the components of this program will teach you to use Office for your own purposes.

Do you want to produce spreadsheets in a snap? Would you like to access the Internet? Do you need to send the same report to a number of people, personalized by name? Would you like to create a presentation with colorful graphics and charts? Do you need to print out a daily schedule or monthly calendar? Office 97 is your answer. Follow the step-by-step instructions in the six textbook sections to see how each function is performed. Then, use the Applications Workbook and companion template files to practice each skill. In no time, you'll be off and computing, using Office to e-mail, to produce your own word-processing documents, spreadsheets, slide shows, and schedules–just like the pros do!

PROGRAM COMPONENTS

The various titles in the Glencoe Visual Series are packaged as three components: the Student Textbook, the Applications Workbook, and the template files. Some days your instructor may use just the textbook in class. More than likely, however, you'll use all three together. How do these three components work together to help you learn to use Office? Read on to find out.

STUDENT TEXTBOOK

The Student Textbook is the component you are currently reading. Flip through the pages briefly. Scan the contents. You might notice that there are six sections of material in your textbook–*Introduction, Word, Excel, PowerPoint, Outlook,* and *Office and the Internet.* Your instructor likely will start teaching with the *Introduction,* followed by the first chapter of *Word,* and guide your class through the table of contents in order, as there is a logical sequence to learning computer skills. However, don't hesitate to skip ahead if you need to apply a particular skill at any time. The easy-to-use format visually walks you through each step you'll need to perform key Office functions.

Note the graphics on each page. This feature alone makes Glencoe Visual Series easier to use than any other instructional approach. Clear, step-by-step instructions are presented mostly as two-page lessons. The computer skill, or function, is identified on each spread in red type in the top right corner. Locate one of the lesson skills now. Isn't it clear and easy to find? Feel confident! Learning Office 97 with the Glencoe Visual Series is really this easy.

Now, take a moment to look at the large graphics (known as "screen dumps," or "screen captures") that are the focal point of each spread. Advanced technology reproduces Office screens with such incredible sharpness that you'll find it a breeze to locate specific functions, icons, features, and menus on your own screen.

Next, look at the numbered steps and bulleted (•) tips printed in red on each page. They provide you with all the information you'll need to perform a specific Office function. By following these steps and tips from Chapter 1 to the end of each lesson, you'll see how another learner just like you used Office to perform a specific skill.

APPLICATIONS WORKBOOK AND TEMPLATE FILES

The Applications Workbook is a hands-on tool to help you use Office 97 to practice specific computer skills and to try your hand at editing and creating your own template, or practice, documents of your own. Think of these two components as the missing links–the important connections between reading about and seeing already-made documents and making your own. First, your instructor will teach class, using your Student Textbook in a variety of useful ways to present the skills you'll be learning. Next, you will be assigned template files on which to practice your newly acquired skills. After completing them, you'll be ready to use Office to produce your own work.

The template files, provided to your instructor on disk, correspond to the chapters of the Student Textbook. (Your template files likely have been pre-loaded on your computer by your instructor so you can access them quickly and easily.) Do you remember the computer skills that you located earlier as you scanned the pages of your textbook?

In most chapters, the first two template files cover about half of these skills. The third activity directs you to apply all the major skills taught in a particular chapter. And, in the fourth activity, you're on your own. You'll use the activity instructions, called *Working Guidelines*, to produce documents as directed, and show that you can independently perform crucial Office functions.

After you complete a specific lesson in your Student Textbook, your instructor will ask you to open the Applications Workbook to a corresponding lesson. There, you'll find an activity for you and step-by-step directions to edit or create your own work using the skills you just learned. In the template activities, you'll be asked to apply your own personal expertise; knowledge of Communications, Business and Social Sciences, Science and Technology, and Mathematics; and years of world experience to complete personally meaningful activities as you practice Office 97.

ON YOUR MARK, GET SET, GO!

Your instructor will monitor your progress with Office, ask thought-provoking questions, and supply you with tips and shortcuts as you work with the Applications Workbook and template files. Feel free to ask for help if you need a little support once in a while. Or, refer on your own to the Student Textbook. All the activities in the Student Textbook, Applications Workbook, and template files correspond to one another, so itís easy to use all three components simultaneously.

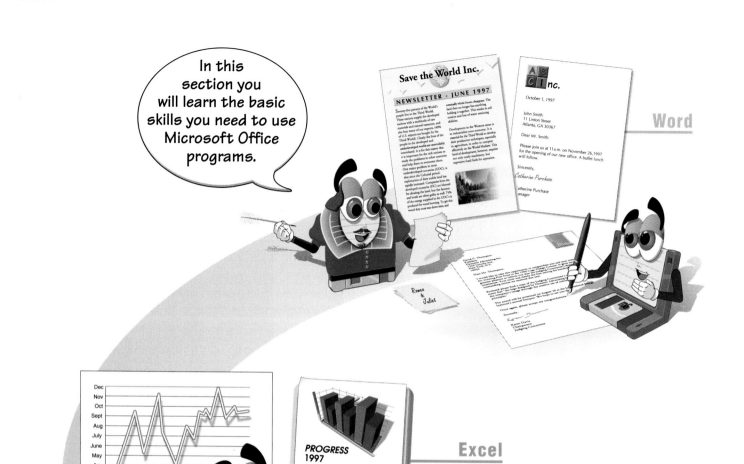

In this section you will learn the basic skills you need to use Microsoft Office programs.

Word

Excel

PowerPoint

2

INTRODUCTION

Outlook

3

Microsoft Office includes several programs to help you accomplish many tasks.

Each Office program has features that make it easy for you to take advantage of the World Wide Web.

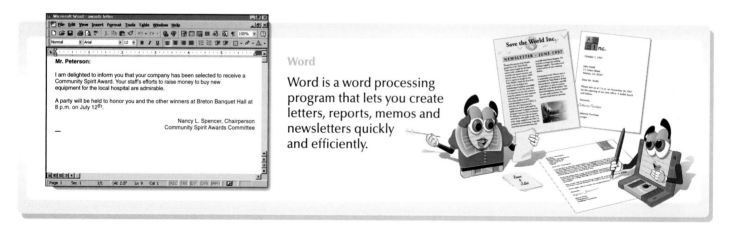

Word

Word is a word processing program that lets you create letters, reports, memos and newsletters quickly and efficiently.

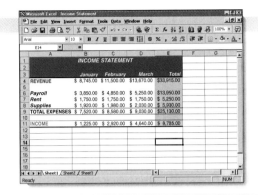

Excel

Excel is a spreadsheet program that helps you organize, analyze and present data.

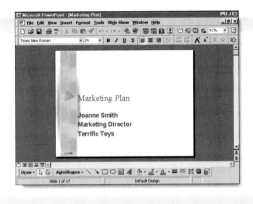

PowerPoint

PowerPoint is a program that helps you plan, organize and design professional presentations.

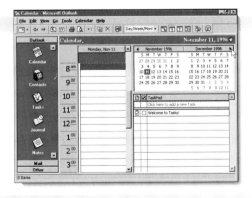

Outlook

Outlook is an information management program that helps you organize messages, appointments, contacts, tasks and activities.

USING THE MOUSE

A mouse is a hand-held device that lets you select and move items on the screen.

Holding the Mouse

Resting your hand on the mouse, use your thumb and two rightmost fingers to move the mouse on your desk. Use your two remaining fingers to press the mouse buttons.

Moving the Mouse

When you move the mouse on your desk, the mouse pointer on the screen moves in the same direction.

The mouse pointer assumes different shapes (examples: ↖, I or ✛), depending on its location on the screen and the task you are performing.

Cleaning the Mouse

A ball under the mouse senses movement. You should occasionally remove and clean this ball to ensure smooth motion of the mouse.

MOUSE ACTIONS

Click

Press and release the left mouse button.

Double-Click

Quickly press and release the left mouse button twice.

Drag and Drop

Move the mouse pointer ($\&$) over an object on your screen and then press and hold down the left mouse button. Still holding down the mouse button, move the mouse to where you want to place the object and then release the mouse button.

MICROSOFT INTELLIMOUSE

The new Microsoft IntelliMouse has a wheel between the left and right mouse buttons. Moving this wheel lets you quickly scroll through information on the screen.

You can also zoom in or out with the Microsoft IntelliMouse by holding down **Ctrl** on your keyboard as you move the wheel.

START A PROGRAM

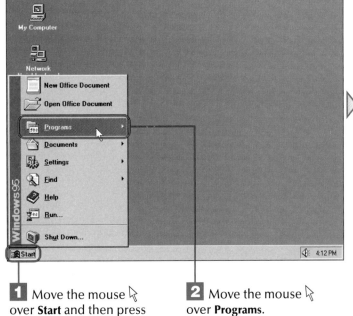

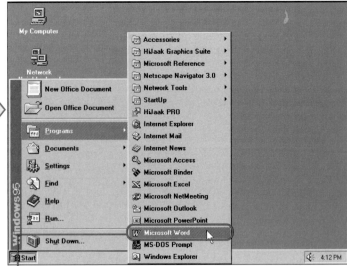

1 Move the mouse over **Start** and then press the left mouse button.

2 Move the mouse over **Programs**.

3 Move the mouse over the program you want to start and then press the left mouse button.

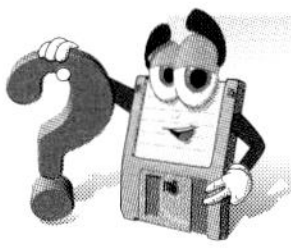

What is the difference between a toolbar and a menu bar?

Each button on a toolbar provides a fast method of selecting a command on a menu. For example, you can use the **Save** button to quickly select the **Save** command.

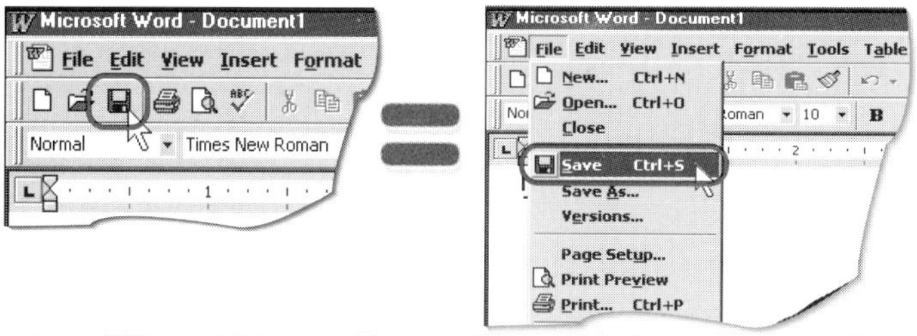

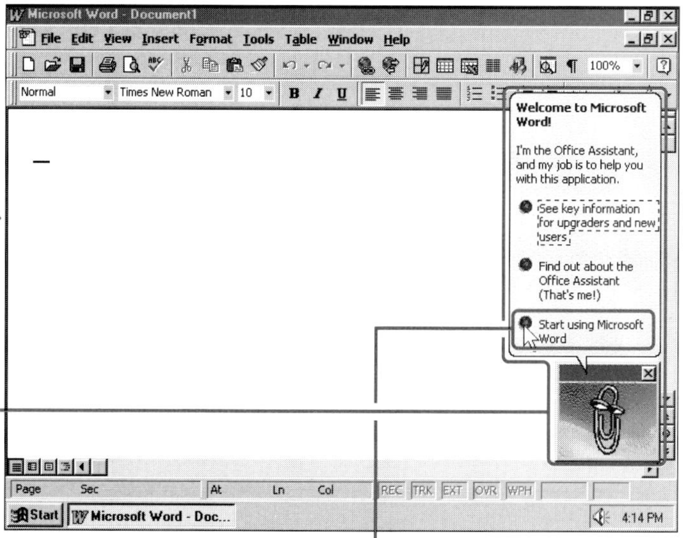

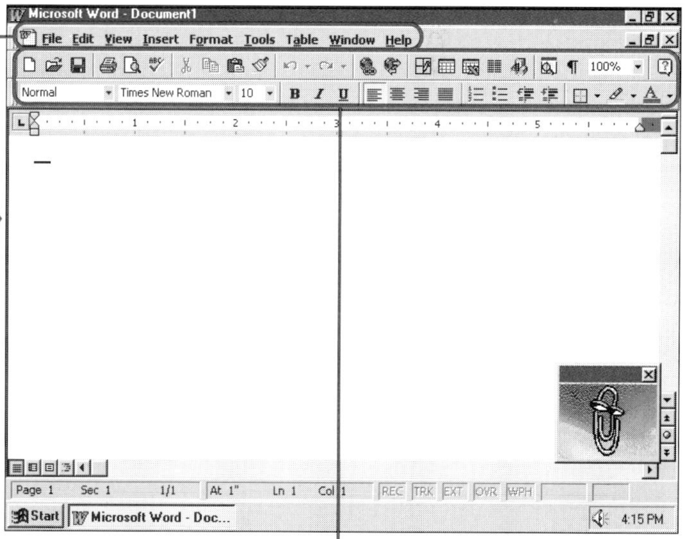

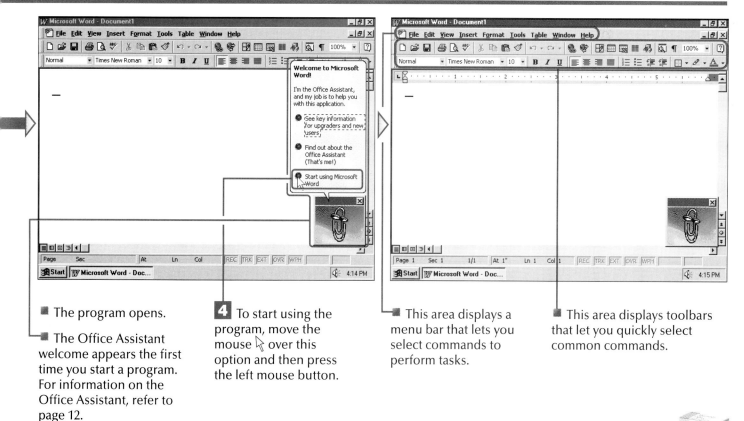

■ The program opens.

■ The Office Assistant welcome appears the first time you start a program. For information on the Office Assistant, refer to page 12.

4 To start using the program, move the mouse over this option and then press the left mouse button.

■ This area displays a menu bar that lets you select commands to perform tasks.

■ This area displays toolbars that let you quickly select common commands.

SWITCH BETWEEN PROGRAMS

You can have more than one program open at a time. You can easily switch between the open programs.

Think of each program as a separate piece of paper. Switching between programs lets you place a different piece of paper at the top of the pile.

SWITCH BETWEEN PROGRAMS

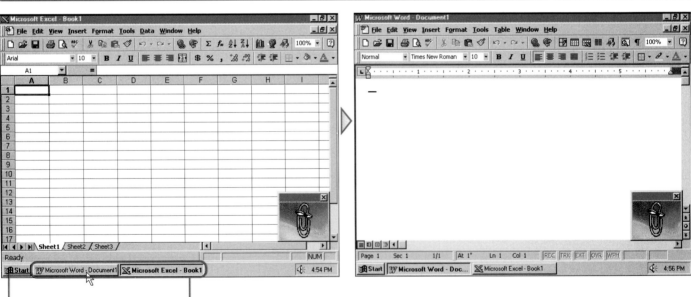

■ The taskbar displays the name of each program you have opened.

Note: To start a program, refer to page 8.

1 To switch to another program, move the mouse ⌖ over the name of the program and then press the left mouse button.

■ The program you selected appears on top of all other open programs.

10

EXIT A PROGRAM

When you finish using a program, exit the program.

You should always exit all programs before turning off your computer.

EXIT A PROGRAM

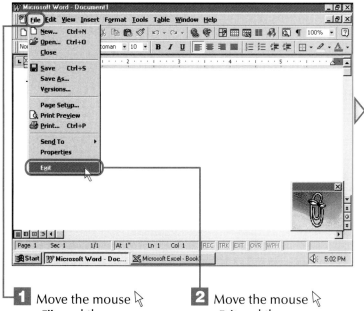

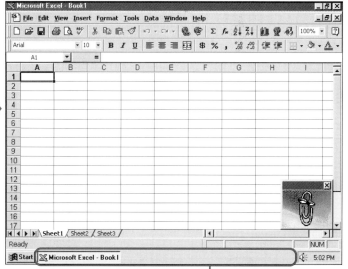

1 Move the mouse ⌖ over **File** and then press the left mouse button.

2 Move the mouse ⌖ over **Exit** and then press the left mouse button.

■ The program disappears from the screen.

■ The name of the program disappears from the taskbar.

GETTING HELP

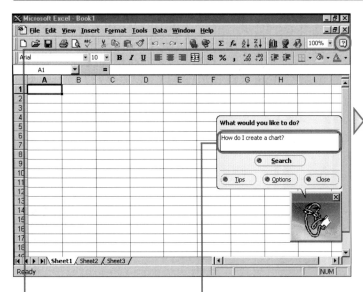

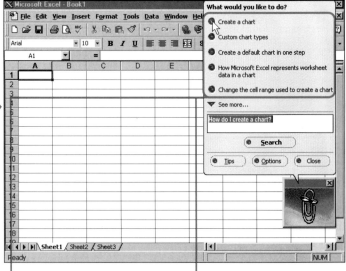

1 To display the Office Assistant, move the mouse ⬚ over 🔲 and then press the left mouse button.

2 Type the question you want to ask and then press **Enter** on your keyboard.

■ The Office Assistant displays a list of help topics that relate to the question you asked.

Note: If you do not see a help topic of interest, try rephrasing your question. Type the new question and then press **Enter** *on your keyboard.*

3 Move the mouse ⬚ over the help topic you want information on and then press the left mouse button.

How do I display the name of each toolbar button?

To display the name of a toolbar button, move the mouse ⃗ over the button. After a few seconds, the name of the button appears.

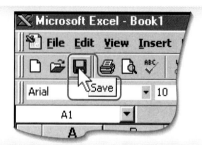

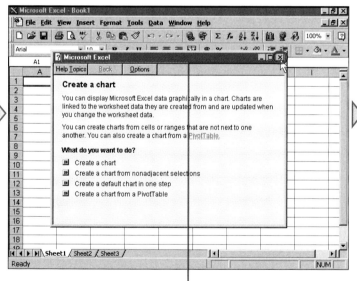

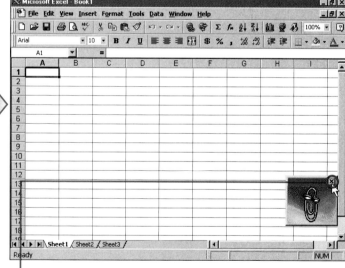

■ The Help window appears, displaying information about the topic you selected.

4 When you finish reading the information, move the mouse ⃗ over ☒ and then press the left mouse button to close the Help window.

5 To hide the Office Assistant, move the mouse ⃗ over ☒ and then press the left mouse button.

Microsoft Word allows you to create letters, reports, memos and newsletters.

Insert a Section Break
Page 90

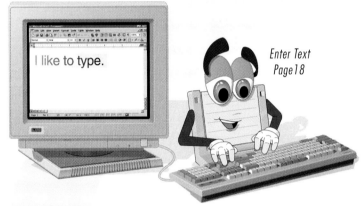

I like to type.

Enter Text
Page 18

Add Bullets or Numbers
Page 72

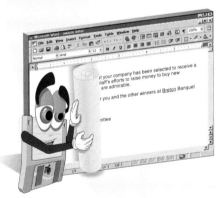

Close a Document
Page 32

Start Word
Page 17

Save a Document
Page 24

Delete Text
Page 44

Dear Susan,

I'm delighted you'll be coming to Chicago
this summer. I've requested the same vacation
time, so we'll be able to spend lots of time
together.

I've enclosed a newspaper article about
upcoming musical events. Be sure to
write to me soon to let me know what you
would like to see so I can order a couple of

have to spend lots of time in Rose Park,
which is one of the city's most beautiful
spots. We can rent bicycles and enjoy the
park's scenic trails. I also know where all the
best restaurants are.

Nancy

WORD

INTRODUCTION TO WORD

Word lets you produce professional documents quickly and efficiently.

You can use Word to create letters, reports, manuals, newsletters and brochures.

Editing

Word offers many features that help you work with text in a document. You can easily edit text, rearrange paragraphs and check for spelling mistakes.

Formatting

Word offers many features that help you change the appearance of a document. You can add page numbers, center text and use various fonts in a document.

Printing

You can produce a paper copy of a Word document. Word lets you see on the screen exactly what the printed document will look like.

When you start Word, a blank document appears. You can type text into this document.

START WORD

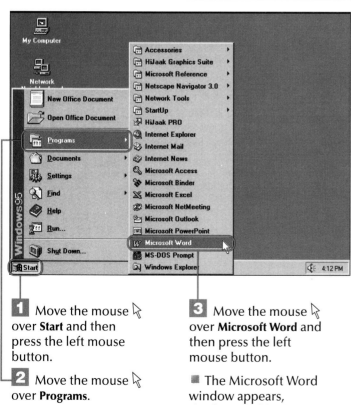

1 Move the mouse over **Start** and then press the left mouse button.

2 Move the mouse over **Programs**.

3 Move the mouse over **Microsoft Word** and then press the left mouse button.

■ The Microsoft Word window appears, displaying a blank document.

■ If you are starting Word for the first time, the Office Assistant welcome appears.

4 To start using Word, move the mouse over this option and then press the left mouse button.

■ To hide the Office Assistant, move the mouse over ☒ and then press the left mouse button.

Note: For more information on the Office Assistant, refer to page 12.

> Word lets you type text into your document quickly and easily.

ENTER TEXT

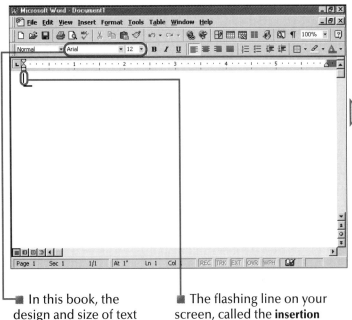

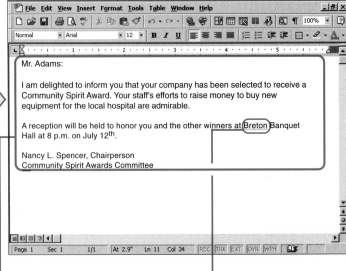

■ In this book, the design and size of text were changed to make the document easier to read. To change the design and size of text, refer to pages 62 and 63.

■ The flashing line on your screen, called the **insertion point**, indicates where the text you type will appear.

1 Type the text.

■ When you reach the end of a line, Word automatically wraps the text to the next line. You only need to press **Enter** when you want to start a new line or paragraph.

■ Word underlines misspelled words in red and grammar mistakes in green.

Note: For information on how to check spelling and grammar, refer to page 56.

THE WORD SCREEN

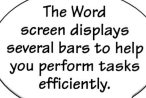

The Word screen displays several bars to help you perform tasks efficiently.

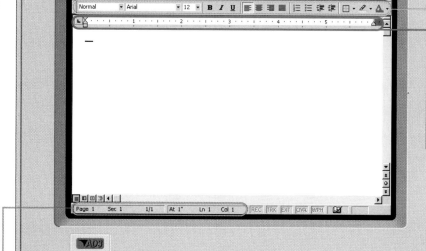

Standard Toolbar

Contains buttons to help you quickly select commonly used commands, such as opening a document.

Formatting Toolbar

Contains buttons to help you quickly select formatting and layout features, such as **bold** and underline.

Ruler

Allows you to change margin and tab settings for your document.

Status Bar

Displays information about the area of the document displayed on your screen and the position of the insertion point.

Page 1

The page displayed on your screen.

Sec 1

The section of the document displayed on your screen.

1/1

The page displayed on the screen and the total number of pages in the document.

At 1"

The distance from the top of the page to the insertion point.

Ln 1

The number of lines from the top of the page to the insertion point.

Col 1

The number of characters from the left margin to the insertion point, including spaces.

SELECT TEXT

Before performing many tasks in Word, you must select the text you want to work with. Selected text appears highlighted on your screen.

SELECT TEXT

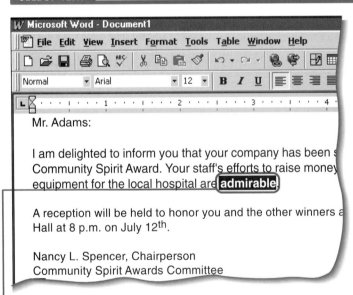

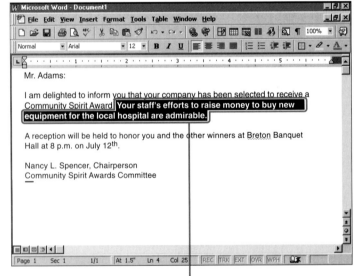

SELECT A WORD

1 Move the mouse I anywhere over the word you want to select and then quickly press the left mouse button twice.

■ To deselect text, move the mouse I outside the selected area and then press the left mouse button.

SELECT A SENTENCE

1 Press and hold down **Ctrl** on your keyboard.

2 Still holding down **Ctrl**, move the mouse I anywhere over the sentence you want to select and then press the left mouse button. Then release **Ctrl**.

How do I select all the text in a document?

To quickly select all the text in your document, press and hold down **Ctrl** and then press **A** on your keyboard. Then release both keys.

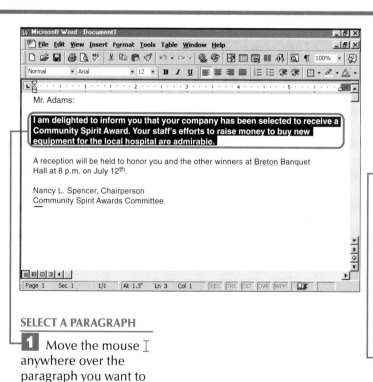

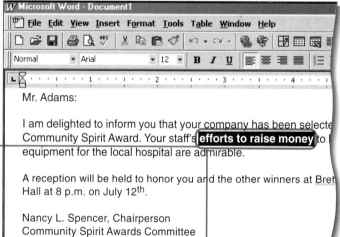

SELECT A PARAGRAPH

1 Move the mouse I anywhere over the paragraph you want to select and then quickly press the left mouse button **three** times.

SELECT ANY AMOUNT OF TEXT

1 Move the mouse I over the first word you want to select.

2 Press and hold down the left mouse button as you move the mouse I over the text you want to select. Then release the mouse button.

MOVE THROUGH A DOCUMENT

You can easily move to another location in your document.

If you create a long document, your computer screen cannot display all the text at the same time. You must scroll up or down to view and edit other parts of the document.

MOVE THE INSERTION POINT

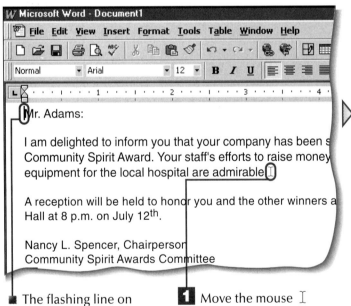

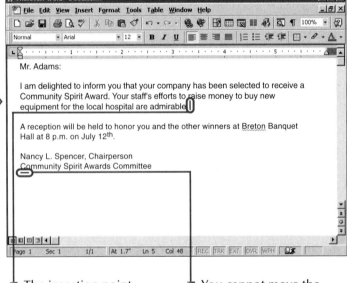

■ The flashing line on the screen, called the **insertion point**, indicates where the text you type will appear.

1 Move the mouse I to where you want to place the insertion point and then press the left mouse button.

■ The insertion point appears in the new position.

Note: You can also press ↑ , ↓ , ← *or* → *on your keyboard to move the insertion point one line or character in any direction.*

■ You cannot move the insertion point below the horizontal line displayed on the screen. To move this line, position the insertion point after the last character in the document and then press Enter several times.

How do I use the new Microsoft IntelliMouse to scroll?

The Microsoft IntelliMouse has a wheel between the left and right mouse buttons. Moving this wheel lets you quickly scroll through a document.

SCROLL UP OR DOWN

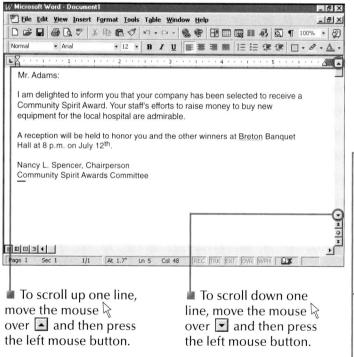

■ To scroll up one line, move the mouse ⤢ over ▲ and then press the left mouse button.

■ To scroll down one line, move the mouse ⤢ over ▼ and then press the left mouse button.

SCROLL TO ANY POSITION

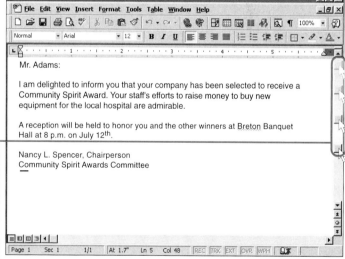

1 To quickly scroll through your document, move the mouse ⤢ over the scroll box ☐.

2 Press and hold down the left mouse button and then move the mouse ⤢ up or down the scroll bar. Then release the mouse button.

■ The location of the scroll box indicates which part of the document you are viewing. To view the middle of the document, move the scroll box halfway down the scroll bar.

SAVE A DOCUMENT

You should save your document to store it for future use. This lets you later retrieve the document for reviewing or editing.

SAVE A DOCUMENT

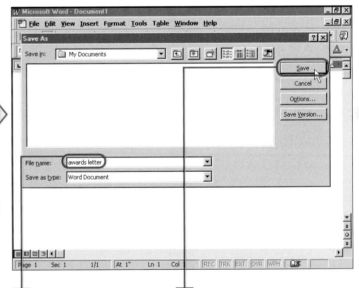

1 Move the mouse ☐ over 🖫 and then press the left mouse button.

■ The **Save As** dialog box appears.

*Note: If you previously saved the document, the **Save As** dialog box will not appear since you have already named the document.*

2 Type a name for the document.

Note: You can use up to 255 characters to name a document.

3 Move the mouse ☐ over **Save** and then press the left mouse button.

24

When you want to make major changes to a document, save the document with a different name before you begin. This gives you two copies of the document—the original document and a document with all the changes.

SAVE A DOCUMENT WITH A NEW NAME

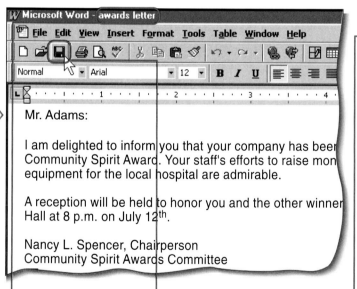

Mr. Adams:

I am delighted to inform you that your company has been
Community Spirit Award. Your staff's efforts to raise mon
equipment for the local hospital are admirable.

A reception will be held to honor you and the other winner
Hall at 8 p.m. on July 12th.

Nancy L. Spencer, Chairperson
Community Spirit Awards Committee

■ Word saves the
document and
displays the name
at the top of the
screen.

SAVE CHANGES

To avoid losing your work,
you should regularly save
changes you make to the
document.

1 Move the mouse ↳
over 🖫 and then press
the left mouse button.

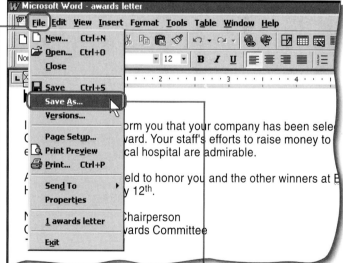

1 Move the mouse ↳
over **File** and then press
the left mouse button.

2 Move the mouse ↳
over **Save As** and then
press the left mouse
button.

3 Perform steps 2
and 3 on page 24.

> You can use the Print Preview feature to see how your document will look when printed.

1 Move the mouse ▷ over 🔍 and then press the left mouse button.

■ The Print Preview window appears.

■ This area tells you which page is displayed and the number of pages in the document. In this example, the document contains one page.

■ If your document contains more than one page, use the scroll bar to view the other pages.

When can I edit my document in the Print Preview window?

Note: To change the shape of the mouse, perform step **3** below.

If the mouse looks like I when over your document, you can edit the document.

If the mouse looks like ⊕ or ⊖ when over your document, you can magnify or shrink the page displayed on your screen.

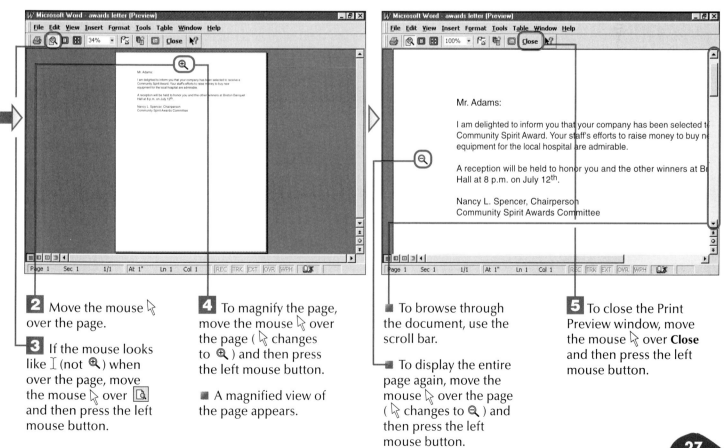

2 Move the mouse ⬚ over the page.

3 If the mouse looks like I (not ⊕) when over the page, move the mouse ⬚ over ▣ and then press the left mouse button.

4 To magnify the page, move the mouse ⬚ over the page (⬚ changes to ⊕) and then press the left mouse button.

■ A magnified view of the page appears.

■ To browse through the document, use the scroll bar.

■ To display the entire page again, move the mouse ⬚ over the page (⬚ changes to ⊖) and then press the left mouse button.

5 To close the Print Preview window, move the mouse ⬚ over **Close** and then press the left mouse button.

PRINT A DOCUMENT

You can produce a paper copy of the document displayed on your screen.

PRINT A DOCUMENT

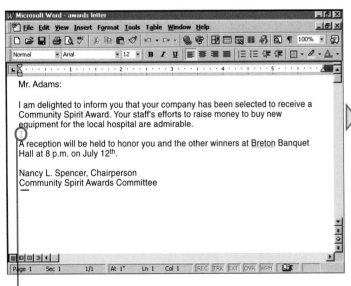

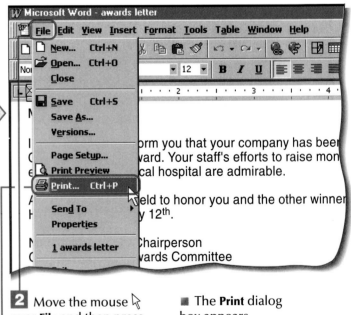

1 Move the mouse I anywhere over the document or page you want to print and then press the left mouse button.

■ To print part of the document, select the text you want to print. To select text, refer to page 20.

2 Move the mouse ⇖ over **File** and then press the left mouse button.

3 Move the mouse ⇖ over **Print** and then press the left mouse button.

■ The **Print** dialog box appears.

28

How do I prepare my printer to print documents?

Before printing, always make sure your printer is turned on and contains paper.

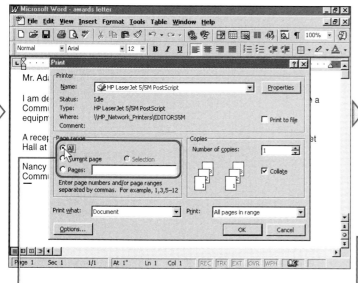

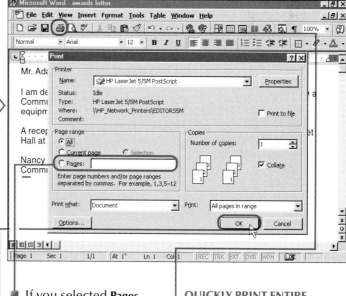

4 Move the mouse ⟍ over the print option you want to use and then press the left mouse button (○ changes to ◉).

All - Prints every page in the document.

Current page - Prints the page containing the insertion point.

Pages - Prints the pages you specify.

Selection - Prints the text you selected.

■ If you selected **Pages** in step **4**, type the pages you want to print (example: **1,3,5** or **2-4**).

5 Move the mouse ⟍ over **OK** and then press the left mouse button.

QUICKLY PRINT ENTIRE DOCUMENT

1 To quickly print an entire document, move the mouse ⟍ over 🖨 and then press the left mouse button.

CREATE A NEW DOCUMENT

You can create a new document to start writing a letter, report or memo.

CREATE A NEW DOCUMENT

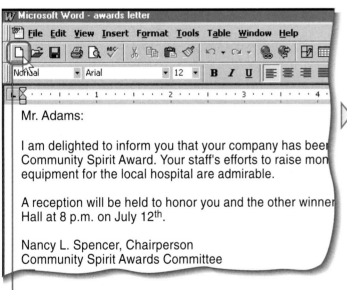

Mr. Adams:

I am delighted to inform you that your company has been Community Spirit Award. Your staff's efforts to raise mon equipment for the local hospital are admirable.

A reception will be held to honor you and the other winner Hall at 8 p.m. on July 12th.

Nancy L. Spencer, Chairperson
Community Spirit Awards Committee

1 Move the mouse over ☐ and then press the left mouse button.

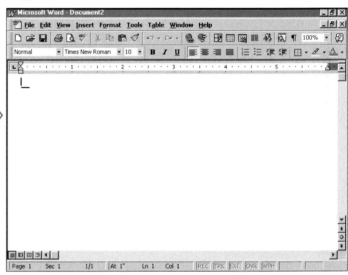

■ A new document appears. The previous document is now hidden behind the new document.

■ Think of each document as a separate piece of paper. When you create a document, you are placing a new piece of paper on the screen.

Word lets you have many documents open at once. You can easily switch from one open document to another.

SWITCH BETWEEN DOCUMENTS

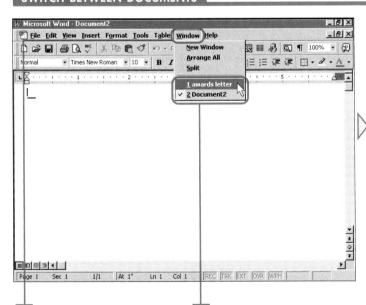

1 To display a list of all open documents, move the mouse ⬡ over **Window** and then press the left mouse button.

2 Move the mouse ⬡ over the document you want to display and then press the left mouse button.

■ The document appears.

■ Word displays the name of the document at the top of your screen.

CLOSE A DOCUMENT

When you finish working with a document, you can close the document to remove it from your screen.

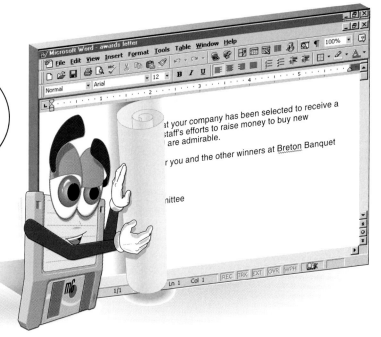

When you close a document, you do not exit the Word program. You can continue to work on other Word documents.

CLOSE A DOCUMENT

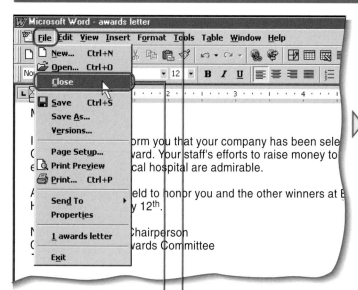

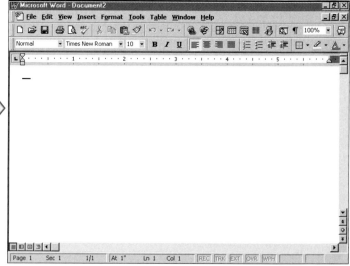

■ To save the document displayed on the screen before closing, refer to page 24.

1 To close the document, move the mouse ⤢ over **File** and then press the left mouse button.

2 Move the mouse ⤢ over **Close** and then press the left mouse button.

■ Word removes the document from the screen.

■ If you had more than one document open, the second last document you worked on appears on the screen.

When you finish using Word, you can exit the program.

You should always exit all programs before turning off your computer.

EXIT WORD

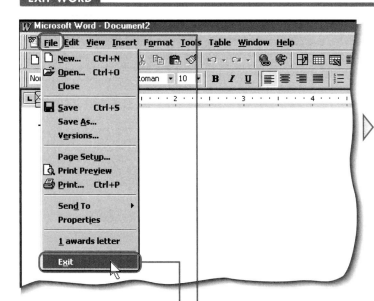

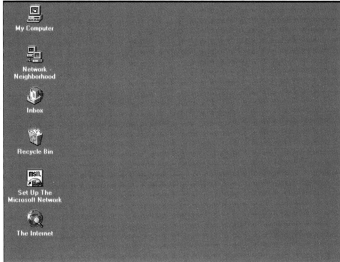

■ Save all open documents before exiting Word. To save a document, refer to page 24.

1 Move the mouse over **File** and then press the left mouse button.

2 Move the mouse over **Exit** and then press the left mouse button.

■ The Word window disappears from the screen.

Note: To restart Word, refer to page 17.

OPEN A DOCUMENT

You can open a saved document and display it on your screen. This allows you to review and make changes to your document.

OPEN A DOCUMENT

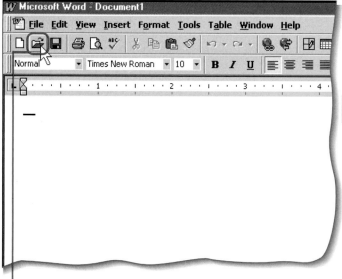

1 Move the mouse over 📂 and then press the left mouse button.

■ The **Open** dialog box appears.

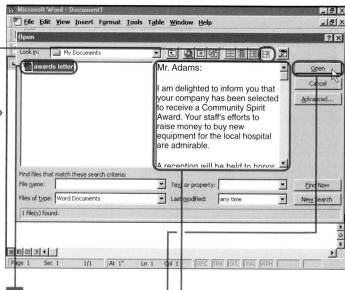

2 Move the mouse over the name of the document you want to open and then press the left mouse button.

3 To see the contents of the document, move the mouse over 📃 and then press the left mouse button.

■ This area displays the contents of the document.

4 To open the document, move the mouse over **Open** and then press the left mouse button.

34

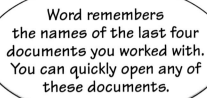

Word remembers
the names of the last four
documents you worked with.
You can quickly open any of
these documents.

QUICKLY OPEN A DOCUMENT

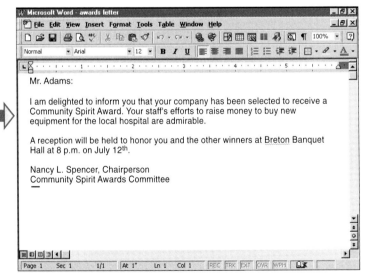

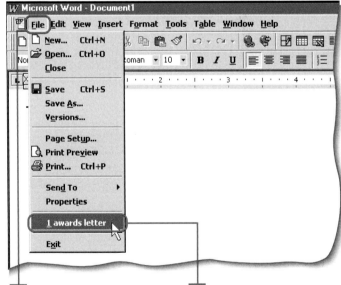

■ Word opens the document and displays it on the screen. You can now review and make changes to the document.

1 Move the mouse over **File** and then press the left mouse button.

2 Move the mouse over the name of the document you want to open and then press the left mouse button.

Word offers four different ways to display your document. You can choose the view that best suits your needs.

CHANGE THE VIEW

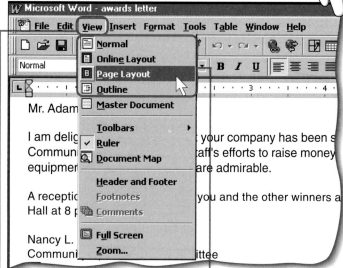

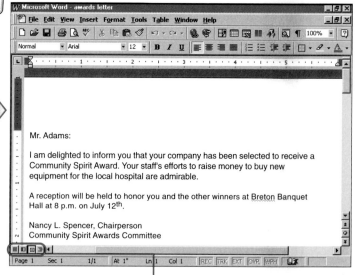

When you first start Word, the document appears in the Normal view.

1 To change the view, move the mouse ⬚ over **View** and then press the left mouse button.

2 Move the mouse ⬚ over the view you want to use and then press the left mouse button.

■ The document appears in the new view.

QUICKLY CHANGE THE VIEW

1 To quickly change the view, move the mouse ⬚ over one of the following options and then press the left mouse button.

▤ Normal	▤ Outline
▤ Online Layout	
▤ Page Layout	

Normal View

This view simplifies the document so you can quickly enter, edit and format text. The Normal view does not display top or bottom margins, headers, footers or page numbers.

Outline View

This view helps you review and work with the structure of a document. You can focus on the main headings by hiding the remaining text.

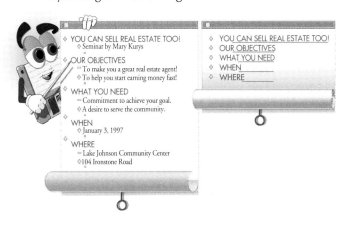

Page Layout View

This view displays the document exactly as it will appear on a printed page. The Page Layout view displays top and bottom margins, headers, footers and page numbers.

Online Layout View

This view displays documents so they are easy to read on the screen. The Online Layout view displays a document map, which lets you move quickly to specific locations in your document.

Word lets you enlarge or reduce the display of text on your screen.

Changing the zoom setting will not affect the way the document appears on a printed page.

ZOOM IN OR OUT

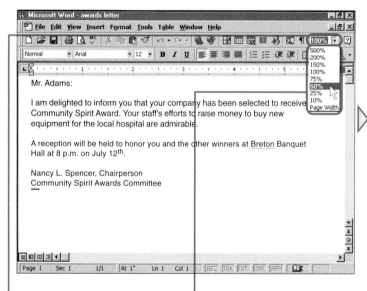

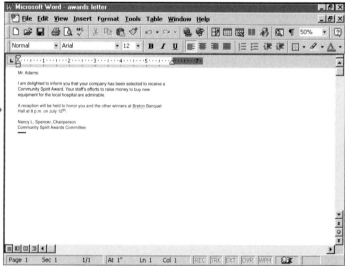

■ When you first start Word, the document appears in the 100% zoom setting.

1 To display a list of zoom settings, move the mouse ⟍ over ▾ in this area and then press the left mouse button.

2 Move the mouse ⟍ over the setting you want to use and then press the left mouse button.

■ The document appears in the new zoom setting. You can edit your document as usual.

■ To return to the normal zoom setting, repeat steps **1** and **2**, selecting **100%** in step **2**.

You can use the ruler to position text on a page. You can display or hide the ruler at any time.

When you first start Word, the ruler is displayed on your screen. Hiding the ruler provides a larger and less cluttered working area.

DISPLAY THE RULER

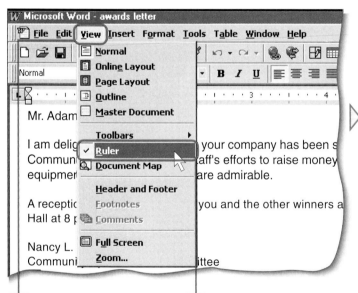

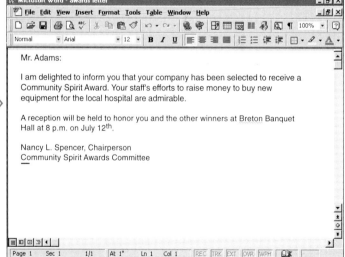

1 To display or hide the ruler, move the mouse over **View** and then press the left mouse button.

2 Move the mouse over **Ruler** and then press the left mouse button. A check mark (✓) beside **Ruler** tells you the ruler is currently displayed.

■ Word displays or hides the ruler.

Word offers several toolbars that you can hide or display at any time. Each toolbar contains buttons that help you quickly perform common tasks.

DISPLAY TOOLBARS

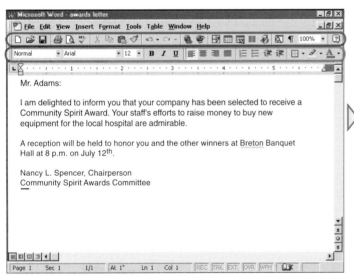

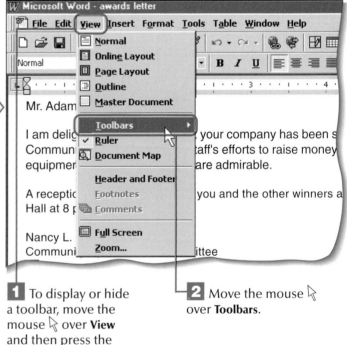

When you first start Word, the Standard and Formatting toolbars appear on the screen.

Standard toolbar

Formatting toolbar

1 To display or hide a toolbar, move the mouse ⌖ over **View** and then press the left mouse button.

2 Move the mouse ⌖ over **Toolbars**.

Why would I want to hide a toolbar?

A screen displaying fewer toolbars provides a larger and less cluttered working area.

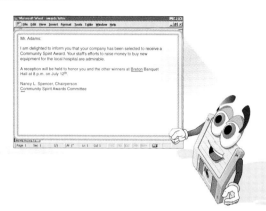

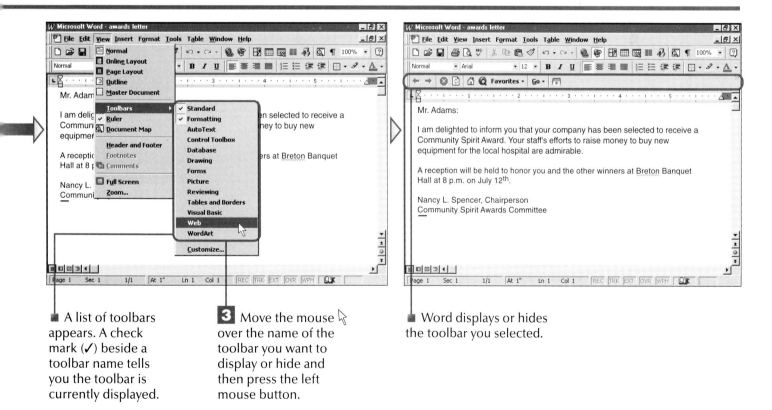

■ A list of toolbars appears. A check mark (✓) beside a toolbar name tells you the toolbar is currently displayed.

3 Move the mouse over the name of the toolbar you want to display or hide and then press the left mouse button.

■ Word displays or hides the toolbar you selected.

INSERT TEXT

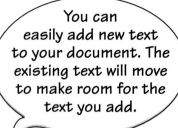
You can easily add new text to your document. The existing text will move to make room for the text you add.

INSERT CHARACTERS

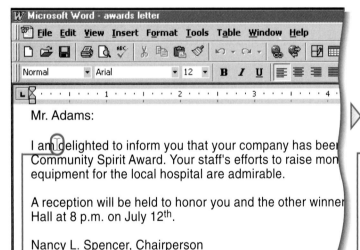

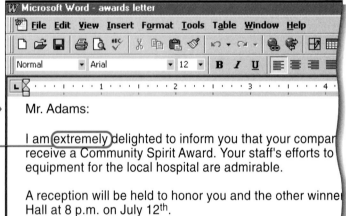

1 Move the mouse I to where you want to insert the new text and then press the left mouse button.

2 Type the text you want to insert. To insert a blank space, press the **Spacebar.**

■ The words to the right of the new text move forward.

42

How do I insert symbols into my document?

Word will automatically replace specific characters you type with symbols. This lets you quickly enter symbols that are not available on your keyboard.

Note: For more information on inserting symbols, refer to page 70.

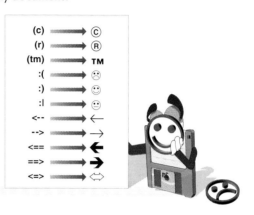

INSERT A BLANK LINE

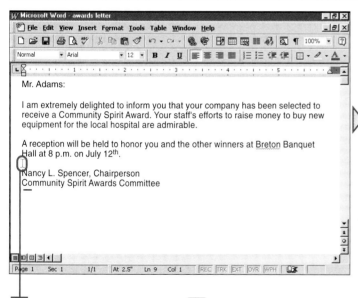

1 Move the mouse I to where you want to insert a blank line and then press the left mouse button.

2 Press **Enter** on your keyboard to insert the blank line.

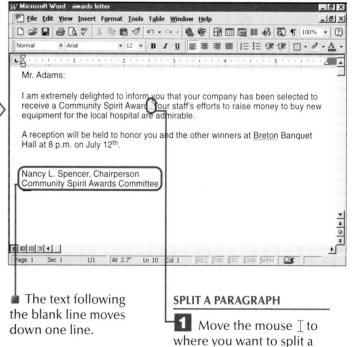

■ The text following the blank line moves down one line.

SPLIT A PARAGRAPH

1 Move the mouse I to where you want to split a paragraph in two and then press the left mouse button.

2 Press **Enter** on your keyboard twice.

DELETE TEXT

You can easily remove text you no longer need. The remaining text moves to fill any empty spaces.

Dear Susan,

I'm delighted you'll be coming to Chicago this summer. I've requested the same vacation time, so we'll be able to spend lots of time together.

I've enclosed a newspaper article about upcoming musical ~~and plays~~. Be sure to write to me so ~~I'll~~ let me know what you would like ~~see~~ so I can order a couple of

~~I~~ have to spend lots of time in Rose Park, which is one of the city's most beautiful spots. We can rent bicycles and enjoy the park's scenic trails. I also know where all the best restaurants are.

Nancy

DELETE CHARACTERS

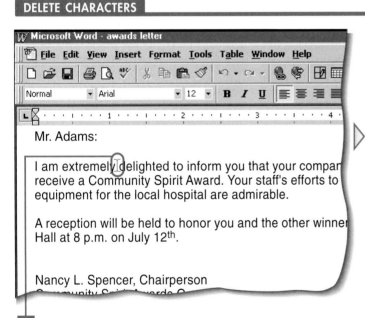

1 Move the mouse I to the **right** of the first character you want to delete and then press the left mouse button.

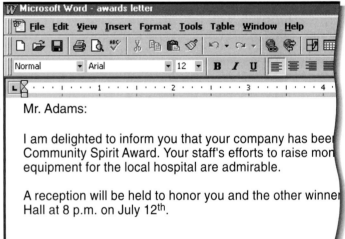

2 Press **+Backspace** on your keyboard once for each character or space you want to delete.

■ You can also use **Delete** on your keyboard to remove characters. Move the mouse I to the **left** of the first character you want to remove and then press the left mouse button. Press **Delete** once for each character or space you want to remove.

44

Can I recover text I accidentally delete?

Word remembers the last changes you made to your document. If you regret deleting text, you can use the Undo feature to undo the change.

Note: For information on the Undo feature, refer to page 47.

DELETE A BLANK LINE

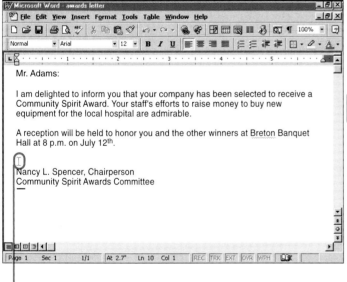

1 Move the mouse I to the beginning of the blank line you want to delete and then press the left mouse button.

2 Press ◆Backspace on your keyboard to remove the blank line.

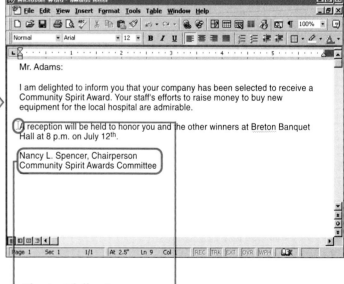

■ The text following the blank line moves up one line.

JOIN TWO PARAGRAPHS

1 Move the mouse I to the left of the first character in the second paragraph and then press the left mouse button.

2 Press ◆Backspace on your keyboard until the paragraphs are joined.

You can quickly delete a section of text you have selected.

DELETE SELECTED TEXT

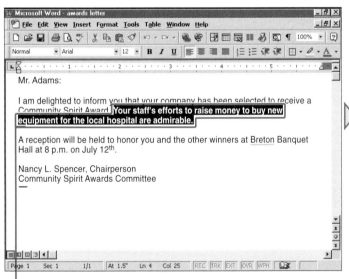

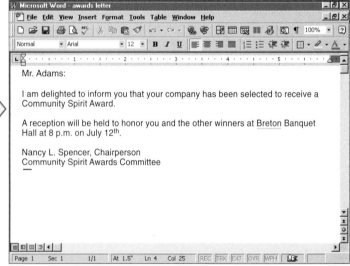

1 Select the text you want to delete. To select text, refer to page 20.

2 Press Delete on your keyboard to remove the text.

Word remembers the last changes you made to your document. If you regret these changes, you can cancel them by using the Undo feature.

UNDO LAST CHANGE

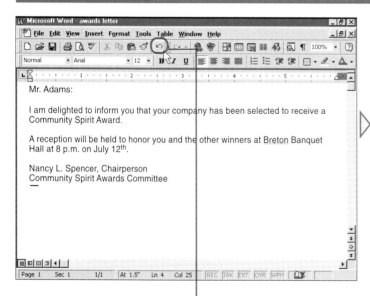

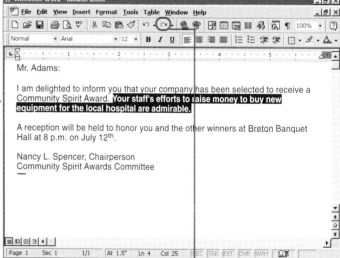

The Undo feature can cancel your last editing and formatting changes.

■1 To undo your last change, move the mouse ⤡ over 🔙 and then press the left mouse button.

■ Word cancels the last change you made to your document.

■ You can repeat step 1 to cancel previous changes you made.

■ To reverse the results of using the Undo feature, move the mouse ⤡ over 🔜 and then press the left mouse button.

You can reorganize your document by moving text from one location to another.

MOVE TEXT

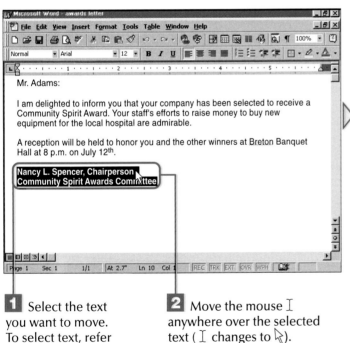

1 Select the text you want to move. To select text, refer to page 20.

2 Move the mouse I anywhere over the selected text (I changes to).

3 Press and hold down the left mouse button as you move the mouse to where you want to place the text.

■ The text will appear where you position the dotted insertion point on your screen.

48

Can moving text help me edit my document?

Moving text lets you easily try out different ways of organizing the text in a document. You can find the most effective structure for your document by experimenting with different placements of sentences and paragraphs.

MOVE TEXT USING TOOLBAR

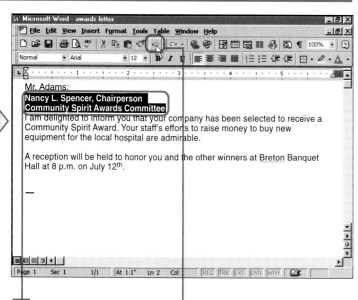

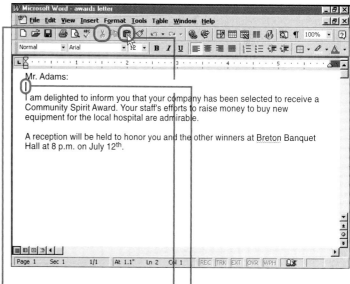

4 Release the left mouse button and the text moves to the new location.

UNDO MOVE

1 To immediately move the text back, move the mouse over ↶ and then press the left mouse button.

1 Select the text you want to move.

2 Move the mouse over ✂ and then press the left mouse button. The text you selected disappears from the screen.

3 Move the mouse I to where you want to place the text and then press the left mouse button.

4 Move the mouse over 📋 and then press the left mouse button. The text appears in the new location.

You can place a copy of text in a different location in your document. This will save you time since you do not have to retype the text.

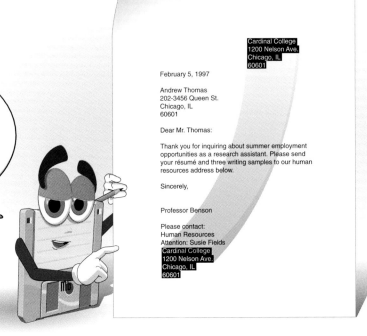

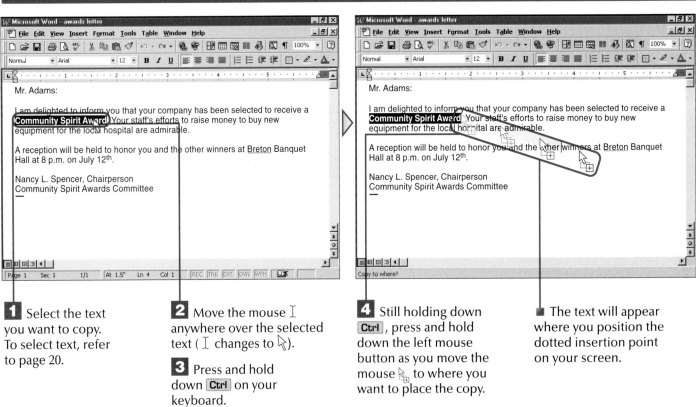

1 Select the text you want to copy. To select text, refer to page 20.

2 Move the mouse I anywhere over the selected text (I changes to ⬚).

3 Press and hold down **Ctrl** on your keyboard.

4 Still holding down **Ctrl**, press and hold down the left mouse button as you move the mouse ⬚ to where you want to place the copy.

■ The text will appear where you position the dotted insertion point on your screen.

50

How can copying text help me edit my document?

If you plan to make major changes to a paragraph, you may want to copy the paragraph before you begin. This gives you two copies of the paragraph—the original paragraph and a paragraph with all the changes.

There is a **10th** anniversary High School Reunion on August 8, 9 and 10 at **Woodblock** High School. We all hope to see you there. **Contact Susan Hughes** for more information.

There is an **11th** anniversary High School Reunion on August 8, 9 and 10 at **Brown** High School. We all hope to see you there. **Call Bob Maki** for more information.

COPY TEXT USING TOOLBAR

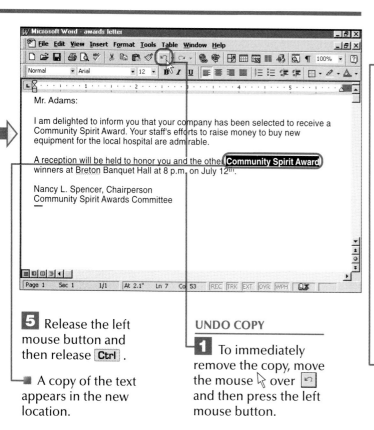

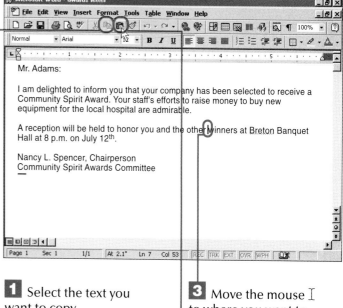

5 Release the left mouse button and then release **Ctrl**.

■ A copy of the text appears in the new location.

UNDO COPY

1 To immediately remove the copy, move the mouse ⍐ over 🔄 and then press the left mouse button.

1 Select the text you want to copy.

2 Move the mouse ⍐ over 📄 and then press the left mouse button. The text you selected remains on the screen.

3 Move the mouse I to where you want to place the copy and then press the left mouse button.

4 Move the mouse ⍐ over 📋 and then press the left mouse button. A copy of the text appears in the new location.

FIND TEXT

You can use the Find feature to locate a word or phrase in your document.

FIND TEXT

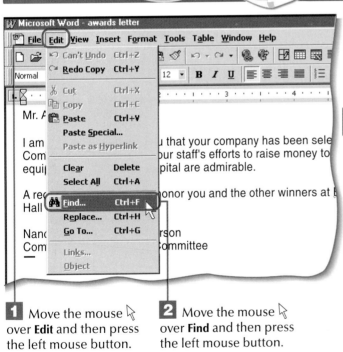

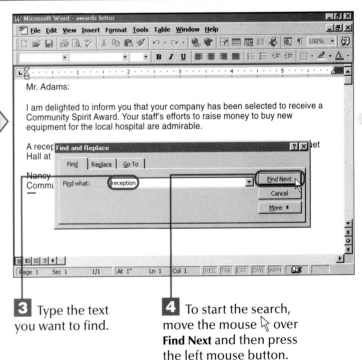

1 Move the mouse over **Edit** and then press the left mouse button.

2 Move the mouse over **Find** and then press the left mouse button.

■ The **Find and Replace** dialog box appears.

3 Type the text you want to find.

4 To start the search, move the mouse over **Find Next** and then press the left mouse button.

52

Can I search for part of a word?

When you search for text in your document, Word will find the text even if it is part of a larger word. For example, if you search for **place**, Word will also find **place**s, **place**ment and common**place**.

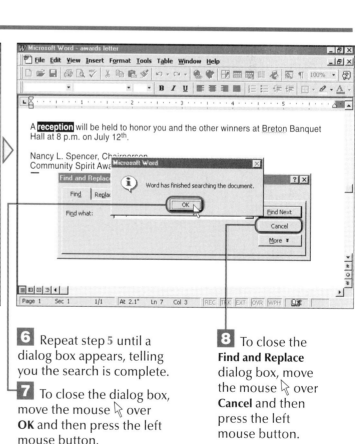

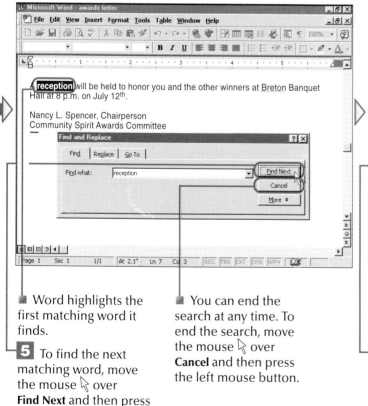

■ Word highlights the first matching word it finds.

5 To find the next matching word, move the mouse ⟍ over **Find Next** and then press the left mouse button.

■ You can end the search at any time. To end the search, move the mouse ⟍ over **Cancel** and then press the left mouse button.

6 Repeat step 5 until a dialog box appears, telling you the search is complete.

7 To close the dialog box, move the mouse ⟍ over **OK** and then press the left mouse button.

8 To close the **Find and Replace** dialog box, move the mouse ⟍ over **Cancel** and then press the left mouse button.

REPLACE TEXT

The Replace feature can locate and replace every occurrence of a word or phrase in your document. This is ideal if you have frequently misspelled a name.

REPLACE TEXT

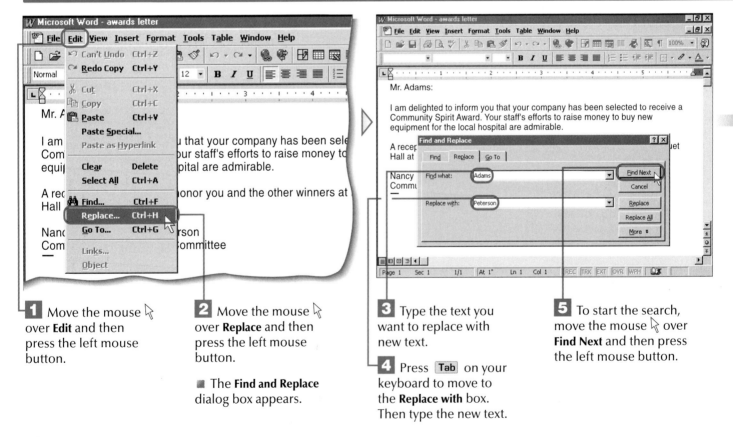

1 Move the mouse ⟋ over **Edit** and then press the left mouse button.

2 Move the mouse ⟋ over **Replace** and then press the left mouse button.

■ The **Find and Replace** dialog box appears.

3 Type the text you want to replace with new text.

4 Press **Tab** on your keyboard to move to the **Replace with** box. Then type the new text.

5 To start the search, move the mouse ⟋ over **Find Next** and then press the left mouse button.

Can I use the Replace feature to enter text more quickly?

The Replace feature is useful if you have to type a long word or phrase (example: University of Massachusetts) many times in a document. You can type a short form of the word or phrase (example: UM) throughout your document and then have Word replace the short form with the full word or phrase.

I attend the University of Massachusetts. The University of Massachusetts is located in Amherst. I work in the University of Massachusetts bookstore.

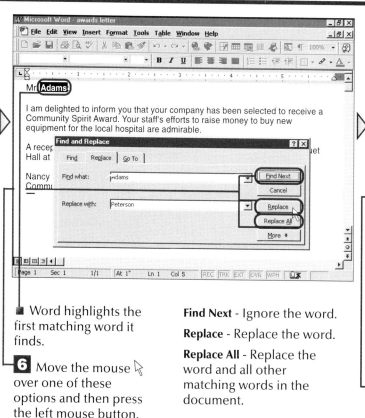

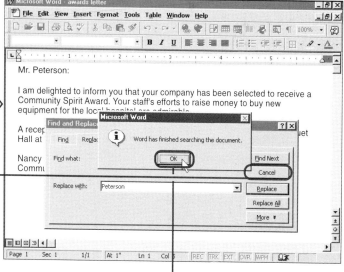

■ Word highlights the first matching word it finds.

6 Move the mouse ⌖ over one of these options and then press the left mouse button.

Find Next - Ignore the word.

Replace - Replace the word.

Replace All - Replace the word and all other matching words in the document.

■ In this example, Word replaces the text and searches for the next matching word.

■ You can end the search at any time. To end the search, move the mouse ⌖ over **Cancel** or **Close** and then press the left mouse button.

7 Repeat step 6 until a dialog box appears, telling you the search is complete.

8 To close the dialog box, move the mouse ⌖ over **OK** and then press the left mouse button.

CHECK SPELLING AND GRAMMAR

Word offers a Spelling and Grammar feature to help you find and correct errors in your document.

Word automatically underlines misspelled words in red and grammar mistakes in green. The red and green underlines will not appear when you print your document.

CHECK SPELLING AND GRAMMAR

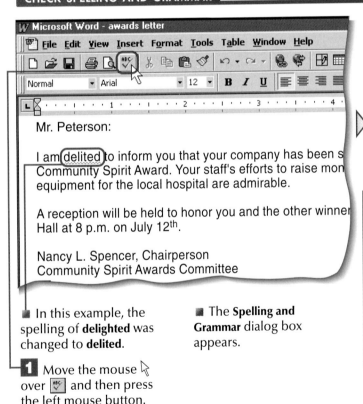

■ In this example, the spelling of **delighted** was changed to **delited**.

1 Move the mouse ⟋ over 🔤 and then press the left mouse button.

■ The **Spelling and Grammar** dialog box appears.

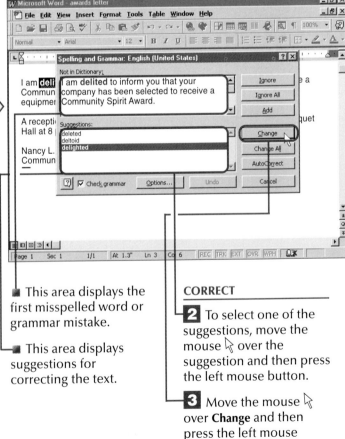

■ This area displays the first misspelled word or grammar mistake.

■ This area displays suggestions for correcting the text.

CORRECT

2 To select one of the suggestions, move the mouse ⟋ over the suggestion and then press the left mouse button.

3 Move the mouse ⟋ over **Change** and then press the left mouse button.

Can Word automatically correct my typing mistakes?

Word automatically corrects common spelling errors as you type.

adn	and
alot	a lot
comittee	committee
don;t	don't
nwe	new
occurence	occurrence
recieve	receive
seperate	separate
teh	the

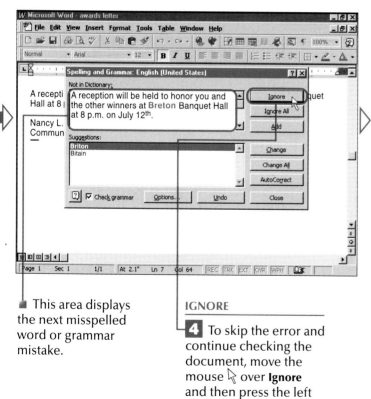

■ This area displays the next misspelled word or grammar mistake.

IGNORE

4 To skip the error and continue checking the document, move the mouse ⬡ over **Ignore** and then press the left mouse button.

*Note: To skip the error and all occurrences of the error, move the mouse ⬡ over **Ignore All** and then press the left mouse button.*

5 Correct or ignore misspelled words and grammar mistakes until this dialog box appears, telling you the spelling and grammar check is complete.

6 To close the dialog box, move the mouse ⬡ over **OK** and then press the left mouse button.

USING THE THESAURUS

You can use the Thesaurus to replace a word in your document with one that is more suitable.

Word ➜ Suggestions

big ➜ large immense huge gigantic

USING THE THESAURUS

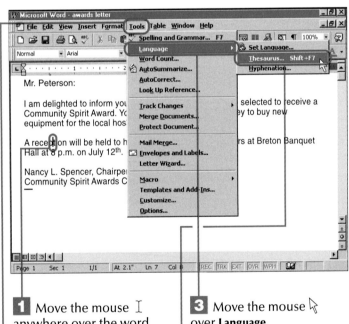

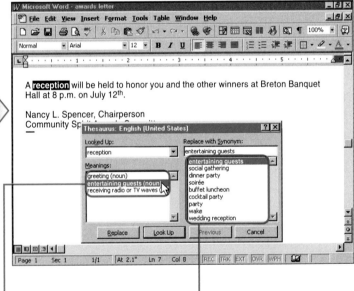

1 Move the mouse I anywhere over the word you want to replace and then press the left mouse button.

2 Move the mouse ↘ over **Tools** and then press the left mouse button.

3 Move the mouse ↘ over **Language**.

4 Move the mouse ↘ over **Thesaurus** and then press the left mouse button.

■ The **Thesaurus** dialog box appears.

5 Move the mouse ↘ over the correct meaning of the word and then press the left mouse button.

■ This area displays words that share the meaning you selected.

58

How can the Thesaurus feature help me?

Using the Thesaurus included with Word is faster and more convenient than searching through a printed thesaurus.

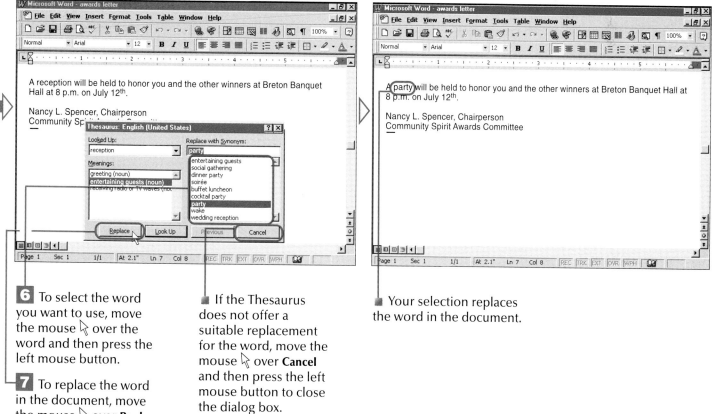

6 To select the word you want to use, move the mouse ⬡ over the word and then press the left mouse button.

7 To replace the word in the document, move the mouse ⬡ over **Replace** and then press the left mouse button.

■ If the Thesaurus does not offer a suitable replacement for the word, move the mouse ⬡ over **Cancel** and then press the left mouse button to close the dialog box.

■ Your selection replaces the word in the document.

BOLD, ITALIC AND UNDERLINE

You can use the Bold, Italic and Underline features to emphasize information in your document.

Bold *Italic* <u>Underline</u>

BOLD, ITALIC AND UNDERLINE

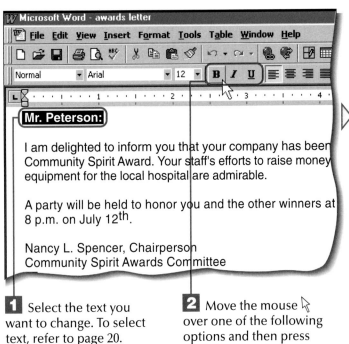

1 Select the text you want to change. To select text, refer to page 20.

2 Move the mouse over one of the following options and then press the left mouse button.

B Bold
I Italic
<u>U</u> Underline

◼ The text you selected appears in the new style.

◼ To deselect text, move the mouse I outside the selected area and then press the left mouse button.

◼ To remove a bold, italic or underline style, repeat steps **1** and **2**.

60

You can enhance the appearance of your document by aligning text in different ways.

CHANGE ALIGNMENT OF TEXT

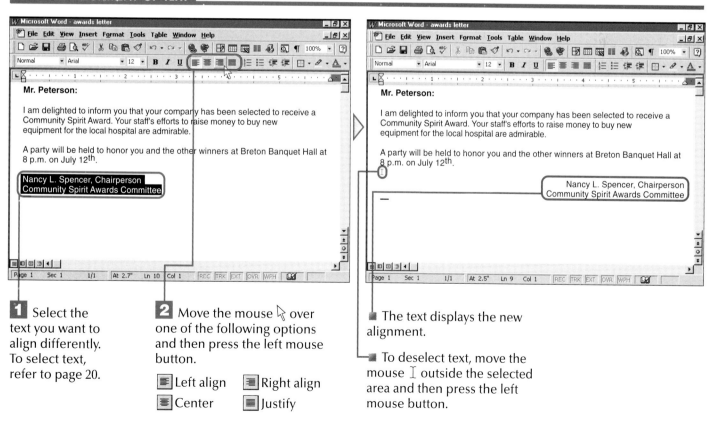

1 Select the text you want to align differently. To select text, refer to page 20.

2 Move the mouse ⌖ over one of the following options and then press the left mouse button.

▤ Left align   ▤ Right align
▤ Center   ▤ Justify

■ The text displays the new alignment.

■ To deselect text, move the mouse Ⅰ outside the selected area and then press the left mouse button.

You can enhance the appearance of your document by changing the design of the text.

CHANGE FONT OF TEXT

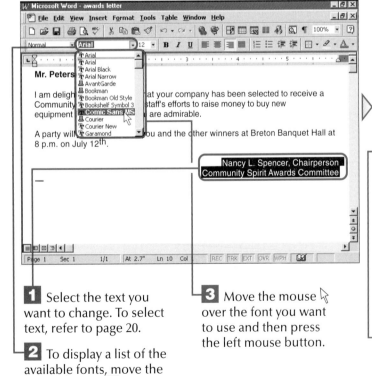

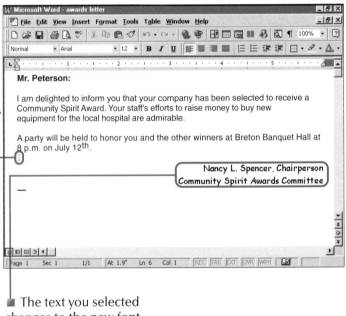

1 Select the text you want to change. To select text, refer to page 20.

2 To display a list of the available fonts, move the mouse ⌖ over ▾ in this area and then press the left mouse button.

3 Move the mouse ⌖ over the font you want to use and then press the left mouse button.

■ The text you selected changes to the new font.

■ To deselect text, move the mouse I outside the selected area and then press the left mouse button.

CHANGE SIZE OF TEXT

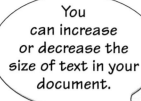

You can increase or decrease the size of text in your document.

8 point

12 point

14 point

18 point

24 point

Word measures the size of text in points. There are approximately 72 points in one inch.

Smaller text lets you fit more information on a page, but larger text is easier to read.

CHANGE SIZE OF TEXT

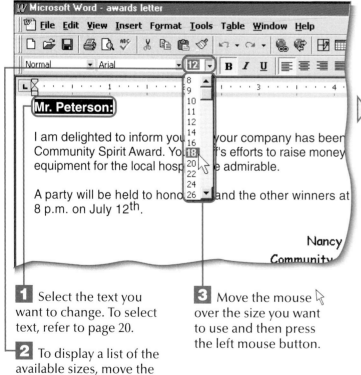

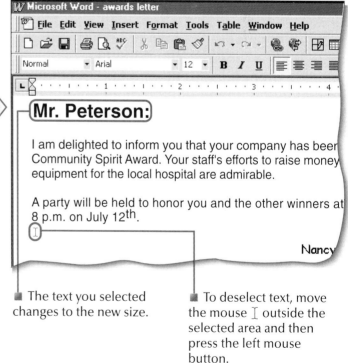

1 Select the text you want to change. To select text, refer to page 20.

2 To display a list of the available sizes, move the mouse over ▾ in this area and then press the left mouse button.

3 Move the mouse over the size you want to use and then press the left mouse button.

■ The text you selected changes to the new size.

■ To deselect text, move the mouse I outside the selected area and then press the left mouse button.

CHANGE APPEARANCE OF TEXT

You can make text in your document look attractive by using various fonts, sizes, styles, underlines and special effects.

CHANGE APPEARANCE OF TEXT

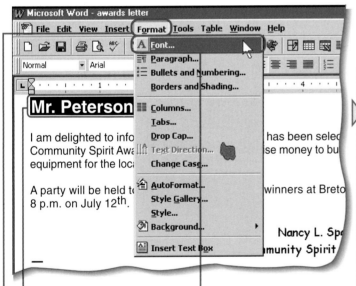

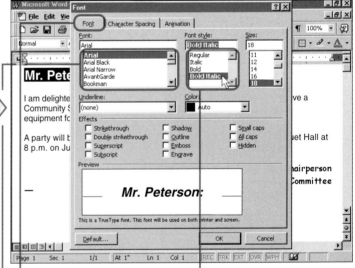

1 Select the text you want to change. To select text, refer to page 20.

2 Move the mouse ⬚ over **Format** and then press the left mouse button.

3 Move the mouse ⬚ over **Font** and then press the left mouse button.

■ The **Font** dialog box appears.

4 Move the mouse ⬚ over the **Font** tab and then press the left mouse button.

5 To change the design of the text, move the mouse ⬚ over the font you want to use and then press the left mouse button.

6 To change the style of the text, move the mouse ⬚ over the style you want to use and then press the left mouse button.

What underline styles and special effects can I add to my document?

Word offers many underline styles and special effects.

Underline Styles	Effects
Single	Strikethrough
Double	Shadow
Dash	Emboss
Wave	Engrave

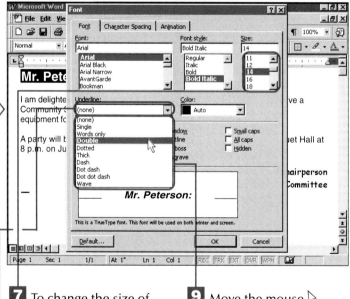

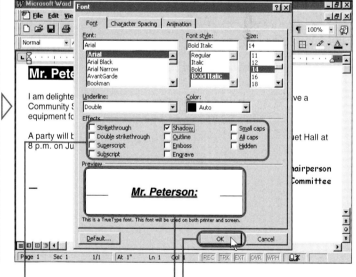

7 To change the size of the text, move the mouse over the size you want to use and then press the left mouse button.

8 To select an underline style, move the mouse over this area and then press the left mouse button.

9 Move the mouse over the underline style you want to use and then press the left mouse button.

10 To select a text effect, move the mouse over the effect you want to use and then press the left mouse button (☐ changes to ☑).

■ This area displays a preview of all the options you selected.

11 To change the selected text, move the mouse over **OK** and then press the left mouse button.

CHANGE TEXT COLOR

You can change the color of text to draw attention to headings or important information in your document.

CHANGE TEXT COLOR

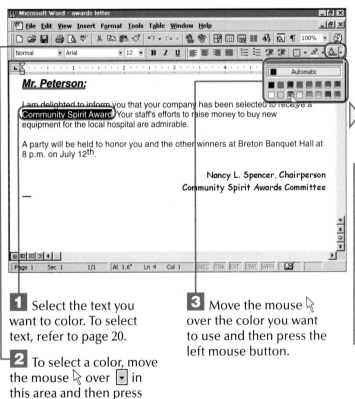

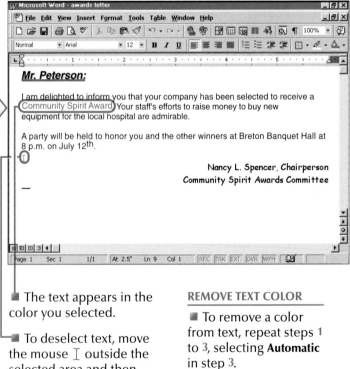

1 Select the text you want to color. To select text, refer to page 20.

2 To select a color, move the mouse ⌖ over ▾ in this area and then press the left mouse button.

3 Move the mouse ⌖ over the color you want to use and then press the left mouse button.

■ The text appears in the color you selected.

■ To deselect text, move the mouse I outside the selected area and then press the left mouse button.

REMOVE TEXT COLOR

■ To remove a color from text, repeat steps **1** to **3**, selecting **Automatic** in step **3**.

You can highlight important text in your document. Highlighting text is useful for marking text you want to verify later.

DEAR MRS. GLEDHILL:

There is a 15th anniversary High School Reunion on August 8, 9 and 10 at Blumlock High School. We all hope to see you there. Contact Susan Hughes for more information.

Susan Hughes

HIGHLIGHT TEXT

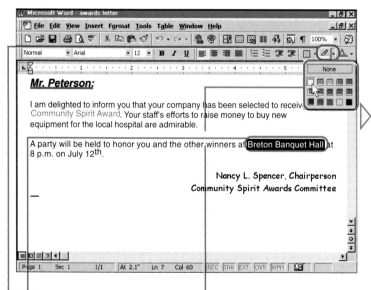

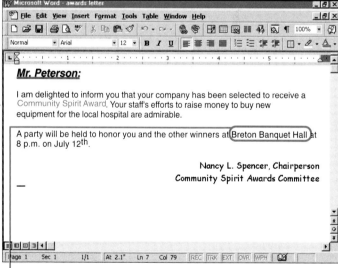

1 Select the text you want to highlight. To select text, refer to page 20.

2 To select a color, move the mouse ⌖ over ⬝ in this area and then press the left mouse button.

3 Move the mouse ⌖ over the color you want to use and then press the left mouse button.

■ The text appears highlighted in the color you selected.

REMOVE HIGHLIGHT

■ To remove a highlight, repeat steps **1** to **3**, selecting **None** in step **3**.

> You can easily make one area of text look exactly like another.

COPY FORMATTING

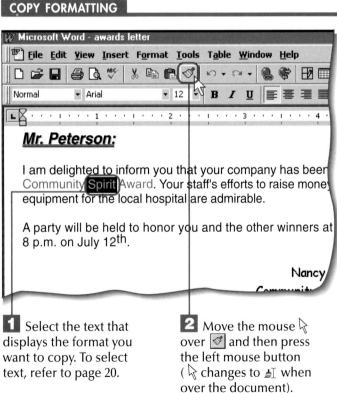

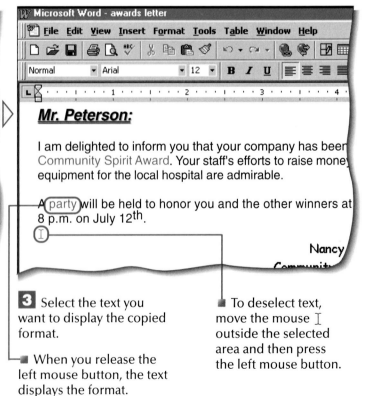

1 Select the text that displays the format you want to copy. To select text, refer to page 20.

2 Move the mouse ⬚ over ⬚ and then press the left mouse button (⬚ changes to ⬚ when over the document).

3 Select the text you want to display the copied format.

■ When you release the left mouse button, the text displays the format.

■ To deselect text, move the mouse ⬚ outside the selected area and then press the left mouse button.

68

You can add a border to emphasize an area of text in your document.

Pasta Perfection

• Order our specialty pasta online for fast delivery.
• Browse through our recipe files.

Our Most Popular Types of Pasta:

• **Cannelloni**
• **Lasagna**
• **Linguine**
• **Manicotti**
• **Ravioli**
• **Spaghetti**

*Perfect pasta
every time!*

ADD A BORDER

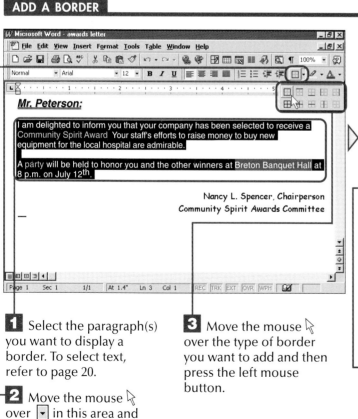

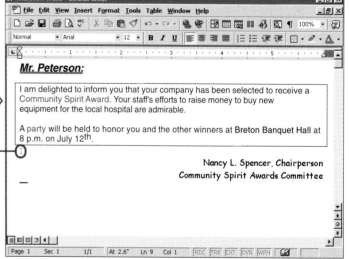

1 Select the paragraph(s) you want to display a border. To select text, refer to page 20.

2 Move the mouse ⏴ over ▾ in this area and then press the left mouse button.

3 Move the mouse ⏴ over the type of border you want to add and then press the left mouse button.

■ The border you selected appears.

■ To deselect text, move the mouse ⏉ outside the selected area and then press the left mouse button.

REMOVE A BORDER

■ Select the paragraph(s) you no longer want to display a border. Then perform steps 2 and 3, selecting ▦ in step 3.

INSERT A SYMBOL

You can insert symbols that do not appear on your keyboard into your document.

INSERT A SYMBOL

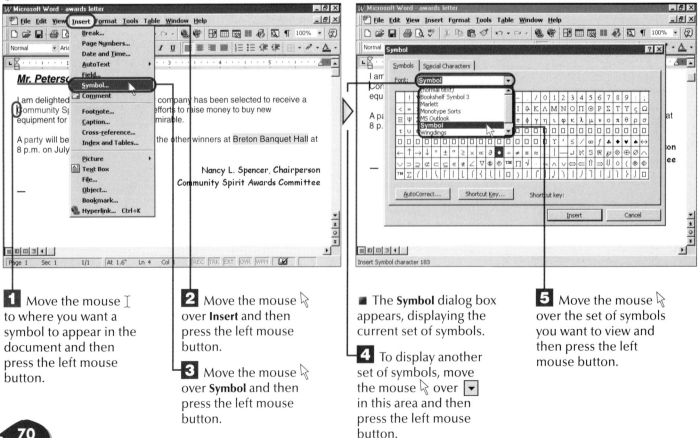

1 Move the mouse I to where you want a symbol to appear in the document and then press the left mouse button.

2 Move the mouse ⬚ over **Insert** and then press the left mouse button.

3 Move the mouse ⬚ over **Symbol** and then press the left mouse button.

■ The **Symbol** dialog box appears, displaying the current set of symbols.

4 To display another set of symbols, move the mouse ⬚ over ▼ in this area and then press the left mouse button.

5 Move the mouse ⬚ over the set of symbols you want to view and then press the left mouse button.

How can I quickly enter symbols into my document?

If you type one of the following sets of characters, Word will instantly replace the characters with a symbol. This lets you quickly enter symbols that are not available on your keyboard.

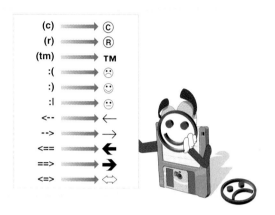

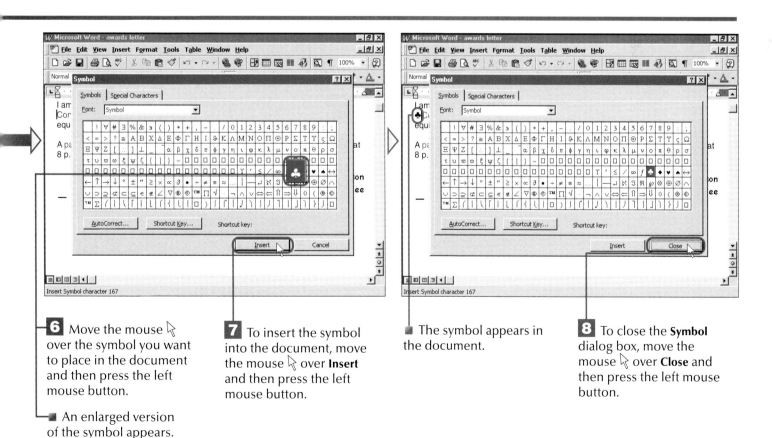

■ **6** Move the mouse ⬚ over the symbol you want to place in the document and then press the left mouse button.

■ An enlarged version of the symbol appears.

7 To insert the symbol into the document, move the mouse ⬚ over **Insert** and then press the left mouse button.

■ The symbol appears in the document.

8 To close the **Symbol** dialog box, move the mouse ⬚ over **Close** and then press the left mouse button.

You can separate items in a list by beginning each item with a bullet or number.

ADD BULLETS OR NUMBERS

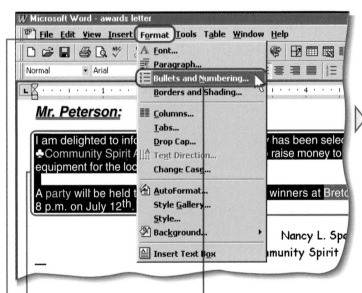

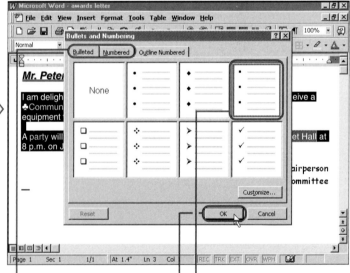

1 Select the text you want to display bullets or numbers. To select text, refer to page 20.

2 Move the mouse ⬚ over **Format** and then press the left mouse button.

3 Move the mouse ⬚ over **Bullets and Numbering** and then press the left mouse button.

■ The **Bullets and Numbering** dialog box appears.

4 Move the mouse ⬚ over the tab for the type of list you want to create and then press the left mouse button.

5 Move the mouse ⬚ over the style you want to use and then press the left mouse button.

6 Move the mouse ⬚ over **OK** and then press the left mouse button.

Should I use bullets or numbers in my list?

Bullets are useful for items in no particular order, such as a shopping list.

Numbers are useful for items in a specific order, such as a recipe.

ADD BULLETS OR NUMBERS AS YOU TYPE

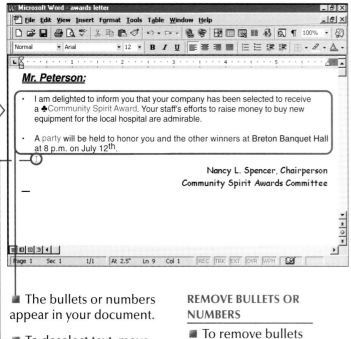

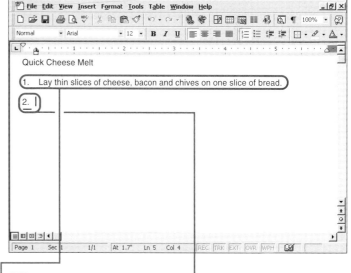

■ The bullets or numbers appear in your document.

■ To deselect text, move the mouse I outside the selected area and then press the left mouse button.

REMOVE BULLETS OR NUMBERS

■ To remove bullets or numbers from the document, perform steps 1 to 6, selecting **None** in step 5.

1 Move the mouse I to where you want the first number or bullet to appear and then press the left mouse button.

2 Type **1.** or * followed by a space. Then type the first item in the list.

3 Press **Enter** on your keyboard and Word automatically starts the next item with a number or bullet.

■ To end the numbered or bulleted list, press **Enter** on your keyboard twice.

CHANGE LINE SPACING

You can change the amount of space between the lines of text in your document to make your document easier to review and edit.

Single
There is a 10th anniversary High School Reunion on August 8, 9 and 10 at Woodblock High School. We all hope to see you there. Contact Susan Hughes for more information.

1.5 Lines
There is a 10th anniversary High School Reunion on August 8, 9 and 10 at Woodblock High School. We all hope to see you there. Contact Susan Hughes for more information.

Double
There is a 10th anniversary High School Reunion on August 8, 9 and 10 at Woodblock High School. We all hope to see you there. Contact Susan Hughes for more information.

CHANGE LINE SPACING

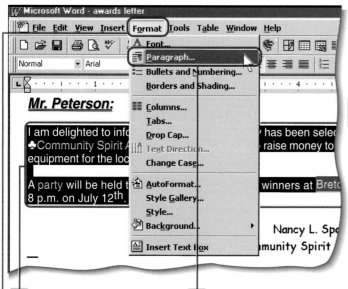

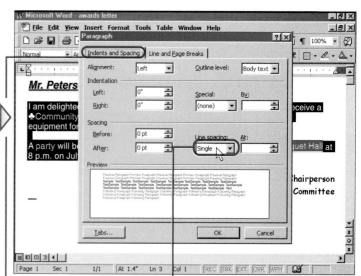

1 Select the paragraph(s) you want to change to a new line spacing. To select text, refer to page 20.

2 Move the mouse over **Format** and then press the left mouse button.

3 Move the mouse over **Paragraph** and then press the left mouse button.

■ The **Paragraph** dialog box appears.

4 Move the mouse over the **Indents and Spacing** tab and then press the left mouse button.

■ This area displays the line spacing for the paragraph(s) you selected.

5 To display a list of the available line spacing options, move the mouse over this area and then press the left mouse button.

Does Word ever automatically adjust the line spacing?

Word automatically increases the spacing of lines that contain large characters.

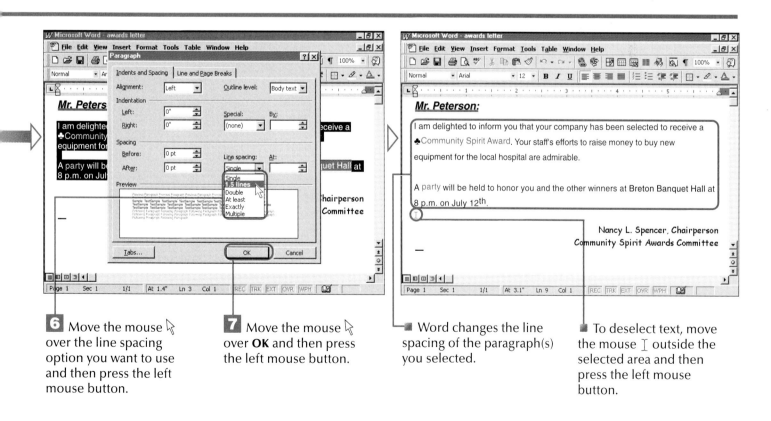

6 Move the mouse ⬚ over the line spacing option you want to use and then press the left mouse button.

7 Move the mouse ⬚ over **OK** and then press the left mouse button.

◼ Word changes the line spacing of the paragraph(s) you selected.

◼ To deselect text, move the mouse ⌶ outside the selected area and then press the left mouse button.

You can use the Indent feature to set off paragraphs in your document.

→| The spacious grounds of Foster City Zoo were established in 1960 on 350 acres of forest and farmland located five miles west of Foster City, NY.

Indent first line

The spacious grounds of Foster City Zoo were
→ established in 1960 on 350 acres of forest
and farmland located five miles west of
Foster City, NY.

Indent all but first line

→ The spacious grounds of Foster City Zoo
were established in 1960 on 350 acres of
forest and farmland located five miles
west of Foster City, NY.

Indent all lines

The spacious grounds of Foster City Zoo
were established in 1960 on 350 acres of
forest and farmland located five miles ←
west of Foster City, NY.

Indent right edge of all lines

INDENT PARAGRAPHS

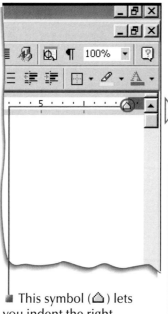

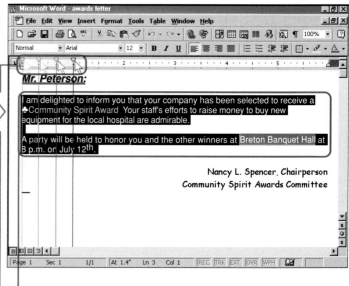

▪ These symbols let you indent the left edge of a paragraph.

▽ Indent first line

△ Indent all but first line

☐ Indent all lines

▪ This symbol (△) lets you indent the right edge of all lines.

Note: If the ruler is not displayed on the screen, refer to page 39 to display the ruler.

1 Select the paragraph(s) you want to indent. To select text, refer to page 20.

2 Move the mouse ⇖ over an indent symbol and then press and hold down the left mouse button as you move the symbol to a new position.

▪ A line shows the new indent position.

What is a hanging indent?

A hanging indent moves all but the first line of a paragraph to the right. Hanging indents are useful when you are creating a résumé, glossary or bibliography.

QUICKLY INDENT ALL LINES IN A PARAGRAPH

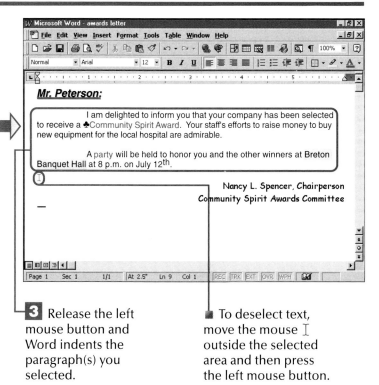

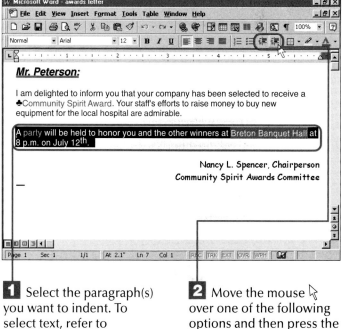

3 Release the left mouse button and Word indents the paragraph(s) you selected.

■ To deselect text, move the mouse I outside the selected area and then press the left mouse button.

1 Select the paragraph(s) you want to indent. To select text, refer to page 20.

2 Move the mouse ⌖ over one of the following options and then press the left mouse button.

🔲 Move paragraph to the left

🔲 Move paragraph to the right

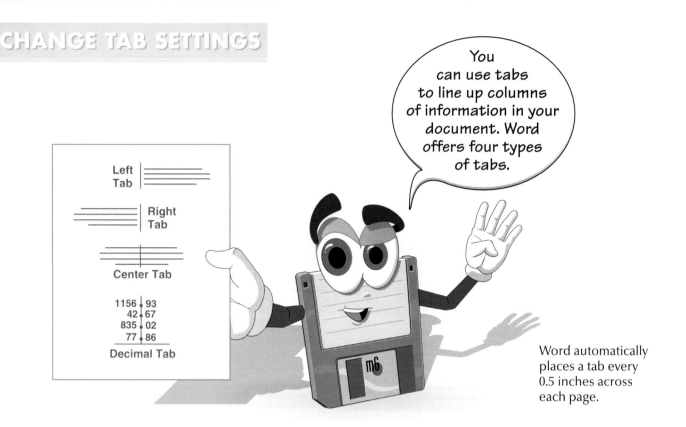

You can use tabs to line up columns of information in your document. Word offers four types of tabs.

Left Tab

Right Tab

Center Tab

1156 93
42 67
835 02
77 86
Decimal Tab

Word automatically places a tab every 0.5 inches across each page.

ADD A TAB

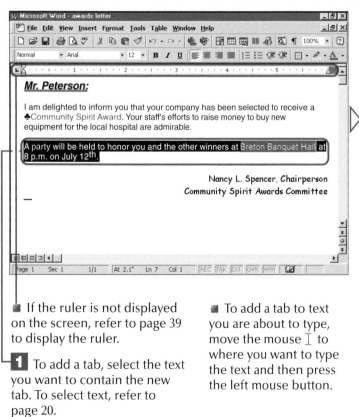

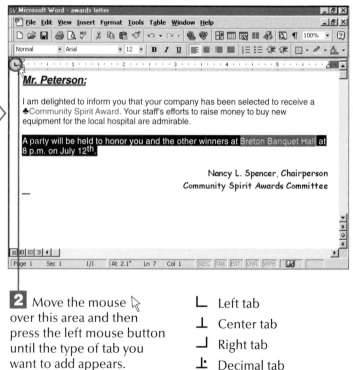

■ If the ruler is not displayed on the screen, refer to page 39 to display the ruler.

1 To add a tab, select the text you want to contain the new tab. To select text, refer to page 20.

■ To add a tab to text you are about to type, move the mouse I to where you want to type the text and then press the left mouse button.

2 Move the mouse ⌖ over this area and then press the left mouse button until the type of tab you want to add appears.

∟ Left tab

⊥ Center tab

⅃ Right tab

⊥ Decimal tab

What happens if I use spaces instead of tabs to line up columns of text?

Your document may not print correctly if you use spaces instead of tabs to line up columns of text.

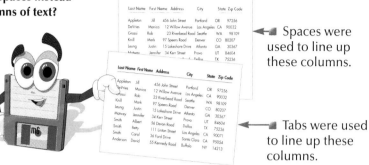

◄ Spaces were used to line up these columns.

◄ Tabs were used to line up these columns.

USING TABS

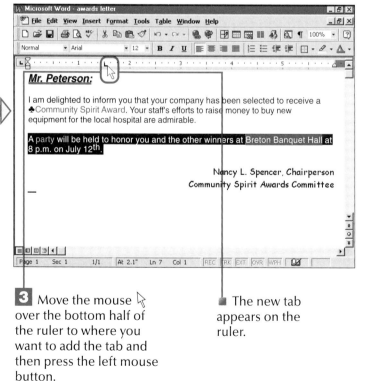

3 Move the mouse over the bottom half of the ruler to where you want to add the tab and then press the left mouse button.

■ The new tab appears on the ruler.

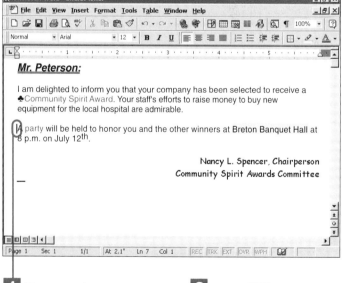

1 To use a tab, move the mouse I to the beginning of the line you want to move across and then press the left mouse button.

2 Press **Tab** on your keyboard and the insertion point moves to the first tab.

CHANGE TAB SETTINGS

You can easily move a tab to a different position on the ruler.

MOVE A TAB

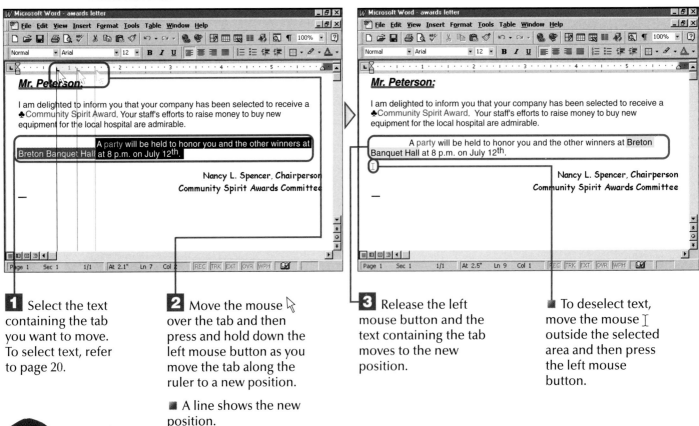

1 Select the text containing the tab you want to move. To select text, refer to page 20.

2 Move the mouse over the tab and then press and hold down the left mouse button as you move the tab along the ruler to a new position.

■ A line shows the new position.

3 Release the left mouse button and the text containing the tab moves to the new position.

■ To deselect text, move the mouse I outside the selected area and then press the left mouse button.

When you no longer need a tab, you can remove it from the ruler.

REMOVE A TAB

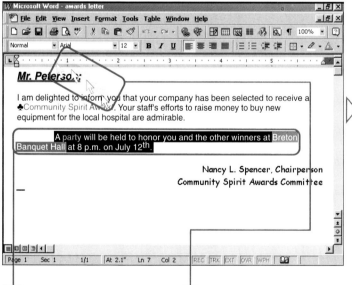

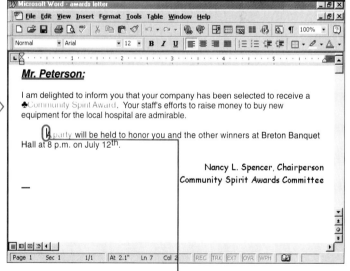

1 Select the text containing the tab you want to remove. To select text, refer to page 20.

2 Move the mouse over the tab and then press and hold down the left mouse button as you move the tab downward off the ruler.

3 Release the left mouse button and the tab disappears from the ruler.

To move text back to the left margin, move the mouse to the left of the first character in the paragraph(s) and then press the left mouse button. Then press **+Backspace** on your keyboard.

81

You can have Word number the pages in your document.

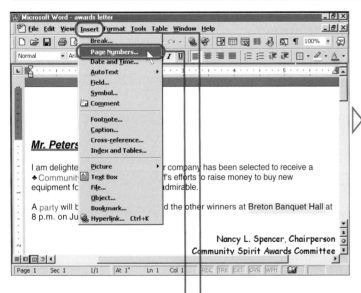

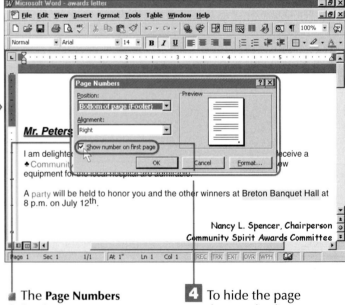

1 Display the document in the Page Layout view. To change the view, refer to page 36.

Note: Word does not display page numbers in the Normal view.

2 Move the mouse over **Insert** and then press the left mouse button.

3 Move the mouse over **Page Numbers** and then press the left mouse button.

■ The **Page Numbers** dialog box appears.

4 To hide the page number on the first page of the document, move the mouse over this option and then press the left mouse button (☑ changes to ☐).

Note: This option is useful if the first page of the document is a title page.

Will Word adjust the page numbers if I change my document?

If you add, remove or rearrange text in your document, Word will automatically adjust the page numbers for you.

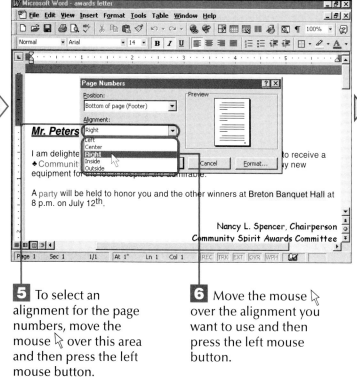

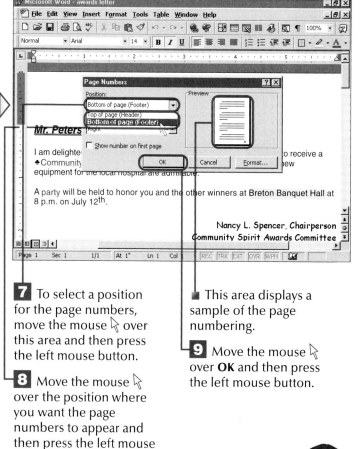

5 To select an alignment for the page numbers, move the mouse over this area and then press the left mouse button.

6 Move the mouse over the alignment you want to use and then press the left mouse button.

7 To select a position for the page numbers, move the mouse over this area and then press the left mouse button.

8 Move the mouse over the position where you want the page numbers to appear and then press the left mouse button.

■ This area displays a sample of the page numbering.

9 Move the mouse over **OK** and then press the left mouse button.

ADD FOOTNOTES

A footnote appears at the bottom of a page to provide additional information about text in your document.

Word ensures that the footnote text always appears on the same page as the footnote number.

ADD FOOTNOTES

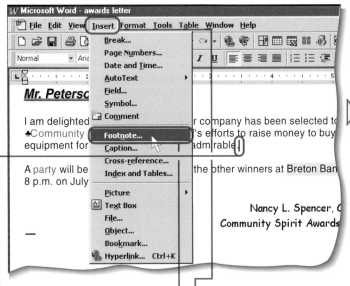

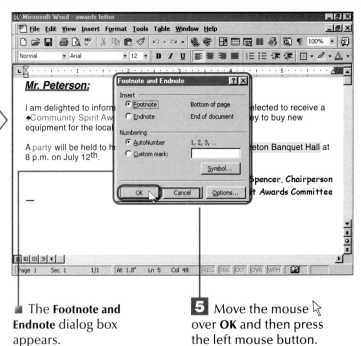

1 Display the document in the Normal view. To change the view, refer to page 36.

2 Move the mouse I to where you want the number of the footnote to appear and then press the left mouse button.

3 Move the mouse ⬦ over **Insert** and then press the left mouse button.

4 Move the mouse ⬦ over **Footnote** and then press the left mouse button.

■ The **Footnote and Endnote** dialog box appears.

5 Move the mouse ⬦ over **OK** and then press the left mouse button.

Will Word adjust the footnote numbers if I add or remove footnotes?

If you add or remove footnotes in your document, Word will automatically renumber the footnotes for you.

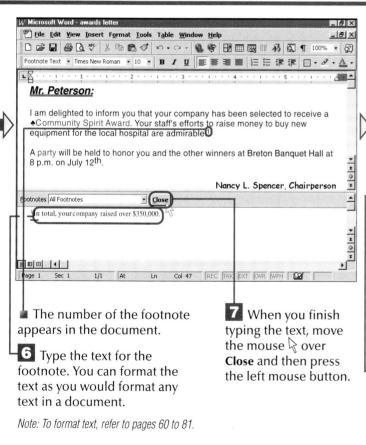

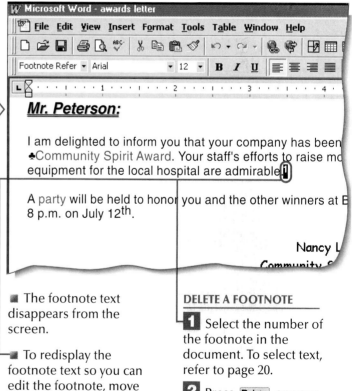

■ The number of the footnote appears in the document.

6 Type the text for the footnote. You can format the text as you would format any text in a document.

Note: To format text, refer to pages 60 to 81.

7 When you finish typing the text, move the mouse ⟦ over **Close** and then press the left mouse button.

■ The footnote text disappears from the screen.

■ To redisplay the footnote text so you can edit the footnote, move the mouse I over the number of the footnote and then quickly press the left mouse button twice.

DELETE A FOOTNOTE

1 Select the number of the footnote in the document. To select text, refer to page 20.

2 Press Delete on your keyboard.

ADD A HEADER AND FOOTER

You can add a header and footer to each page of your document.

A header appears at the top of each page.

A footer appears at the bottom of each page.

ADD A HEADER AND FOOTER

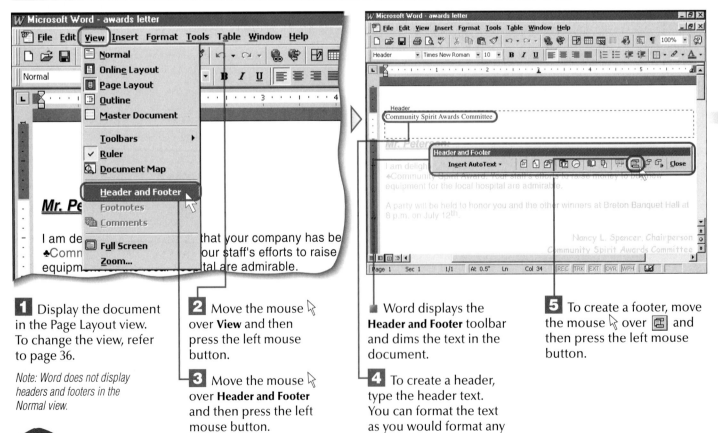

1 Display the document in the Page Layout view. To change the view, refer to page 36.

Note: Word does not display headers and footers in the Normal view.

2 Move the mouse ▷ over **View** and then press the left mouse button.

3 Move the mouse ▷ over **Header and Footer** and then press the left mouse button.

■ Word displays the **Header and Footer** toolbar and dims the text in the document.

4 To create a header, type the header text. You can format the text as you would format any text in a document.

5 To create a footer, move the mouse ▷ over 🗐 and then press the left mouse button.

What information can a header or footer contain?

A header or footer can contain information such as the company name, author's name, chapter title or date.

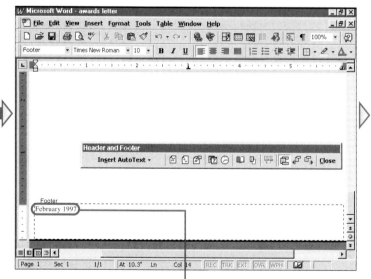

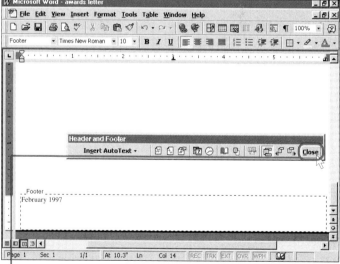

■ The **Footer** area appears.

Note: To return to the header area at any time, repeat step 5.

6 Type the footer text. You can format the text as you would format any text in a document.

Note: To format text, refer to pages 60 to 81.

7 When you have finished creating the header and footer, move the mouse over **Close** and then press the left mouse button.

EDIT A HEADER OR FOOTER

1 To edit a header or footer, repeat steps 1 to 7.

INSERT A PAGE BREAK

If you want to start a new page at a specific place in your document, you can insert a page break. A page break shows where one page ends and another begins.

INSERT A PAGE BREAK

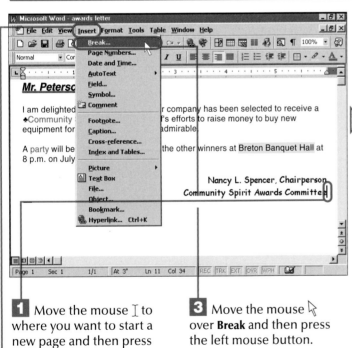

1 Move the mouse I to where you want to start a new page and then press the left mouse button.

2 Move the mouse ⬧ over **Insert** and then press the left mouse button.

3 Move the mouse ⬧ over **Break** and then press the left mouse button.

■ The **Break** dialog box appears.

4 Move the mouse ⬧ over **OK** and then press the left mouse button.

Will Word ever insert page breaks automatically?

When you fill a page with text, Word automatically starts a new page by inserting a page break for you.

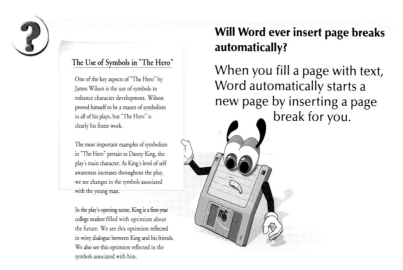

REMOVE A PAGE BREAK

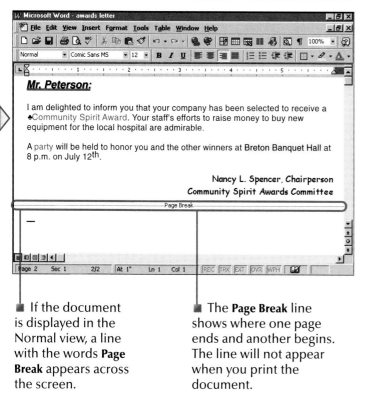

■ If the document is displayed in the Normal view, a line with the words **Page Break** appears across the screen.

■ The **Page Break** line shows where one page ends and another begins. The line will not appear when you print the document.

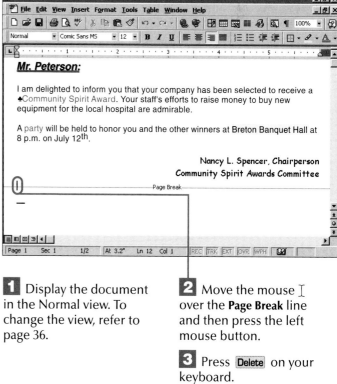

1 Display the document in the Normal view. To change the view, refer to page 36.

2 Move the mouse I over the **Page Break** line and then press the left mouse button.

3 Press Delete on your keyboard.

INSERT A SECTION BREAK

You can divide your document into sections so you can format each section separately.

You need to divide a document into sections to change margins, create columns or vertically center text for only part of your document.

INSERT A SECTION BREAK

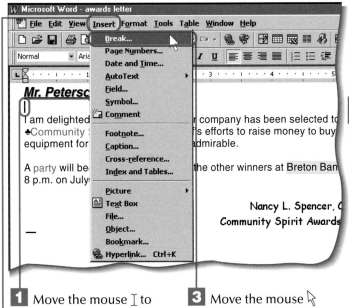

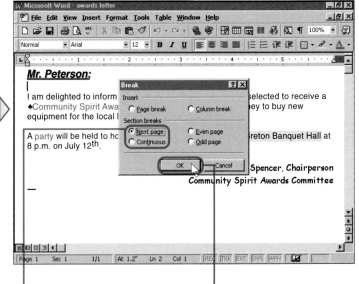

1 Move the mouse I to where you want to start a new section and then press the left mouse button.

2 Move the mouse ⩗ over **Insert** and then press the left mouse button.

3 Move the mouse ⩗ over **Break** and then press the left mouse button.

■ The **Break** dialog box appears.

4 Move the mouse ⩗ over one of the following options and then press the left mouse button (○ changes to ◉).

Next page - Creates a new section on a new page.

Continuous - Creates a new section on the current page.

5 Move the mouse ⩗ over **OK** and then press the left mouse button.

If I remove a section break will my document change?

When you remove a section break, the text above the break assumes the appearance of the following section.

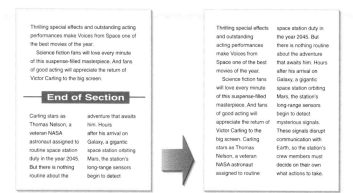

REMOVE A SECTION BREAK

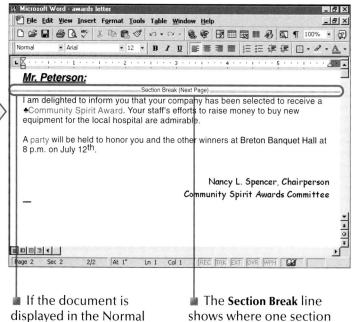

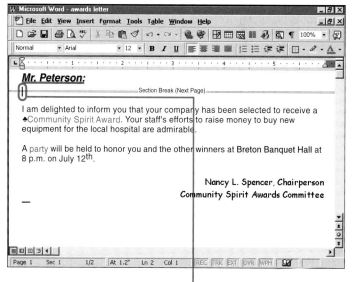

■ If the document is displayed in the Normal view, a double line with the words **Section Break** appears across the screen.

■ The **Section Break** line shows where one section ends and another begins. The line will not appear when you print the document.

1 Display the document in the Normal view. To change the view, refer to page 36.

2 Move the mouse I over the **Section Break** line and then press the left mouse button.

3 Press Delete on your keyboard.

You can vertically center text on each page of a document. This is useful for creating title pages or short memos.

CENTER TEXT ON A PAGE

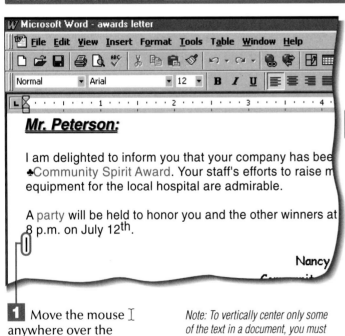

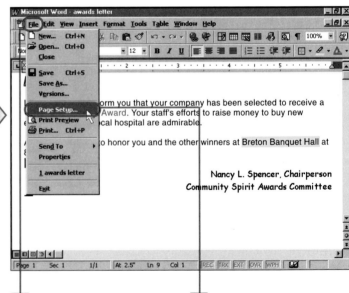

1 Move the mouse I anywhere over the document or section you want to vertically center and then press the left mouse button.

Note: To vertically center only some of the text in a document, you must divide the document into sections. To divide a document into sections, refer to page 90.

2 Move the mouse ⍅ over **File** and then press the left mouse button.

3 Move the mouse ⍅ over **Page Setup** and then press the left mouse button.

■ The **Page Setup** dialog box appears.

How can I see what text centered on a page will look like when printed?

You can use the Print Preview feature to display a page on your screen. This lets you see how the page will look when printed.

Note: For information on using Print Preview, refer to page 26.

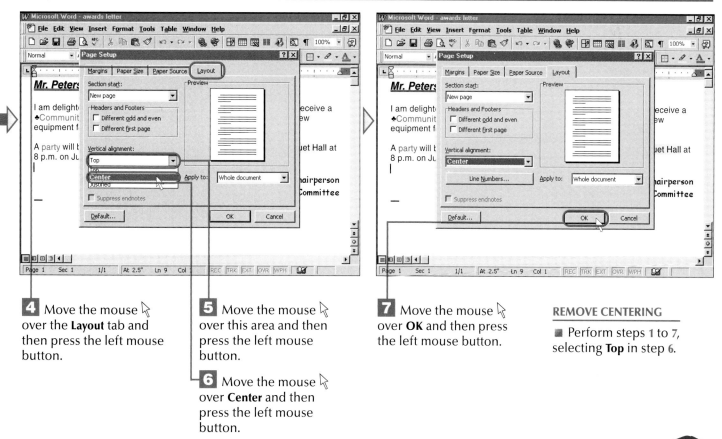

4 Move the mouse over the **Layout** tab and then press the left mouse button.

5 Move the mouse over this area and then press the left mouse button.

6 Move the mouse over **Center** and then press the left mouse button.

7 Move the mouse over **OK** and then press the left mouse button.

REMOVE CENTERING

■ Perform steps **1** to **7**, selecting **Top** in step **6**.

A margin is the amount of space between text and an *edge* of your paper. You can easily change the margins to suit your document.

Changing margins lets you accommodate letterhead and other specialty paper.

CHANGE MARGINS

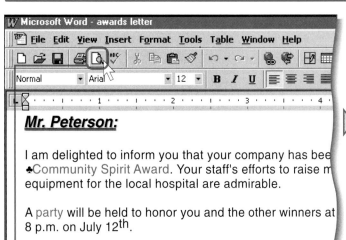

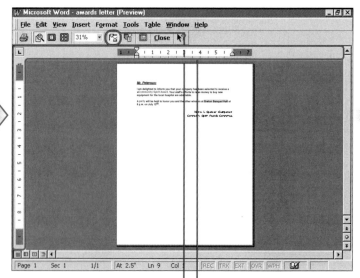

1 To change the margins for the entire document, move the mouse ⬚ over 🔍 and then press the left mouse button.

Note: To change the margins for only part of the document, refer to the top of page 95.

■ The document appears in the Print Preview window. For more information on using Print Preview, refer to page 26.

■ This area displays the ruler.

■ If the ruler is not displayed, move the mouse ⬚ over 🔲 and then press the left mouse button.

How can I change the margins for part of my document?

If you want to change the left and right margins for part of your document, change the indentation of paragraphs. To indent paragraphs, refer to page 76.

If you want to change the top and bottom margins for a few pages in your document, you must divide the document into sections. To divide a document into sections, refer to page 90.

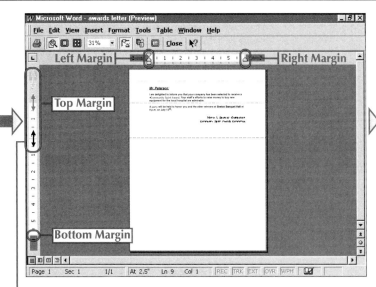

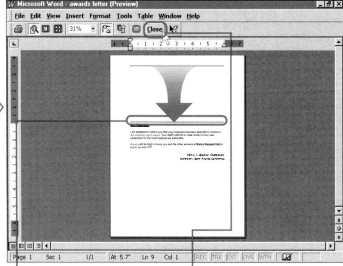

2 Move the mouse ↕ over the margin you want to move (↕ changes to ↕ or ↔) and then press and hold down the left mouse button as you move the margin to a new location.

■ A line shows the new location.

Note: To view the exact measurement of a margin from the edge of the page, press and hold down **Alt** *on your keyboard as you perform step* **2**.

3 Release the left mouse button and the margin moves to the new location.

4 Repeat steps **2** and **3** for each margin you want to move.

5 To close the Print Preview window, move the mouse ↕ over **Close** and then press the left mouse button.

CREATE NEWSPAPER COLUMNS

You can display your text in columns like those found in a newspaper. This is useful for creating documents such as newsletters and brochures.

CREATE NEWSPAPER COLUMNS

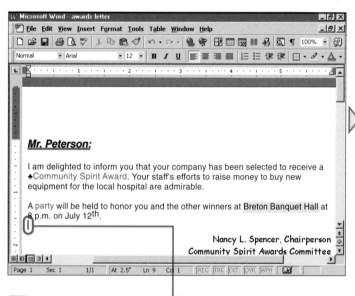

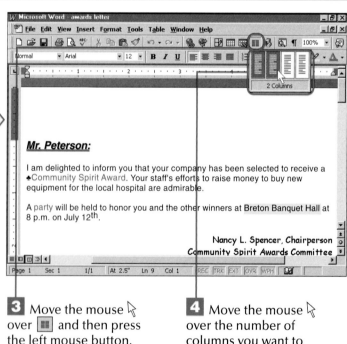

1 Display the document in the Page Layout view. To change the view, refer to page 36.

Note: Word does not display newspaper columns side-by-side in the Normal view.

2 Move the mouse I anywhere over the document or section you want to display in newspaper columns and then press the left mouse button.

Note: To create newspaper columns for only part of the document, you must divide the document into sections. To divide a document into sections, refer to page 90.

3 Move the mouse over ▦ and then press the left mouse button.

4 Move the mouse over the number of columns you want to display and then press the left mouse button.

Why is there text in only one of my columns?

Word fills one column with text before starting a new column.

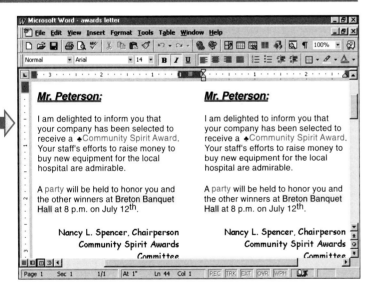

■ The text in the document appears in newspaper columns.

Note: In this example, the existing text was copied to show the newspaper columns. To copy text, refer to page 50.

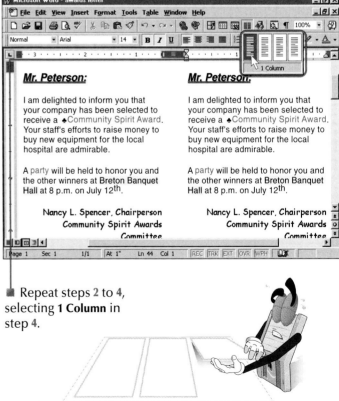

■ Repeat steps **2** to **4**, selecting **1 Column** in step **4**.

You can create a table to neatly display information in your document.

Word lets you draw a table on the screen as you would draw a table with a pen and paper.

CREATE A TABLE

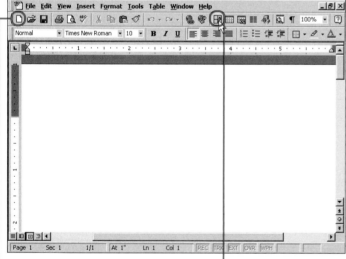

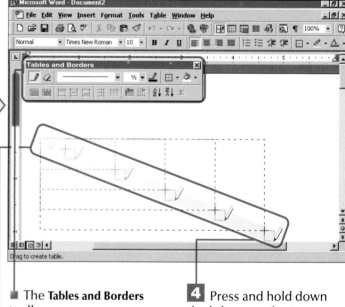

■ In this example, a new document was created. To create a new document, move the mouse ⬚ over ⬚ and then press the left mouse button.

1 Display the document in the Page Layout view. To change the view, refer to page 36.

2 To create a table, move the mouse ⬚ over ⬚ and then press the left mouse button.

■ The **Tables and Borders** toolbar appears.

3 Move the mouse ⬚ to where you want the top left corner of the table to appear.

4 Press and hold down the left mouse button as you move the mouse ⬚ until the outline of the table displays the size you want. Then release the mouse button.

98

Can I move a toolbar out of the way?

If a toolbar is in the way, you can easily move the toolbar to a new location.

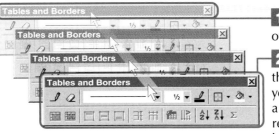

1 Move the mouse ⬚ over the title bar.

2 Press and hold down the left mouse button as you move the toolbar to a new location. Then release the mouse button.

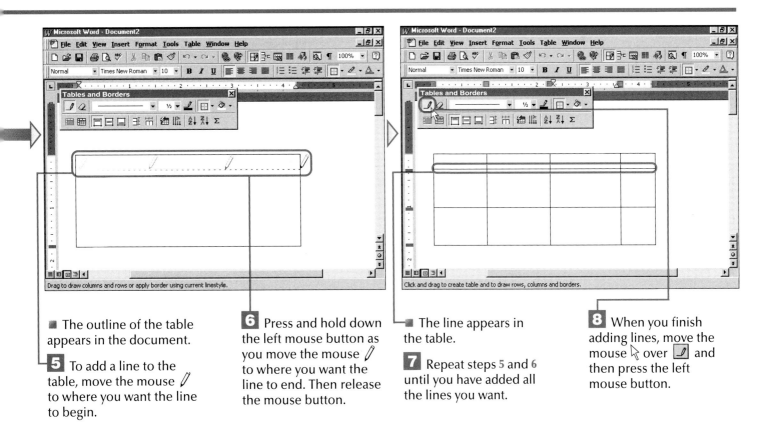

■ The outline of the table appears in the document.

5 To add a line to the table, move the mouse ⬚ to where you want the line to begin.

6 Press and hold down the left mouse button as you move the mouse ⬚ to where you want the line to end. Then release the mouse button.

■ The line appears in the table.

7 Repeat steps 5 and 6 until you have added all the lines you want.

8 When you finish adding lines, move the mouse ⬚ over ⬚ and then press the left mouse button.

CHANGE ROW HEIGHT OR COLUMN WIDTH

After you have created a table, you can change the height of rows or the width of columns.

CHANGE ROW HEIGHT

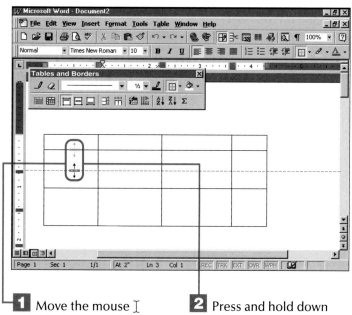

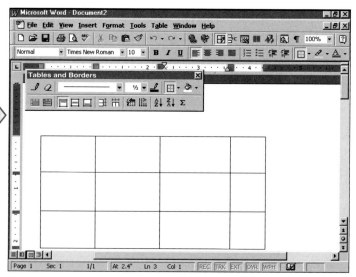

1 Move the mouse I over the bottom edge of the row you want to change (I changes to ÷).

2 Press and hold down the left mouse button as you move the row edge to a new position.

■ A line shows the new position.

3 Release the left mouse button and the row displays the new height.

What are rows, columns and cells?

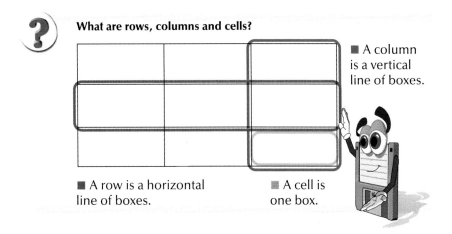

■ A column is a vertical line of boxes.

■ A row is a horizontal line of boxes.

■ A cell is one box.

CHANGE COLUMN WIDTH

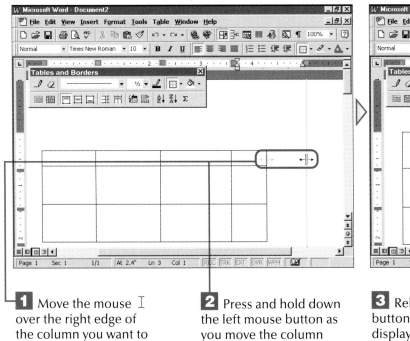

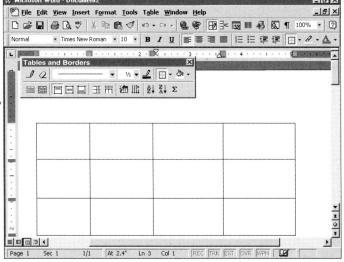

1 Move the mouse I over the right edge of the column you want to change (I changes to ↔).

2 Press and hold down the left mouse button as you move the column edge to a new position.

■ A line shows the new position.

3 Release the mouse button and the column displays the new width.

You can erase lines you do not need in your table.

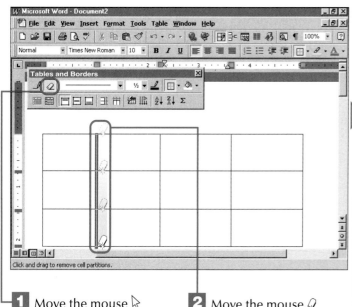

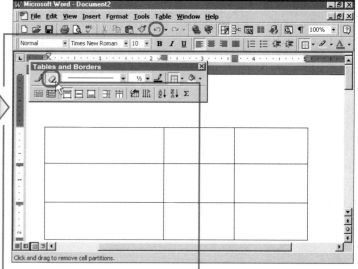

1 Move the mouse ⌖ over 🖉 and then press the left mouse button.

*Note: If the **Tables and Borders** toolbar is not displayed, move the mouse ⌖ over 🖼 and then press the left mouse button to display the toolbar.*

2 Move the mouse 🖉 over the line you want to erase and then press and hold down the left mouse button as you move the mouse 🖉 along the line.

3 Release the left mouse button and the line disappears.

■ To immediately return the line to the table, move the mouse ⌖ over ↶ and then press the left mouse button.

4 Repeat steps 2 and 3 for all the lines you want to erase.

5 When you finish erasing lines, move the mouse ⌖ over 🖉 and then press the left mouse button.

ENTER TEXT

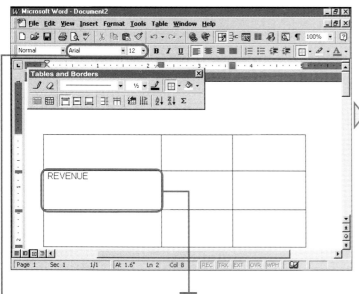

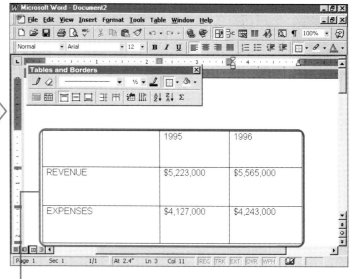

■ In this example, the design and size of text were changed to make the text easier to read. To change the design and size of text, refer to pages 62 and 63.

1 Move the mouse I over the cell where you want to type text and then press the left mouse button. Then type the text.

Note: To quickly move through the cells in a table, press ← , ↑ , ↓ *or* → *on your keyboard.*

2 Repeat step 1 until you have typed all the text.

■ You can edit and format the text in a table as you would edit and format any text in a document.

You can add a row or column to your table if you want to insert additional information.

January	February	Total Boxes Sold
9000	8000	17000
7000	700	14000
8500		10000
2050		11050
7800		16800
4500		13550

ADD A ROW

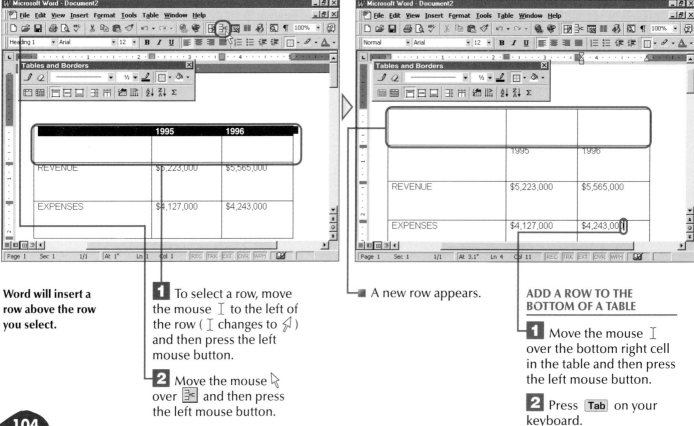

Word will insert a row above the row you select.

1 To select a row, move the mouse I to the left of the row (I changes to ⇗) and then press the left mouse button.

2 Move the mouse ⇗ over ⌹ and then press the left mouse button.

■ A new row appears.

ADD A ROW TO THE BOTTOM OF A TABLE

1 Move the mouse I over the bottom right cell in the table and then press the left mouse button.

2 Press **Tab** on your keyboard.

Is there another way to add a row or column to a table?

You can add a row or column by drawing a line for the new row or column.

1 Move the mouse over on the **Tables and Borders** toolbar and then press the left mouse button.

2 To draw the line in your table, perform steps **5** and **6** on page 99.

ADD A COLUMN

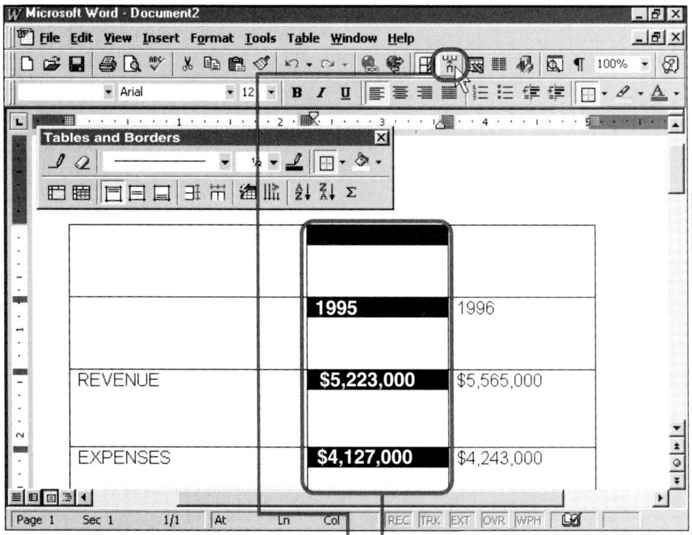

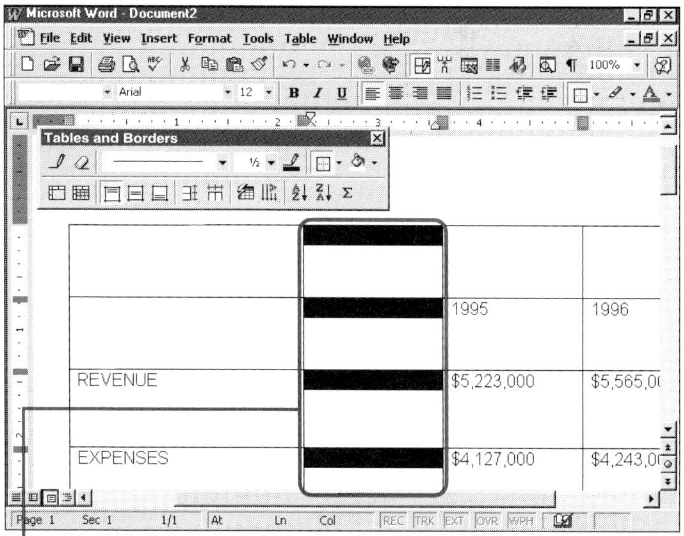

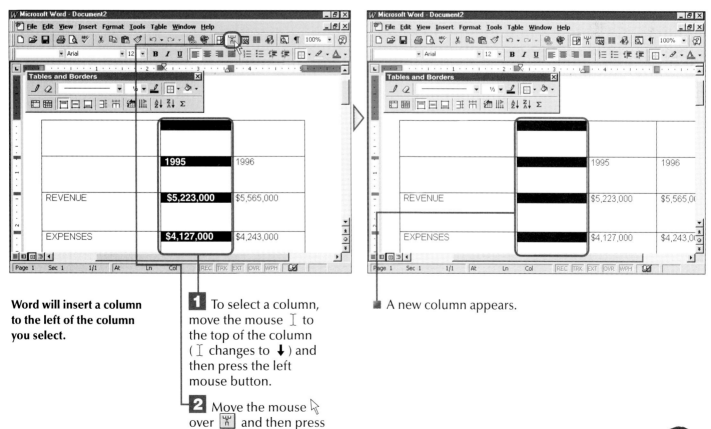

Word will insert a column to the left of the column you select.

1 To select a column, move the mouse to the top of the column (changes to) and then press the left mouse button.

2 Move the mouse over and then press the left mouse button.

■ A new column appears.

DELETE A ROW OR COLUMN

You can delete a row or column you no longer need.

DELETE A ROW OR COLUMN

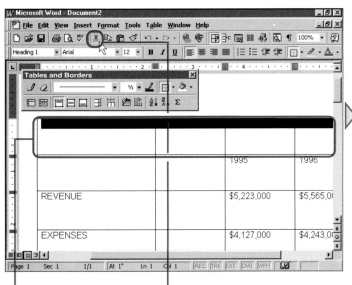

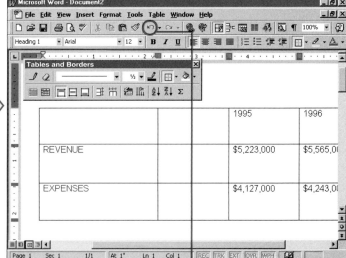

1 To select the row you want to delete, move the mouse I to the left of the row (I changes to ⇗) and then press the left mouse button.

■ To select the column you want to delete, move the mouse I to the top of the column (I changes to ↓) and then press the left mouse button.

2 Move the mouse ⇗ over 🔏 and then press the left mouse button.

■ The row or column disappears.

■ To immediately return the row or column to the table, move the mouse ⇗ over 🔄 and then press the left mouse button.

106

DELETE A TABLE

You can quickly remove an entire table from your document.

DELETE A TABLE

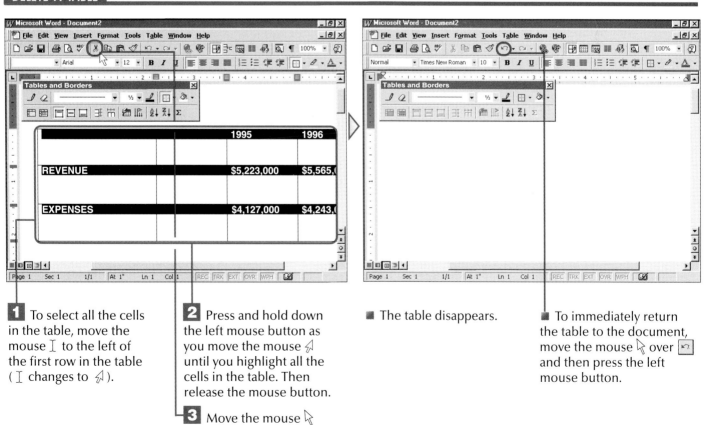

1 To select all the cells in the table, move the mouse I to the left of the first row in the table (I changes to ⇗).

2 Press and hold down the left mouse button as you move the mouse ⇗ until you highlight all the cells in the table. Then release the mouse button.

3 Move the mouse ⇗ over ✄ and then press the left mouse button.

■ The table disappears.

■ To immediately return the table to the document, move the mouse ⇗ over ↶ and then press the left mouse button.

FORMAT A TABLE

Word offers many ready-to-use designs that you can choose from to give your table a new appearance.

FORMAT A TABLE

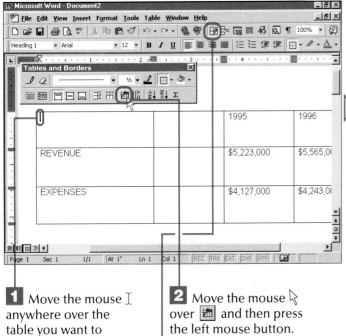

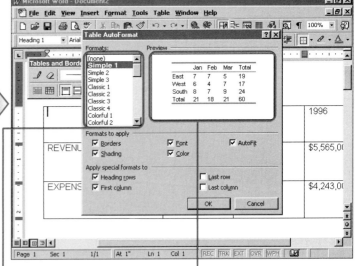

1 Move the mouse I anywhere over the table you want to change and then press the left mouse button.

2 Move the mouse ⇖ over 🔲 and then press the left mouse button.

■ If the **Tables and Borders** toolbar is not displayed, move the mouse ⇖ over 🔲 and then press the left mouse button to display the toolbar.

■ The **Table AutoFormat** dialog box appears.

■ This area displays a list of the available table designs.

■ This area displays a sample of the highlighted table design.

3 Press ↓ or ↑ on your keyboard until a design you like appears.

108

What are some table designs offered by Word?

	Jan	Feb	Mar	Total
East	7	7	5	19
West	6	4	7	17
South	8	7	9	24
Total	21	18	21	60

Colorful 1

	Jan	Feb	Mar	Total
East	7	7	5	19
West	6	4	7	17
South	8	7	9	24
Total	21	18	21	60

Grid 8

	Jan	Feb	Mar	Total
East	7	7	5	19
West	6	4	7	17
South	8	7	9	24
Total	21	18	21	60

Classic 3

	Jan	Feb	Mar	Total
East	7	7	5	19
West	6	4	7	17
South	8	7	9	24
Total	21	18	21	60

Columns 5

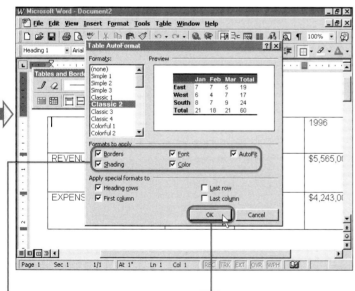

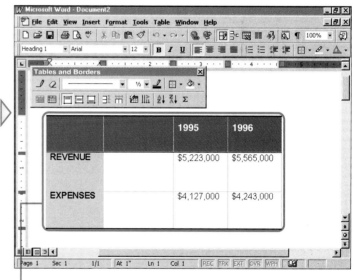

■ A check mark (☑) beside an option tells you that Word will apply the option to the table.

4 To add or remove a check mark (☑) for an option, move the mouse ⬚ over the check box beside the option and then press the left mouse button.

5 To apply the design to the table, move the mouse ⬚ over **OK** and then press the left mouse button.

■ The table displays the design you selected.

REMOVE AUTOFORMAT

■ Perform steps 1 to 3, selecting **Grid 1** in step 3. Then press **Enter** on your keyboard.

Microsoft Excel is a spreadsheet program that lets you organize, analyze and present data easily and efficiently.

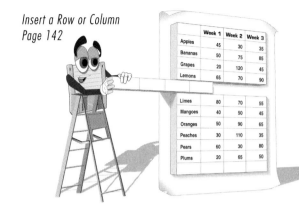

Insert a Row or Column
Page 142

Start Excel
Page 113

Introduction to Excel
Page 112

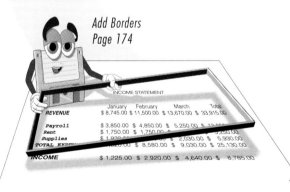

Add Borders
Page 174

Enter a Function
Page 150

EXCEL

Insert a Worksheet
Page 196

Copy Data
Page 140

Excel helps you organize, analyze and attractively present data.

Formulas and Functions

Excel provides powerful tools to calculate and analyze data in your worksheets.

Edit and Format Data

Excel lets you efficiently enter, edit and change the appearance of data in your worksheets.

Charts

Excel helps you create colorful charts using your worksheet data.

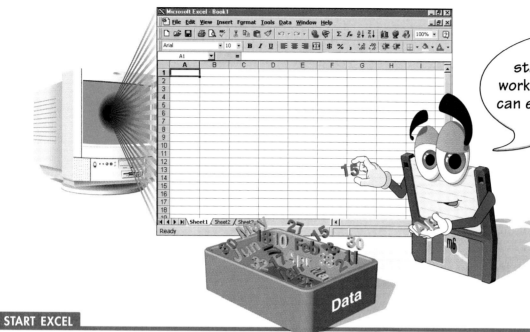

When you start Excel, a blank worksheet appears. You can enter data into this worksheet.

START EXCEL

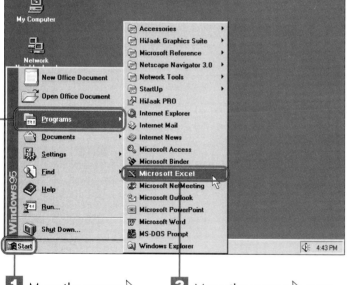

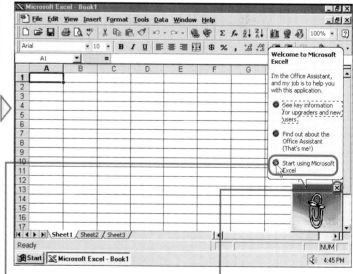

1 Move the mouse ⯆ over **Start** and then press the left mouse button.

2 Move the mouse ⯆ over **Programs**.

3 Move the mouse ⯆ over **Microsoft Excel** and then press the left mouse button.

■ The Microsoft Excel window appears, displaying a blank worksheet.

■ If you are starting Excel for the first time, the Office Assistant welcome appears.

4 To start using Excel, move the mouse ⯆ over this option and then press the left mouse button.

■ To hide the Office Assistant, move the mouse ⯆ over **X** and then press the left mouse button.

Note: For more information on the Office Assistant, refer to page 12.

WORKSHEET BASICS

A worksheet consists of rows, columns and cells.

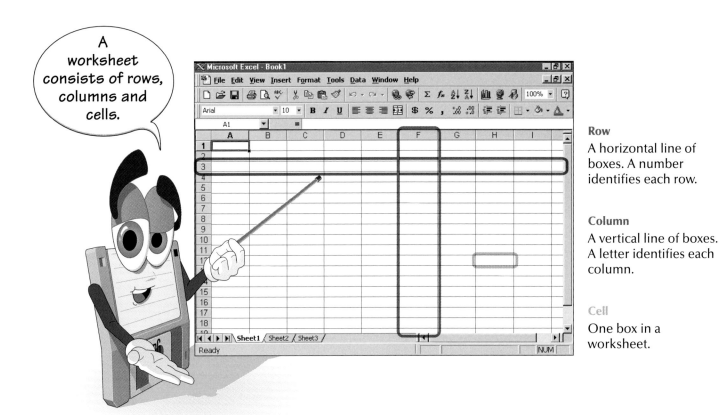

Row

A horizontal line of boxes. A number identifies each row.

Column

A vertical line of boxes. A letter identifies each column.

Cell

One box in a worksheet.

Cell Reference

A cell reference defines the location of each cell in a worksheet. A cell reference consists of a column letter followed by a row number (example: B3).

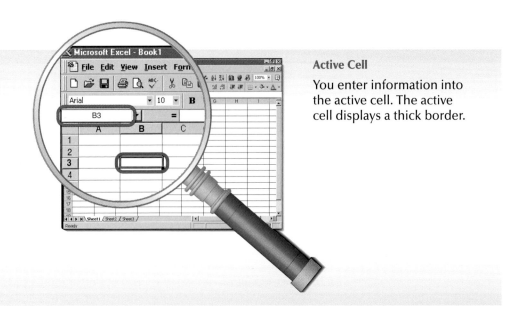

Active Cell

You enter information into the active cell. The active cell displays a thick border.

THE EXCEL SCREEN

The Excel screen displays several items to help you perform tasks efficiently.

Menu Bar

Contains commands that let you perform tasks.

Toolbars

Contain buttons to help you quickly select common commands.

Formula Bar

Displays the cell reference and contents of the active cell.

Status Bar

Displays information about the task you are performing.

Worksheet Tabs

An Excel file is called a workbook. Each workbook is divided into several worksheets. Excel displays a tab for each worksheet.

A workbook is similar to a three-ring binder that contains several sheets of paper.

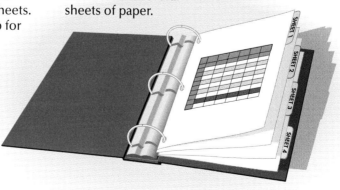

> You can enter data into your worksheet quickly and easily.

ENTER DATA

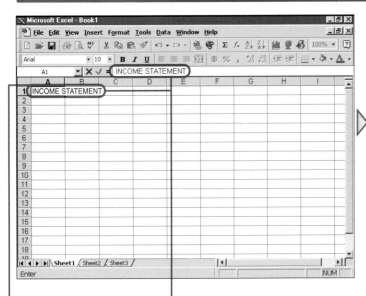

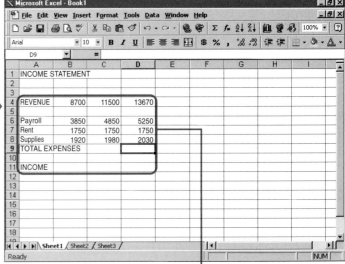

1 Move the mouse ⊕ over the cell where you want to enter data and then press the left mouse button. Then type the data.

■ If you make a typing mistake, press **◆Backspace** on your keyboard to remove the incorrect data and then type the correct data.

■ The data you type appears in the active cell and in the formula bar.

2 To enter the data and move down one cell, press **Enter** on your keyboard.

Note: To enter the data and move one cell in any direction, press ↑ , ↓ , ← *or* → *on your keyboard.*

3 Repeat steps 1 and 2 until you finish entering all the data.

How do I use the number keys on the right side of my keyboard?

When **NUM** appears at the bottom of your screen, you can use the number keys on the right side of your keyboard to enter numbers.

■ To turn on or off the display of **NUM** on your screen, press **Num Lock** on your keyboard.

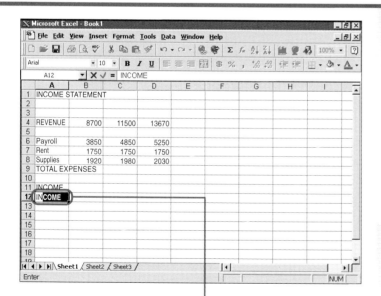

4	TOTAL EXPENSES	
5		
6		

4	TOTAL EX	227
5		
6		

Long Words

If text is too long to fit in a cell, the text will spill into the neighboring cell.

If the neighboring cell contains data, Excel will display as much of the text as the column width will allow. To change the column width, refer to page 166.

4	1.22E+10	
5		
6		

4	#####	
5		
6		

Long Numbers

If a number is too long to fit in a cell, Excel will display the number in scientific form or as number signs (#). To change the column width, refer to page 166.

AUTOCOMPLETE

If the first few letters you type match another cell in the column, Excel will complete the text for you.

■ To keep the text Excel provides, press **Enter** on your keyboard.

■ To enter different text, continue typing.

COMPLETE A SERIES

Excel can save you time by completing a text or number series for you.

COMPLETE A SERIES

Text Series

Mon	Tue	Wed	Thu
Product 1	Product 2	Product 3	Product 4
1st Quarter	2nd Quarter	3rd Quarter	4th Quarter

■ Excel completes a text series based on the text in the first cell.

Number Series

1995	1996	1997	1998
5	10	15	20
202	204	206	208

■ Excel completes a number series based on the numbers in the first two cells.

These numbers tell Excel how much to add to each number to complete the series.

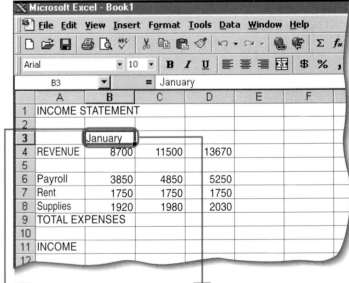

1 Enter the text or the first two numbers you want to start the series.

2 Select the cell(s) containing the text or numbers you entered. To select cells, refer to page 120.

Can I change the color of data in my worksheet?

You can easily change the color of data to make your worksheet more attractive. To do so, refer to page 176.

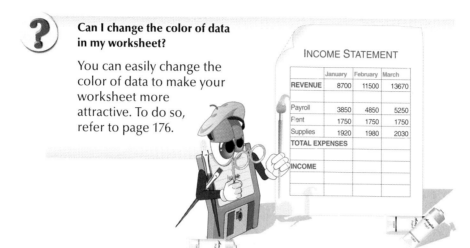

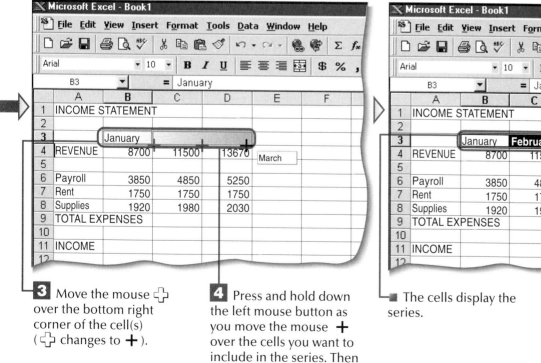

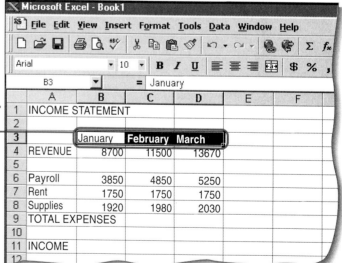

3 Move the mouse ⬚ over the bottom right corner of the cell(s) (⬚ changes to ✚).

4 Press and hold down the left mouse button as you move the mouse ✚ over the cells you want to include in the series. Then release the mouse button.

■ The cells display the series.

Note: You can also perform steps 1 to 4 to complete a series in a column.

SELECT CELLS

Before performing many tasks in Excel, you must select the cells you want to work with. Selected cells appear highlighted on your screen.

SELECT ONE CELL

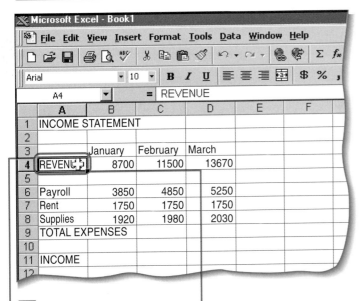

1 Move the mouse ✛ over the cell you want to select and then press the left mouse button.

■ The cell becomes the active cell and displays a thick border.

SELECT GROUPS OF CELLS

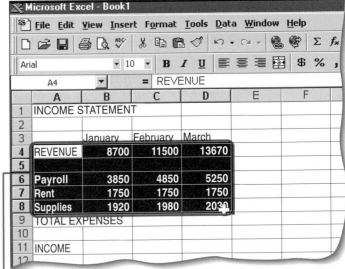

1 Move the mouse ✛ over the first cell you want to select.

2 Press and hold down the left mouse button as you move the mouse ✛ to highlight all the cells you want to select. Then release the mouse button.

■ To select multiple groups of cells, press and hold down **Ctrl** on your keyboard as you repeat steps **1** and **2** for each group.

■ To deselect cells, move the mouse ✛ over any cell and then press the left mouse button.

**How do I select all the cells
in my worksheet?**

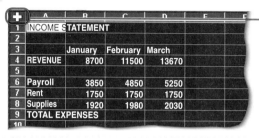

■ To select all the cells
in your worksheet, move
the mouse ⊹ over the
area where the row and
column headings meet
and then press the left
mouse button.

SELECT A ROW

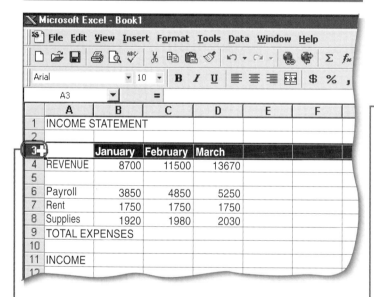

1 Move the mouse ⊹ over
the number of the row you
want to select and then press
the left mouse button.

SELECT A COLUMN

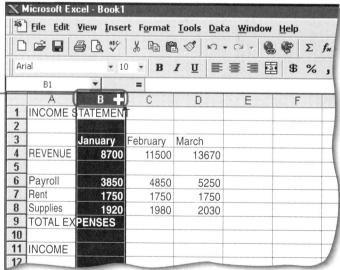

1 Move the mouse ⊹ over
the letter of the column you
want to select and then press
the left mouse button.

If your worksheet contains a lot of data, your computer screen cannot display all the data at once. You must scroll through the worksheet to view other areas.

SCROLL UP OR DOWN

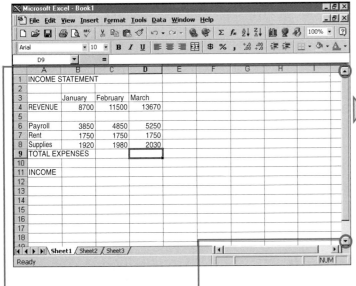

■ To scroll up one row, move the mouse ⌖ over ▲ and then press the left mouse button.

■ To scroll down one row, move the mouse ⌖ over ▼ and then press the left mouse button.

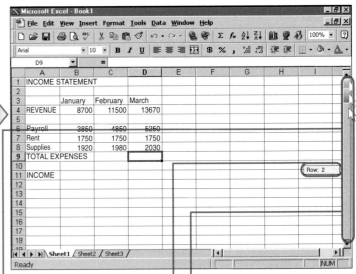

QUICKLY SCROLL

1 To quickly scroll to any row in the worksheet, move the mouse ⌖ over the scroll box.

2 Press and hold down the left mouse button as you move the mouse ⌖ up or down the scroll bar.

3 When this box displays the number of the row you want to view, release the mouse button.

How do I use the new Microsoft IntelliMouse to scroll through a worksheet?

The Microsoft IntelliMouse has a wheel between the left and right mouse buttons. Moving this wheel lets you quickly scroll up and down through a worksheet.

SCROLL LEFT OR RIGHT

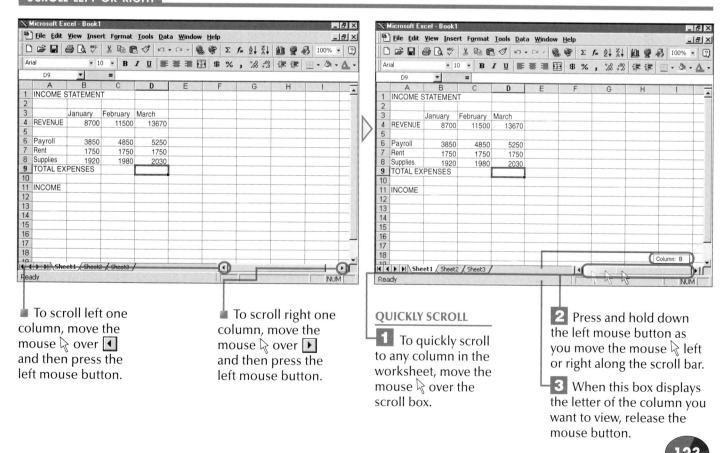

■ To scroll left one column, move the mouse ⤢ over ◄ and then press the left mouse button.

■ To scroll right one column, move the mouse ⤢ over ► and then press the left mouse button.

QUICKLY SCROLL

1 To quickly scroll to any column in the worksheet, move the mouse ⤢ over the scroll box.

2 Press and hold down the left mouse button as you move the mouse ⤢ left or right along the scroll bar.

3 When this box displays the letter of the column you want to view, release the mouse button.

Excel lets you enlarge or reduce the display of data on your screen.

Changing the zoom setting will not affect the way data appears on a printed page.

ZOOM IN OR OUT

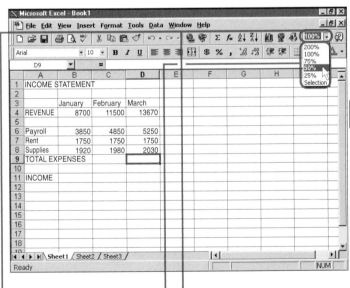

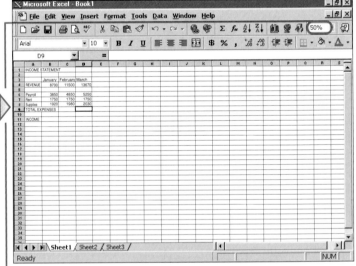

■ When you first start Excel, the worksheet appears in the 100% zoom setting.

1 To display a list of zoom settings, move the mouse over ▾ in this area and then press the left mouse button.

2 Move the mouse ▾ over the zoom setting you want to use and then press the left mouse button.

■ The worksheet appears in the new zoom setting. You can edit your worksheet as usual.

■ To return to the normal zoom setting, repeat steps **1** and **2**, selecting **100%** in step **2**.

Excel offers several toolbars that you can hide or display at any time. Each toolbar contains a series of buttons that help you quickly perform tasks.

Standard
Formatting

When you first start Excel, the Standard and Formatting toolbars appear on your screen.

DISPLAY TOOLBARS

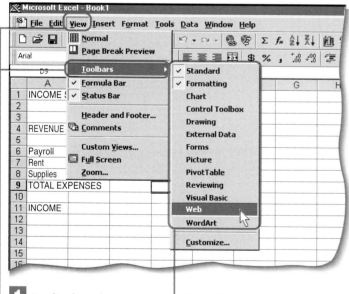

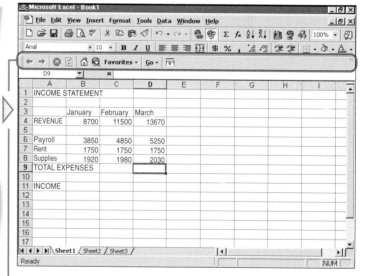

1 To display a list of toolbars, move the mouse ⟍ over **View** and then press the left mouse button.

2 Move the mouse ⟍ over **Toolbars**.

■ A check mark (✓) beside a toolbar name tells you the toolbar is currently displayed.

3 To display or hide a toolbar, move the mouse ⟍ over the name of the toolbar and then press the left mouse button.

■ Excel displays or hides the toolbar you selected.

SAVE A WORKBOOK

You should save your workbook to store it for future use. This lets you later review and make changes to the workbook.

SAVE A WORKBOOK

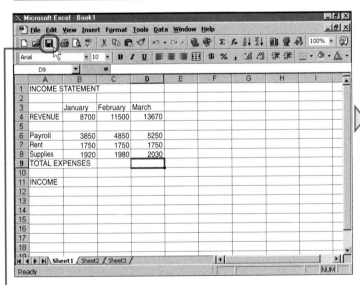

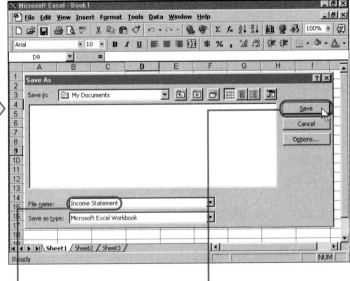

1 Move the mouse 🅺 over 🖫 and then press the left mouse button.

■ The **Save As** dialog box appears.

*Note: If you previously saved the workbook, the **Save As** dialog box will not appear since you have already named the workbook.*

2 Type a name for the workbook.

Note: You can use up to 218 characters, including spaces, to name a workbook.

3 Move the mouse 🅺 over **Save** and then press the left mouse button.

What is the difference between a workbook and a worksheet?

An Excel file is called a workbook. Each workbook is divided into several worksheets. A workbook is similar to a three-ring binder that contains several sheets of paper.

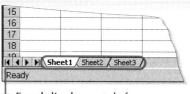

■ Excel displays a tab for each worksheet in your workbook.

Note: To use multiple worksheets in a workbook, refer to pages 194 to 199.

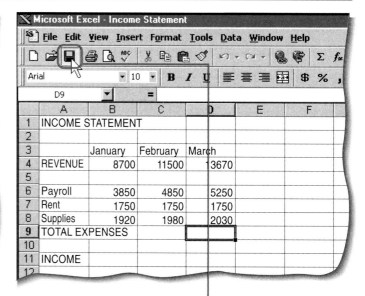

■ Excel saves the workbook and displays the name at the top of the screen.

SAVE CHANGES

To avoid losing your work, you should regularly save changes you make to a workbook.

1 Move the mouse ⌕ over 🖫 and then press the left mouse button.

CREATE A NEW WORKBOOK

You can easily create another workbook to store new data.

CREATE A NEW WORKBOOK

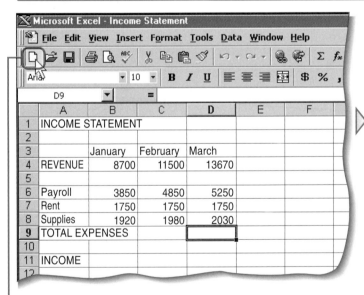

1 Move the mouse ⇗ over 🗋 and then press the left mouse button.

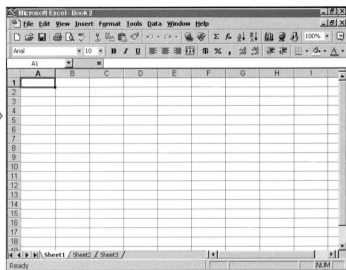

■ A new workbook appears. The previous workbook is now hidden behind the new workbook.

SWITCH BETWEEN WORKBOOKS

Excel lets you have many workbooks open at once. You can easily switch between all of your open workbooks.

SWITCH BETWEEN WORKBOOKS

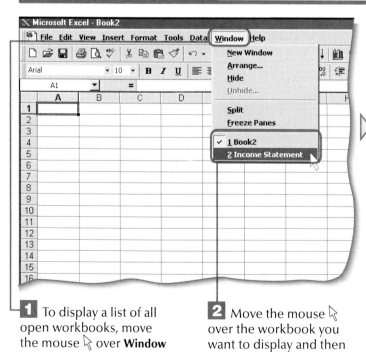

1 To display a list of all open workbooks, move the mouse over **Window** and then press the left mouse button.

2 Move the mouse over the workbook you want to display and then press the left mouse button.

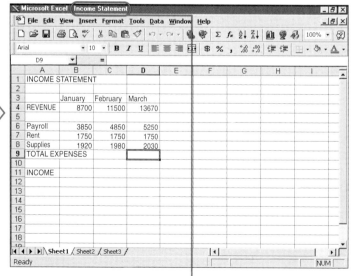

■ The workbook appears.

■ Excel displays the name of the workbook at the top of the screen.

CLOSE A WORKBOOK

When you finish using a workbook, you can close the workbook to remove it from your screen.

When you close a workbook, you do not exit the Excel program. You can continue to work on other workbooks.

CLOSE A WORKBOOK

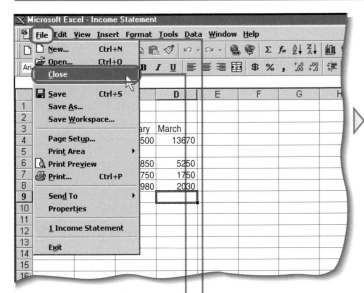

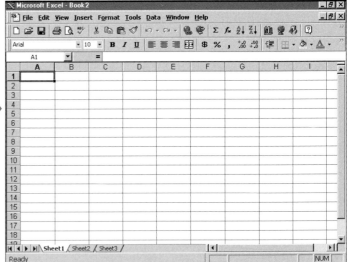

■ To save the workbook before closing, refer to page 126.

1 To close the workbook, move the mouse ⌖ over **File** and then press the left mouse button.

2 Move the mouse ⌖ over **Close** and then press the left mouse button.

■ Excel removes the workbook from the screen.

■ If you had more than one workbook open, the second last workbook you worked on appears on the screen.

EXIT EXCEL

When you finish using Excel, you can exit the program.

You should exit all programs before turning off your computer.

EXIT EXCEL

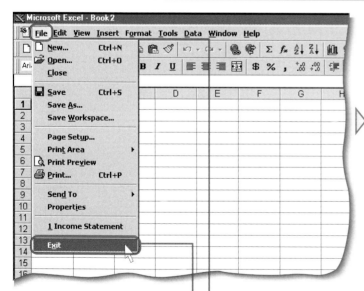

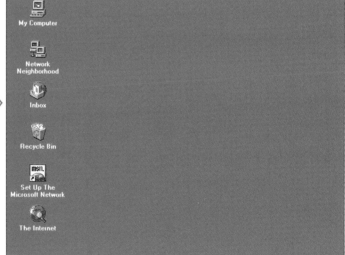

■ Save all open workbooks before exiting Excel. To save a workbook, refer to page 126.

1 Move the mouse ⊳ over **File** and then press the left mouse button.

2 Move the mouse ⊳ over **Exit** and then press the left mouse button.

■ The Excel window disappears from the screen.

Note: To restart Excel, refer to page 113.

OPEN A WORKBOOK

You can open a saved workbook and display it on your screen. This lets you review and make changes to the workbook.

OPEN A WORKBOOK

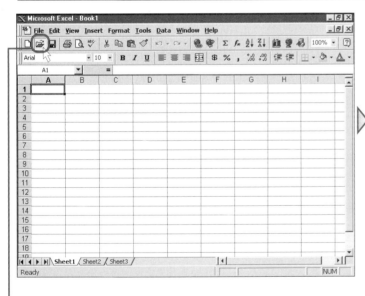

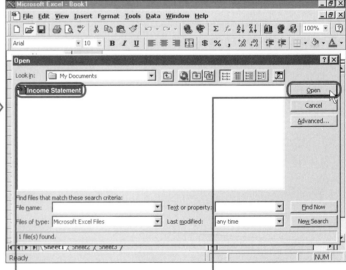

1 Move the mouse over 📂 and then press the left mouse button.

■ The **Open** dialog box appears.

2 Move the mouse over the name of the workbook you want to open and then press the left mouse button.

3 To open the workbook, move the mouse over **Open** and then press the left mouse button.

Excel remembers the names of the last four workbooks you opened. You can quickly open any of these workbooks.

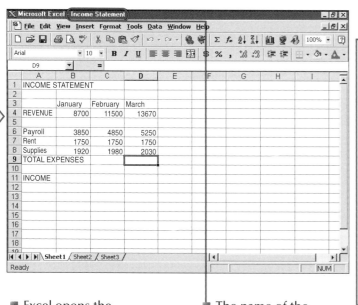

QUICKLY OPEN A WORKBOOK

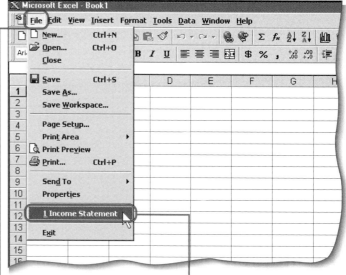

■ Excel opens the workbook and displays it on the screen. You can now review and make changes to the workbook.

■ The name of the workbook appears at the top of the screen.

1 Move the mouse ⤢ over **File** and then press the left mouse button.

2 Move the mouse ⤢ over the name of the workbook you want to open and then press the left mouse button.

After you enter data into your worksheet, you can change the data to correct a mistake or update the data.

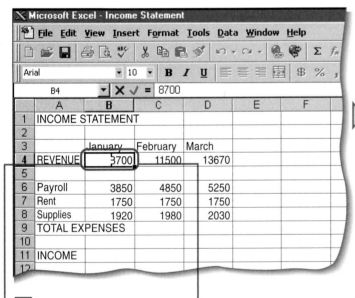

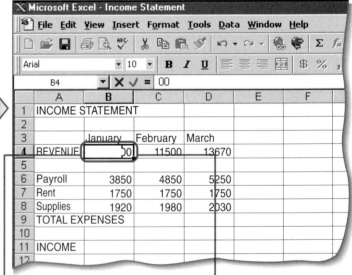

1 Move the mouse ⊹ over the cell containing the data you want to edit and then quickly press the left mouse button twice.

■ A flashing insertion point appears in the cell.

2 Press ← or → on your keyboard to move the insertion point to where you want to add or remove characters.

3 To remove the character to the left of the insertion point, press ◆Backspace on your keyboard.

Can Excel automatically correct my typing mistakes?

Excel automatically corrects common spelling errors as you type.

adn	→	and
alot	→	a lot
comittee	→	committee
don;t	→	don't
nwe	→	new
occurence	→	occurrence
recieve	→	receive
seperate	→	separate
teh	→	the

REPLACE ALL DATA IN A CELL

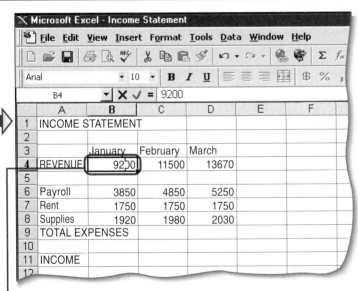

4 To insert data where the insertion point flashes on the screen, type the data.

5 When you finish making changes to the data, press **Enter** on your keyboard.

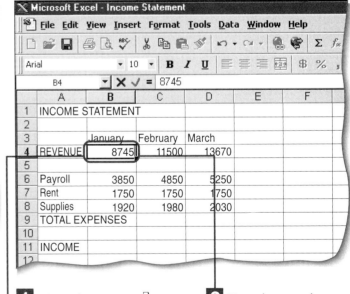

1 Move the mouse ⇧ over the cell containing the data you want to replace with new data and then press the left mouse button.

2 Type the new data and then press **Enter** on your keyboard.

DELETE DATA

You can easily remove data you no longer need from cells in your worksheet.

DELETE DATA

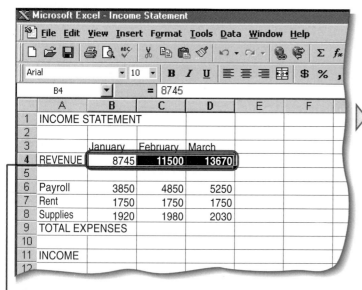

1 Select the cell(s) containing the data you want to delete. To select cells, refer to page 120.

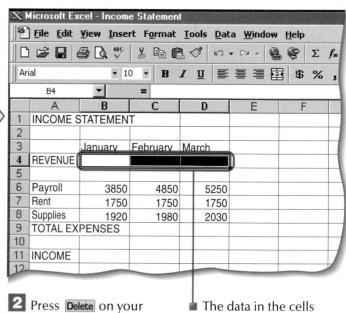

2 Press `Delete` on your keyboard.

■ The data in the cells you selected disappears.

136

UNDO LAST CHANGE

UNDO LAST CHANGE

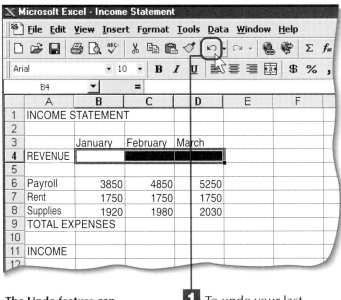 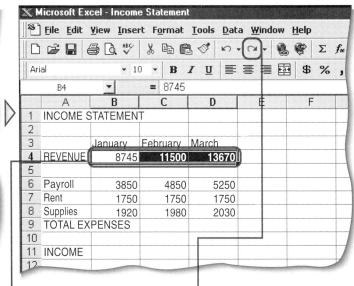

The Undo feature can cancel your last editing and formatting changes.

1 To undo your last change, move the mouse over and then press the left mouse button.

■ Excel cancels the last change you made to the worksheet.

■ You can repeat step **1** to cancel previous changes you made.

■ To reverse the results of using the Undo feature, move the mouse over and then press the left mouse button.

MOVE DATA

You can reorganize the data in your worksheet by moving data from one location to another.

MOVE DATA

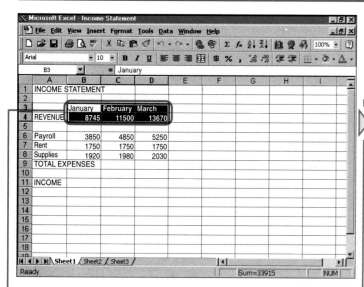

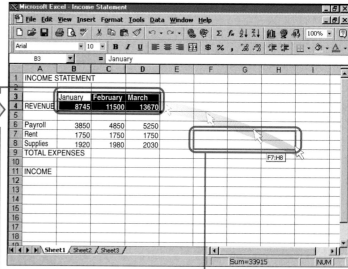

1 Select the cells containing the data you want to move. To select cells, refer to page 120.

2 Move the mouse ⊕ over a border of the selected cells (⊕ changes to ⬉).

3 Press and hold down the left mouse button as you move the mouse ⬉ to where you want to place the data.

Why does this message appear when I try to move data?

This message may appear when you try to move data to a location that already contains data.

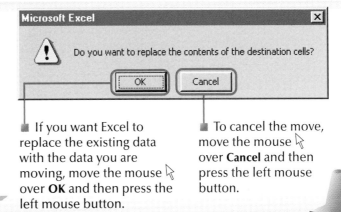

■ If you want Excel to replace the existing data with the data you are moving, move the mouse ⬩ over **OK** and then press the left mouse button.

■ To cancel the move, move the mouse ⬩ over **Cancel** and then press the left mouse button.

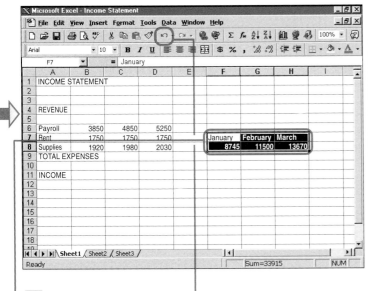

4 Release the mouse button and the data moves to the new location.

UNDO THE MOVE

■ To immediately move the data back, move the mouse ⬩ over ↺ and then press the left mouse button.

MOVE DATA USING TOOLBAR

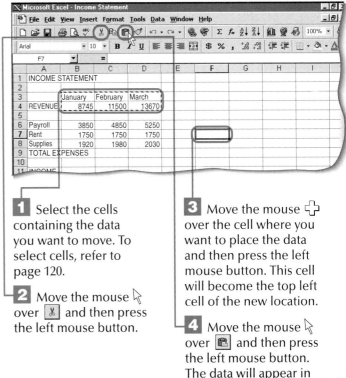

1 Select the cells containing the data you want to move. To select cells, refer to page 120.

2 Move the mouse ⬩ over ✂ and then press the left mouse button.

3 Move the mouse ⬩ over the cell where you want to place the data and then press the left mouse button. This cell will become the top left cell of the new location.

4 Move the mouse ⬩ over 📋 and then press the left mouse button. The data will appear in the new location.

You can place a copy of data in a different location in your worksheet. This will save you time since you do not have to retype the data.

COPY DATA

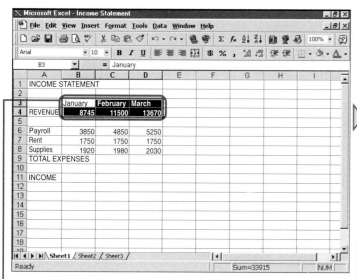

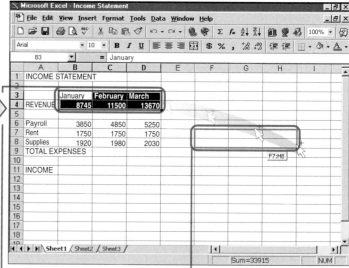

1 Select the cells containing the data you want to copy. To select cells, refer to page 120.

2 Move the mouse 🖑 over a border of the selected cells (🖑 changes to ⬉).

3 Press and hold down **Ctrl** on your keyboard.

4 Still holding down **Ctrl**, press and hold down the left mouse button as you move the mouse ⬉⁺ to where you want to place the copy.

How can I quickly copy data to the active cell?

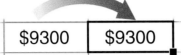

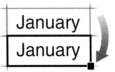

■ To quickly copy the contents of the cell on the left of the active cell, press and hold down **Ctrl** as you press **R** on your keyboard.

■ To quickly copy the contents of the cell above the active cell, press and hold down **Ctrl** as you press **D** on your keyboard.

COPY DATA USING TOOLBAR

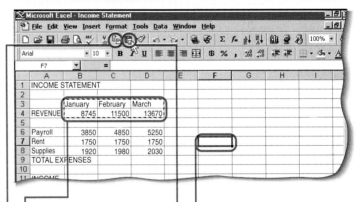

5 Release the mouse button and then release **Ctrl**.

■ A copy of the data appears in the new location.

UNDO COPY

■ To immediately remove the copy, move the mouse ⟍ over ↶ and then press the left mouse button.

1 Select the cells containing the data you want to copy. To select cells, refer to page 120.

2 Move the mouse ⟍ over 🗐 and then press the left mouse button.

3 Move the mouse ⊹ over the cell where you want to place the data and then press the left mouse button. This cell will become the top left cell of the new location.

4 Move the mouse ⟍ over 🗒 and then press the left mouse button. A copy of the data will appear in the new location.

INSERT A ROW OR COLUMN

You can add a row or column to your worksheet when you want to insert additional data.

	Week 1	Week 2	Week 3
Apples	45	30	35
Bananas	50	75	85
Grapes	20	120	45
Lemons	65	70	90
Limes	80	70	55
Mangoes	40	50	45
Oranges	50	90	65
Peaches	30	110	35
Pears	60	30	80
Plums	20	65	50

INSERT A ROW

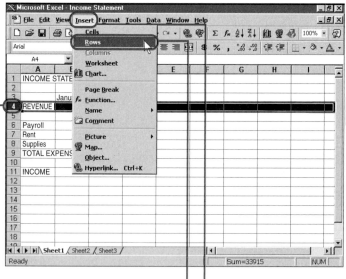

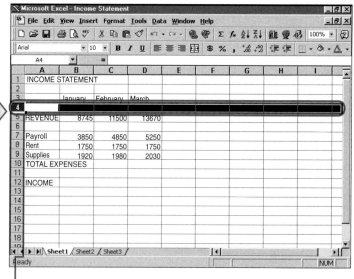

Excel will insert a row above the row you select.

1 To select a row, move the mouse ⊹ over the row number and then press the left mouse button.

2 Move the mouse over **Insert** and then press the left mouse button.

3 Move the mouse over **Rows** and then press the left mouse button.

■ The new row appears and all the rows that follow shift downward.

142

Do I need to adjust my formulas when I insert a row or column?

When you insert a row or column, Excel updates any formulas affected by the insertion.

Note: For information on formulas, refer to page 146.

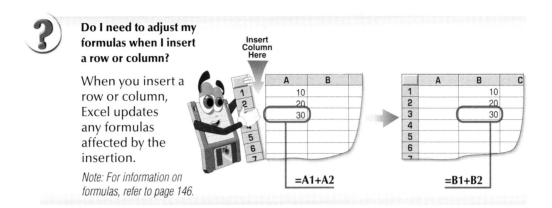

=A1+A2   =B1+B2

INSERT A COLUMN

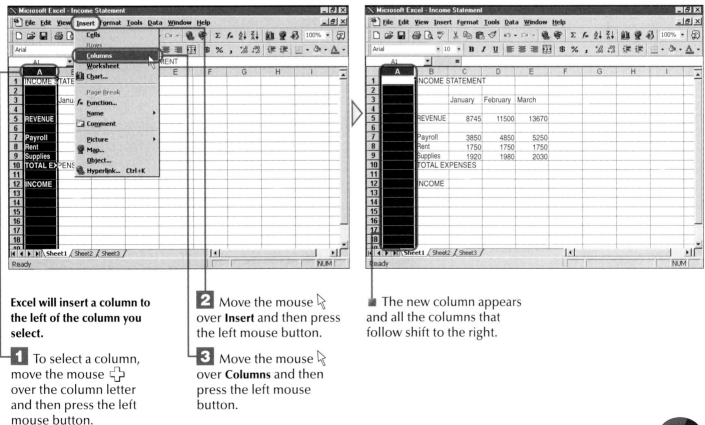

Excel will insert a column to the left of the column you select.

1 To select a column, move the mouse ⬧ over the column letter and then press the left mouse button.

2 Move the mouse ⬧ over **Insert** and then press the left mouse button.

3 Move the mouse ⬧ over **Columns** and then press the left mouse button.

■ The new column appears and all the columns that follow shift to the right.

DELETE A ROW OR COLUMN

You can delete a row or column from your worksheet to remove cells you no longer need.

DELETE A ROW

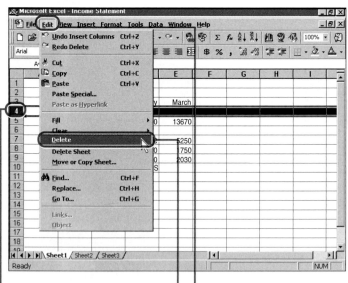

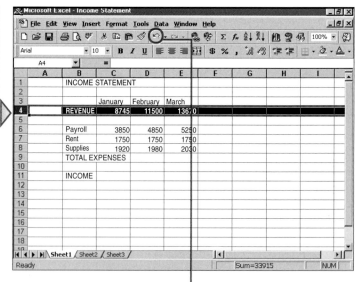

1 To select the row you want to delete, move the mouse ⊕ over the row number and then press the left mouse button.

2 Move the mouse ⊳ over **Edit** and then press the left mouse button.

3 Move the mouse ⊳ over **Delete** and then press the left mouse button.

■ The row disappears and all the rows that follow shift upward.

■ To immediately return the row to the worksheet, move the mouse ⊳ over 🔄 and then press the left mouse button.

Why did #REF! appear in a cell after I deleted a row or column?

If **#REF!** appears in a cell in your worksheet, you deleted data needed to calculate a formula.

Note: For information on formulas, refer to page 146.

DELETE A COLUMN

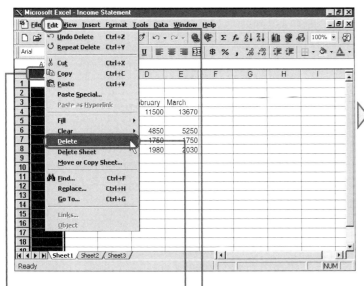

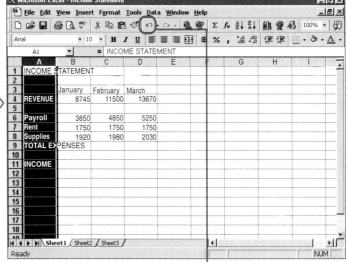

1 To select the column you want to delete, move the mouse ⊡ over the column letter and then press the left mouse button.

2 Move the mouse ⊡ over **Edit** and then press the left mouse button.

3 Move the mouse ⊡ over **Delete** and then press the left mouse button.

■ The column disappears and all the columns that follow shift to the left.

■ To immediately return the column to the worksheet, move the mouse ⊡ over ⊡ and then press the left mouse button.

A formula helps you calculate and analyze data in your worksheet.

A formula always begins with an equal sign (=).

INTRODUCTION TO FORMULAS

$$45-3+4*5 = 62$$

OR

$$45-(3+4)*5 = 10$$

Order of Calculations

Excel performs calculations in the following order:

1 Exponents ($\wedge$)

2 Multiplication (*) and Division (/)

3 Addition (+) and Subtraction (-)

You can use parentheses ( ) to change the order that Excel performs calculations. Excel will calculate the data inside the parentheses first.

Cell References

When entering formulas, use cell references (example: **=A1+A2**) instead of actual data (example: **=10+30**) whenever possible. When you use cell references and you change a number used in a formula, Excel will automatically redo the calculations for you.

EXAMPLES OF FORMULAS

	A	B	
1	10		
2	20		
3	30		
4	40		
5			
6	1230		
7			

■ This cell contains the formula:

=A1+A2+A3*A4

=10+20+30*40

=1230

	A	B	
1	10		
2	20		
3	30		
4	40		
5			
6	2010		
7			

■ This cell contains the formula:

=A1+(A2+A3)*A4

=10+(20+30)*40

=2010

	A	B	
1	10		
2	20		
3	30		
4	40		
5			
6	320		
7			

■ This cell contains the formula:

=A1*A3-A2+A4

=10*30-20+40

=320

	A	B	
1	10		
2	20		
3	30		
4	40		
5			
6	140		
7			

■ This cell contains the formula:

=A1*(A3-A2)+A4

=10*(30-20)+40

=140

	A	B	
1	10		
2	20		
3	30		
4	40		
5			
6	63		
7			

■ This cell contains the formula:

=A3/A1+A2+A4

=30/10+20+40

=63

	A	B	
1	10		
2	20		
3	30		
4	40		
5			
6	41		
7			

■ This cell contains the formula:

=A3/(A1+A2)+A4

=30/(10+20)+40

=41

ENTER A FORMULA

mG's Pizza Parlor

ORDERS

	A	B
1	Pizza	600
2	Spaghetti	200
3	Garlic Bread	400
4	TOTAL	1200

=B1+B2+B3

You can enter a formula into any cell in your worksheet.

ENTER A FORMULA

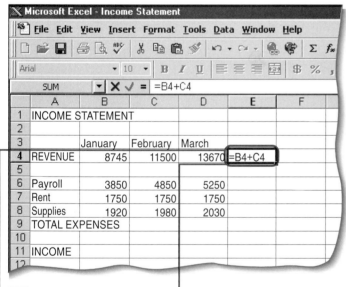

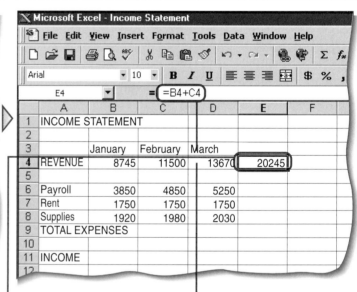

1 Move the mouse ⇧ over the cell where you want to enter a formula and then press the left mouse button.

2 Type an equal sign (=) to begin the formula.

3 Type the formula and then press **Enter** on your keyboard.

■ The result of the calculation appears in the cell.

4 To view the formula you entered, move the mouse ⇧ over the cell containing the formula and then press the left mouse button.

■ The formula for the cell appears in the formula bar.

? What happens if I change a number used in a formula?

If you change a number used in a formula, Excel will automatically calculate a new result.

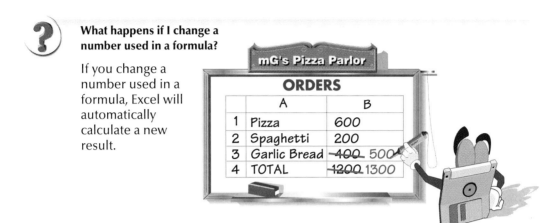

EDIT A FORMULA

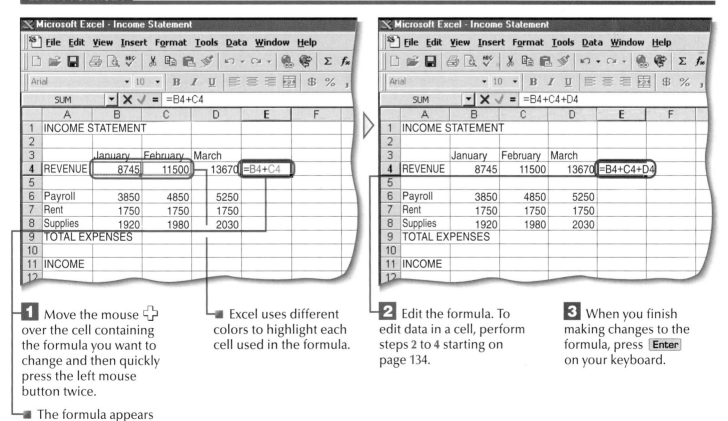

1 Move the mouse ⊹ over the cell containing the formula you want to change and then quickly press the left mouse button twice.

■ The formula appears in the cell.

■ Excel uses different colors to highlight each cell used in the formula.

2 Edit the formula. To edit data in a cell, perform steps 2 to 4 starting on page 134.

3 When you finish making changes to the formula, press `Enter` on your keyboard.

ENTER A FUNCTION

A function is a ready-to-use formula that performs a specialized calculation on your worksheet data.

AVERAGE
MAX
ROUND

INTRODUCTION TO FUNCTIONS

■ A function always begins with an equal sign (=).

■ The data Excel will use to calculate a function is enclosed in parentheses ( ).

=SUM(A1,A2,A3)

=AVERAGE(C1,C2,C3)

=MAX(B7,C7,D7,E7)

=COUNT(D12,D13,D14)

=SUM(A1:A3)

=AVERAGE(C1:C3)

=MAX(B7:E7)

=COUNT(D12:D14)

Specify Individual Cells

When there is a comma (,) between cell references in a function, Excel uses each cell to perform the calculation.

For example, =SUM(A1,A2,A3) is the same as the formula =A1+A2+A3.

Specify Group of Cells

When there is a colon (:) between cell references in a function, Excel uses the specified cells and all cells between them to perform the calculation.

For example, =SUM(A1:A3) is the same as the formula =A1+A2+A3.

150

COMMON FUNCTIONS

	A	B	C
1	10		
2	20		
3	30		
4	40		
5			
6	25		
7			

Average

Calculates the average value of a list of numbers.

■ This cell contains the function:

=AVERAGE(A1:A4)

=(A1+A2+A3+A4)/4

=(10+20+30+40)/4

=25

	A	B	C
1	10		
2	20		
3	30		
4	40		
5			
6	4		
7			

Count

Calculates the number of values in a list.

■ This cell contains the function:

=COUNT(A1:A4)

=4

	A	B	C
1	10		
2	20		
3	30		
4	40		
5			
6	40		
7			

Max

Finds the largest value in a list of numbers.

■ This cell contains the function:

=MAX(A1:A4)

=40

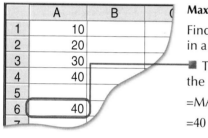

	A	B	C
1	10		
2	20		
3	30		
4	40		
5			
6	10		
7			

Min

Finds the smallest value in a list of numbers.

■ This cell contains the function:

=MIN(A1:A4)

=10

	A	B	C
1	10		
2	20		
3	30		
4	40		
5			
6	100		
7			

Sum

Adds a list of numbers.

■ This cell contains the function:

=SUM(A1:A4)

=A1+A2+A3+A4

=10+20+30+40

=100

	A	B	C
1	42.3617		
2			
3			
4			
5			
6	42.36		
7			

Round

Rounds a value to a specific number of digits.

■ This cell contains the function:

=ROUND(A1,2)

=42.36

ENTER A FUNCTION

Excel helps you enter functions in your worksheet. This lets you perform calculations without typing long, complex formulas.

ENTER A FUNCTION

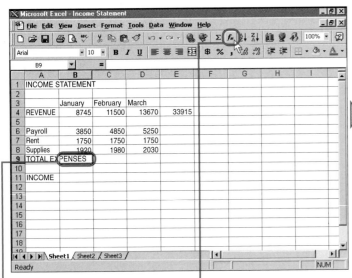

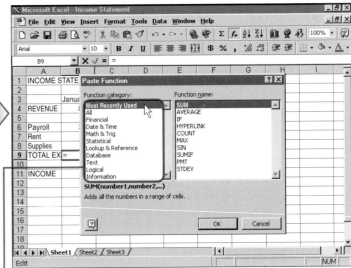

1 Move the mouse ⊹ over the cell where you want to enter a function and then press the left mouse button.

2 Move the mouse ⍦ over 𝑓ₓ and then press the left mouse button.

■ The **Paste Function** dialog box appears.

3 Move the mouse ⍦ over the category that contains the function you want to use and then press the left mouse button.

*Note: If you do not know which category contains the function you want to use, select **All** to display a list of all the functions.*

How many functions does Excel offer?

Excel offers over 200 functions to help you analyze data in your worksheet. There are financial functions, math and trigonometry functions, date and time functions, statistical functions and many more.

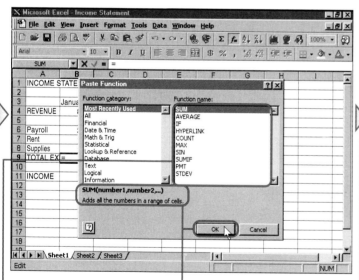

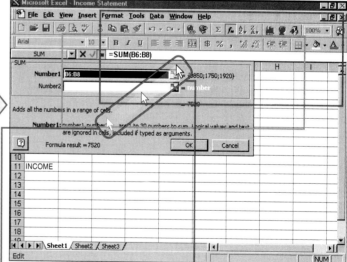

■ This area displays the functions in the category you selected.

4 Move the mouse ⬧ over a function of interest and then press the left mouse button.

■ This area describes the function you selected.

5 To enter the function in the worksheet, move the mouse ⬧ over **OK** and then press the left mouse button.

■ A dialog box appears. If the dialog box covers data you want to use in the calculation, you can move it to a new location.

6 To move the dialog box, position the mouse ⬧ over a blank area in the dialog box.

7 Press and hold down the left mouse button as you move the dialog box to a new location. Then release the mouse button.

CONTINUED➡

When entering a function, you must specify which numbers you want to use in the calculation.

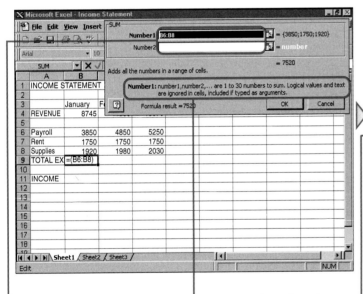

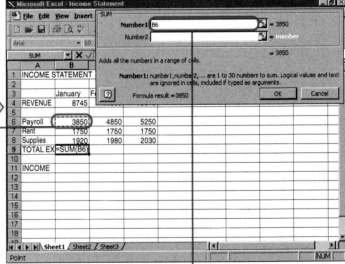

■ This area displays boxes where you enter the numbers you want to use in the calculation.

■ This area describes the number you need to enter.

8 To enter a number, move the mouse ✛ over the cell in the worksheet that contains the number and then press the left mouse button.

Note: If the number you want to enter does not appear in the worksheet, type the number.

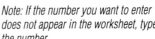

■ The area now displays the cell you selected.

Can I enter a function by myself?

You can easily enter a function yourself by typing the entire function into a cell.

=COUNT(D1:D

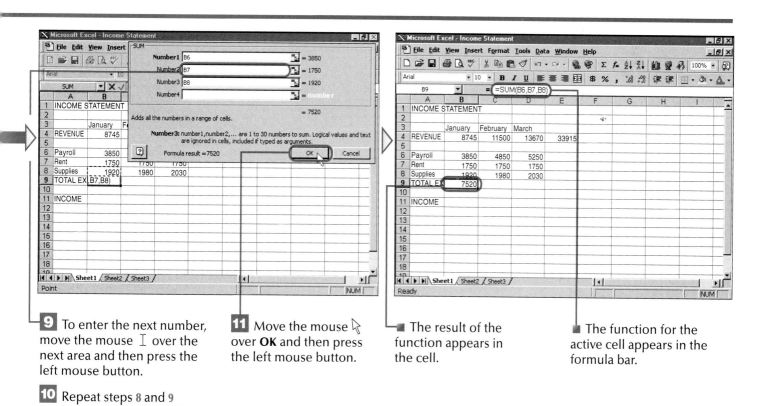

9 To enter the next number, move the mouse I over the next area and then press the left mouse button.

10 Repeat steps 8 and 9 until you have entered all the numbers you want to use in the calculation.

11 Move the mouse ▷ over **OK** and then press the left mouse button.

■ The result of the function appears in the cell.

■ The function for the active cell appears in the formula bar.

USING AUTOCALCULATE

You can quickly view the results of common calculations without entering a formula into your worksheet.

USING AUTOCALCULATE

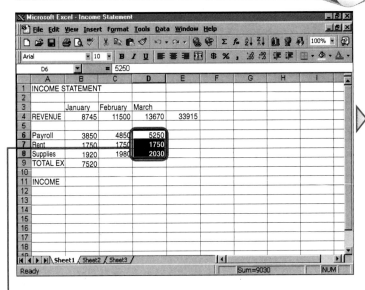

1 Select the cells you want to include in the calculation. To select cells, refer to page 120.

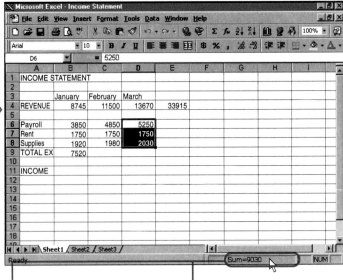

■ This area displays the sum of the cells you selected.

2 To display the result for a different calculation, move the mouse ⟋ over this area and then press the **right** mouse button.

156

What calculations can AutoCalculate perform?

Average
Calculates the average value of a list of numbers.

Count
Calculates the number of items in a list, including text.

Count Nums
Calculates the number of values in a list.

Max
Finds the largest value in a list.

Min
Finds the smallest value in a list.

Sum
Adds a list of numbers.

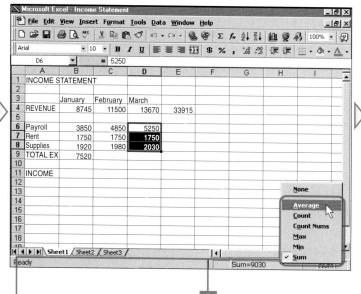

■ A list appears, displaying the calculations you can perform.

3 Move the mouse ⬚ over the calculation you want to perform and then press the left mouse button.

■ This area displays the result for the new calculation.

ADD NUMBERS

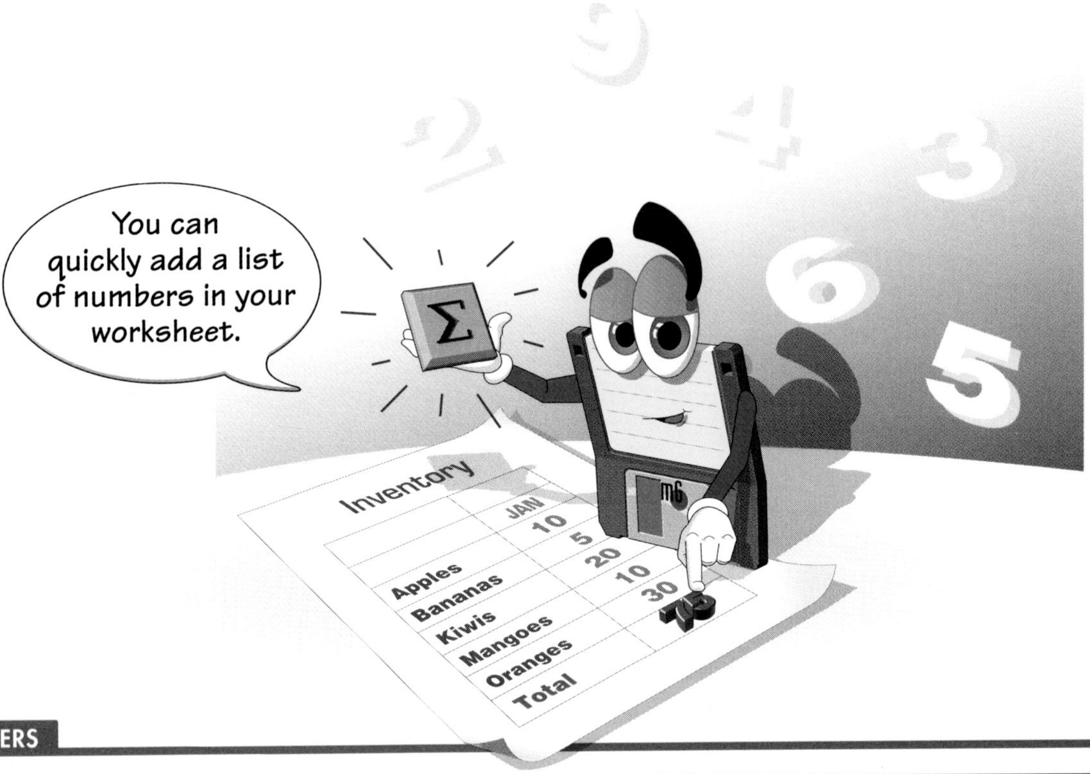
You can quickly add a list of numbers in your worksheet.
Inventory
JAN
Apples
Bananas
Kiwis
Mangoes
Oranges
Total
10
5
20
10
30

ADD NUMBERS

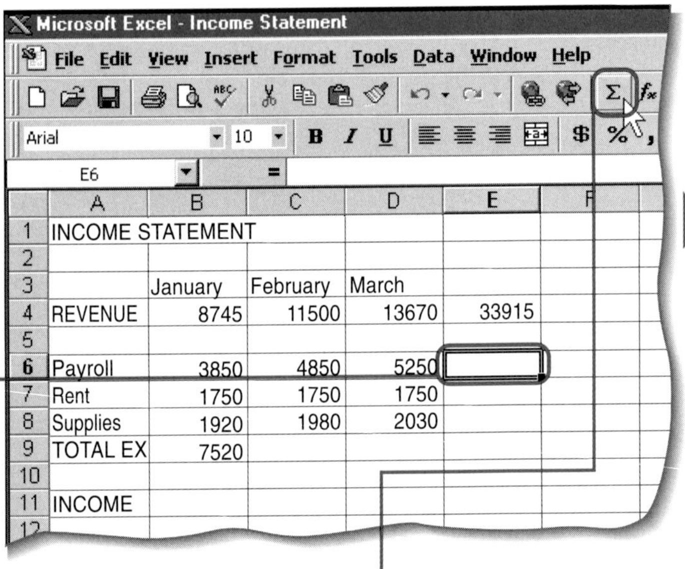
Microsoft Excel - Income Statement
File Edit View Insert Format Tools Data Window Help
Arial
10
E6
=
INCOME STATEMENT
January February March
REVENUE 8745 11500 13670 33915
Payroll 3850 4850 5250
Rent 1750 1750 1750
Supplies 1920 1980 2030
TOTAL EX 7520
INCOME

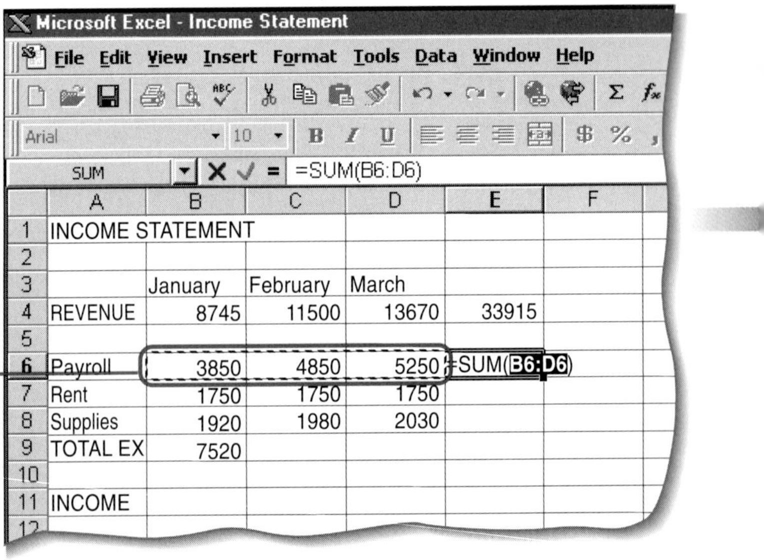
Microsoft Excel - Income Statement
File Edit View Insert Format Tools Data Window Help
Arial
10
SUM
=SUM(B6:D6)
INCOME STATEMENT
January February March
REVENUE 8745 11500 13670 33915
Payroll 3850 4850 5250 =SUM(B6:D6)
Rent 1750 1750 1750
Supplies 1920 1980 2030
TOTAL EX 7520
INCOME

1 Move the mouse ✚ over the cell below or to the right of the cells you want to add and then press the left mouse button.

2 Move the mouse ↖ over Σ and then press the left mouse button.

■ Excel outlines the cells it will use in the calculation with a dotted line.

■ If Excel does not outline the correct cells, select the cells containing the numbers you want to add. To select cells, refer to page 120.

Why did number signs (#) appear in a cell?

If number signs (#) appear in a cell, the result of a calculation is too long to fit in the cell. To display the result, you need to change the column width. To do so, refer to page 166.

#####

CALCULATE A GRAND TOTAL

Microsoft Excel - Income Statement

File Edit View Insert Format Tools Data Window Help

Arial ▼ 10 ▼ **B** *I* U ≡ ≡ ≡ ⊞ $ %

E7 =

	A	B	C	D	E	F
1	INCOME STATEMENT					
2						
3		January	February	March		
4	REVENUE	8745	11500	13670	33915	
5						
6	Payroll	3850	4850	5250	13950	
7	Rent	1750	1750	1750		
8	Supplies	1920	1980	2030		
9	TOTAL EX	7520				
10						
11	INCOME					
12						

Microsoft Excel - Total Sales

File Edit View Insert Format Tools Data Window Help

Arial ▼ 10 ▼ **B** *I* U ≡ ≡ ≡ ⊞ $ %

SUM ▼ X ✓ = =SUM(E8,E4)

	A	B	C	D	E	F
1	Seattle Office		January Sales		$52,000.00	
2			February Sales		$69,400.00	
3			March Sales		$74,100.00	
4				TOTAL	$195,500.00	
5	New York Office		January Sales		$74,500.00	
6			February Sales		$86,900.00	
7			March Sales		$96,900.00	
8				TOTAL	$258,300.00	
9				GRAND TOTAL	=SUM(E8,E4)	
10						
11						
12						

3 Press **Enter** on your keyboard to perform the calculation.

■ The result appears.

■ If the worksheet contains several subtotals, you can quickly calculate a grand total.

1 Move the mouse ✛ over the cell below or to the right of the cells that contain the subtotals and then press the left mouse button.

2 Move the mouse ▷ over Σ and then press the left mouse button.

3 Press **Enter** on your keyboard.

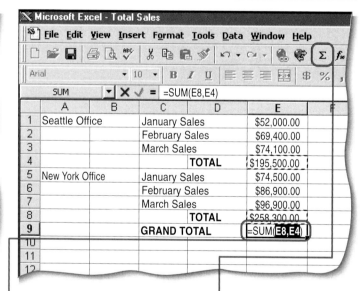

ERRORS IN FORMULAS

An error message appears when Excel cannot properly calculate a formula.

ERROR

Errors in formulas are often the result of typing mistakes. You can correct an error by editing the cell containing the error. To edit data in a cell, refer to page 134.

#####

The column is too narrow to display the result of the calculation. To display the result, refer to page 166 to change the column width.

	A	B	C
1	9924		
2	5521		
3			
4	#####		
5			
6			

■ This cell contains the formula:

=A1*A2

#DIV/0!

The formula divides a number by zero (0). Excel considers a blank cell to contain a value of zero.

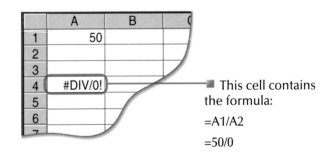

	A	B	C
1	50		
2			
3			
4	#DIV/0!		
5			
6			

■ This cell contains the formula:

=A1/A2

=50/0

#NAME?

The formula contains a function name or cell reference Excel does not recognize.

	A	B	
1	10		
2	20		
3	30		
4	#NAME?		
5			
6			

◼ This cell contains the formula:

=SUMM(A1:A3)

In this example, the name of the SUM function was misspelled.

#REF!

The formula refers to a cell that is not valid.

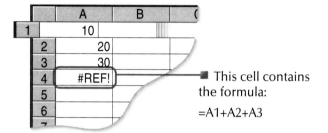

	A	B	
1	10		
2	20		
3	30		
4	#REF!		
5			
6			

◼ This cell contains the formula:

=A1+A2+A3

In this example, a row containing a cell used in the formula was deleted.

#VALUE!

The formula refers to a cell that Excel cannot use in a calculation.

	A	B	
1	10		
2	20		
3	January		
4	#VALUE!		
5			
6			

◼ This cell contains the formula:

=A1+A2+A3

In this example, a cell used in the formula contains text.

Circular Reference

A warning message appears when a formula refers to the cell that contains the formula. This is called a circular reference.

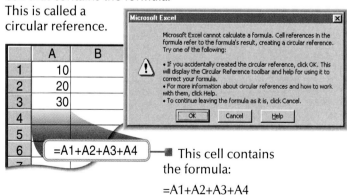

Microsoft Excel

Microsoft Excel cannot calculate a formula. Cell references in the formula refer to the formula's result, creating a circular reference. Try one of the following:

• If you accidentally created the circular reference, click OK. This will display the Circular Reference toolbar and help for using it to correct your formula.
• For more information about circular references and how to work with them, click Help.
• To continue leaving the formula as it is, click Cancel.

[OK] [Cancel] [Help]

	A	B	
1	10		
2	20		
3	30		
4			
5			
6	=A1+A2+A3+A4		

◼ This cell contains the formula:

=A1+A2+A3+A4

COPY A FORMULA

If you want to use the same formula several times in your worksheet, you can save time by copying the formula.

COPY A FORMULA—USING RELATIVE REFERENCES

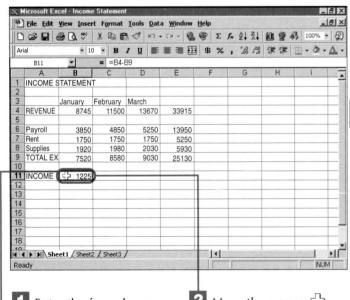

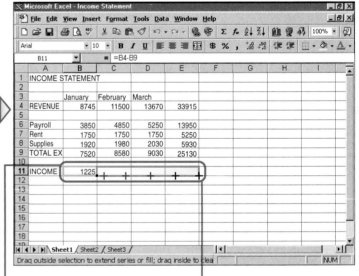

1 Enter the formula you want to copy to other cells. To enter a formula, refer to page 148.

Note: In this example, enter the formula =B4-B9 in cell B11 to calculate INCOME.

2 Move the mouse ⇧ over the cell containing the formula you want to copy and then press the left mouse button.

3 Move the mouse ⇧ over the bottom right corner of the cell (⇧ changes to ✛).

4 Press and hold down the left mouse button as you move the mouse ✛ over the cells you want to receive a copy of the formula. Then release the mouse button.

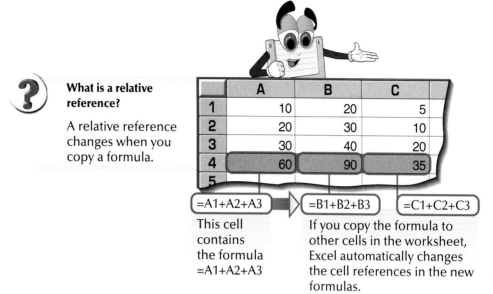

What is a relative reference?

A relative reference changes when you copy a formula.

	A	B	C
1	10	20	5
2	20	30	10
3	30	40	20
4	60	90	35
5			

=A1+A2+A3   =B1+B2+B3   =C1+C2+C3

This cell contains the formula =A1+A2+A3

If you copy the formula to other cells in the worksheet, Excel automatically changes the cell references in the new formulas.

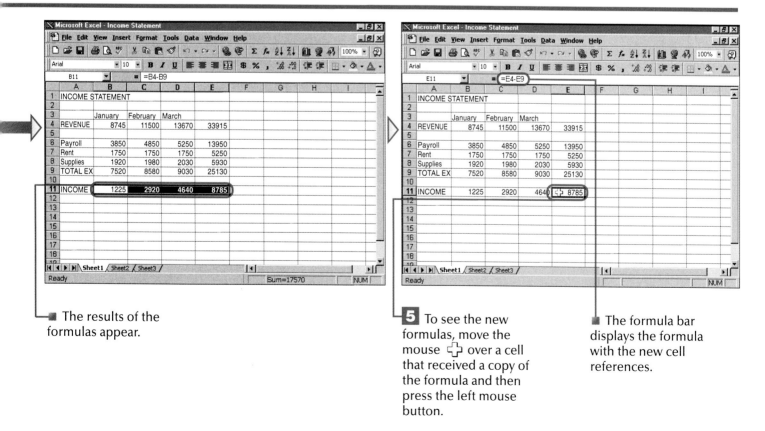

■ The results of the formulas appear.

5 To see the new formulas, move the mouse ✛ over a cell that received a copy of the formula and then press the left mouse button.

■ The formula bar displays the formula with the new cell references.

COPY A FORMULA

You can copy a formula to other cells in your worksheet to save time. If you do not want Excel to change a cell reference when you copy a formula, you can use an absolute reference.

COPY A FORMULA—USING ABSOLUTE REFERENCES

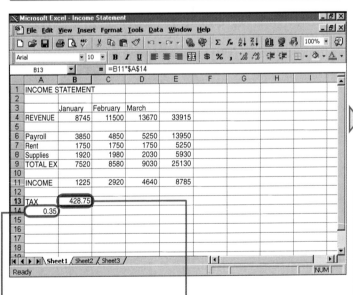

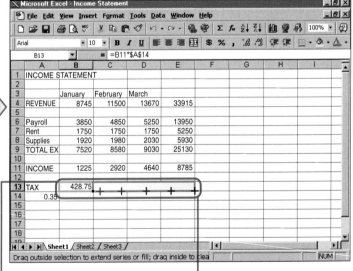

1 Enter the data you want to remain the same in all the formulas.

2 Enter the formula you want to copy to other cells. To enter a formula, refer to page 146.

Note: In this example, enter the formula =B11*$A$14 in cell B13 to calculate TAX. For information on absolute references, refer to the top of page 165.

3 Move the mouse ⊹ over the cell containing the formula you want to copy and then press the left mouse button.

4 Move the mouse ⊹ over the bottom right corner of the cell (⊹ changes to ✛).

5 Press and hold down the left mouse button as you move the mouse ✛ over the cells you want to receive a copy of the formula. Then release the mouse button.

What is an absolute reference?

An absolute reference does not change when you copy a formula. To make a cell reference absolute, type a dollar sign ($) before both the column letter and row number (example: $A$7).

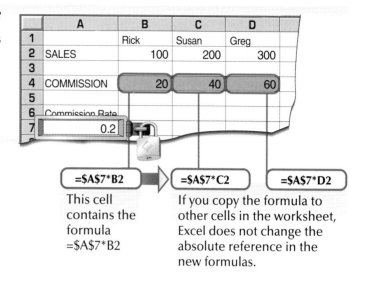

	A	B	C	D
1		Rick	Susan	Greg
2	SALES	100	200	300
3				
4	COMMISSION	20	40	60
5				
6	Commission Rate			
7	0.2			

=$A$7*B2   =$A$7*C2   =$A$7*D2

This cell contains the formula =$A$7*B2

If you copy the formula to other cells in the worksheet, Excel does not change the absolute reference in the new formulas.

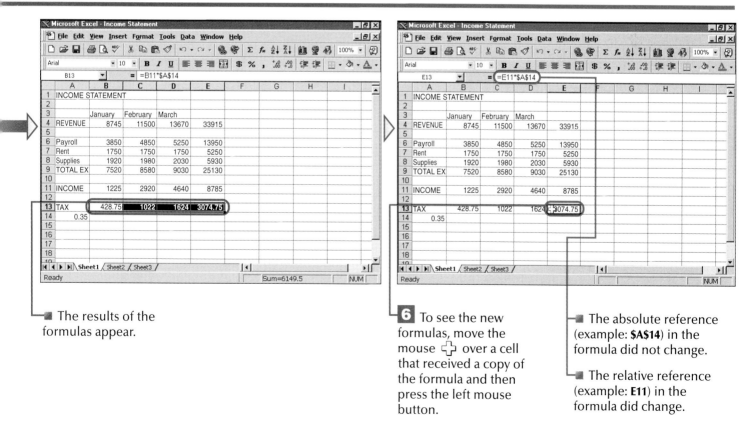

■ The results of the formulas appear.

6 To see the new formulas, move the mouse ⊕ over a cell that received a copy of the formula and then press the left mouse button.

■ The absolute reference (example: **$A$14**) in the formula did not change.

■ The relative reference (example: **E11**) in the formula did change.

CHANGE COLUMN WIDTH

You can improve the appearance of your worksheet and display hidden data by changing the width of columns.

FRUIT SALES		
Fruit	Jan	Feb
Waterme	100	180
Apples	120	150
Bananas	200	220
Cherries	300	200
Strawberr	100	150
Mangoes	110	110

CHANGE COLUMN WIDTH

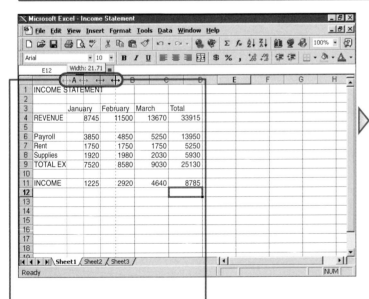

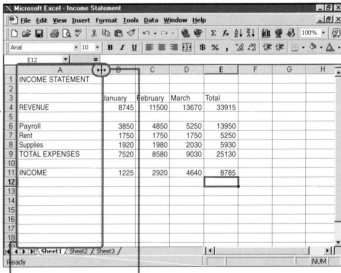

1 To change the width of a column, move the mouse 🔲 over the right edge of the column heading (🔲 changes to ↔).

2 Press and hold down the left mouse button as you move the column edge until the dotted line displays the column width you want. Then release the mouse button.

■ The column displays the new width.

FIT LONGEST ITEM

You can have Excel change a column width to fit the longest item in the column.

■ Move the mouse 🔲 over the right edge of the column heading (🔲 changes to ↔) and then quickly press the left mouse button twice.

166

CHANGE ROW HEIGHT

You can change the height of rows to add space between the rows of data in your worksheet.

FRUIT SALES

Fruit	Jan	Feb
Watermelon	100	180
Apples	120	150
Bananas	200	220
Cherries	300	200
Strawberries	100	150
Mangoes	110	110

CHANGE ROW HEIGHT

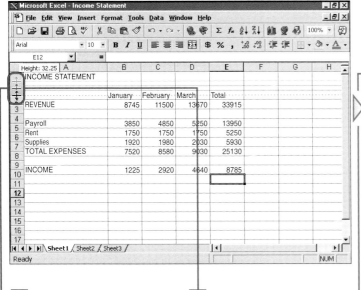

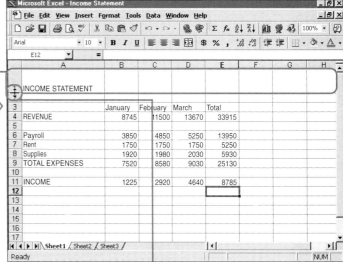

1 To change the height of a row, move the mouse ⊕ over the bottom edge of the row heading (⊕ changes to ✚).

2 Press and hold down the left mouse button as you move the row edge until the dotted line displays the row height you want. Then release the mouse button.

■ The row displays the new height.

FIT TALLEST ITEM

You can have Excel change a row height to fit the tallest item in the row.

■ Move the mouse ⊕ over the bottom edge of the row heading (⊕ changes to ✚) and then quickly press the left mouse button twice.

167

You can quickly change the appearance of numbers in your worksheet without retyping the numbers.

Option		Example
$	Change to dollar value	10 → $10.00
%	Change to percentage	0.15 → 15%
,	Add comma and display two decimal places	1000 → 1,000.00
.00→.0	Add decimal place	10.19 → 10.190
.00→.0	Remove decimal place	10.19 → 10.2

When you change the appearance of numbers, you do not change the value of the numbers.

CHANGE APPEARANCE OF NUMBERS

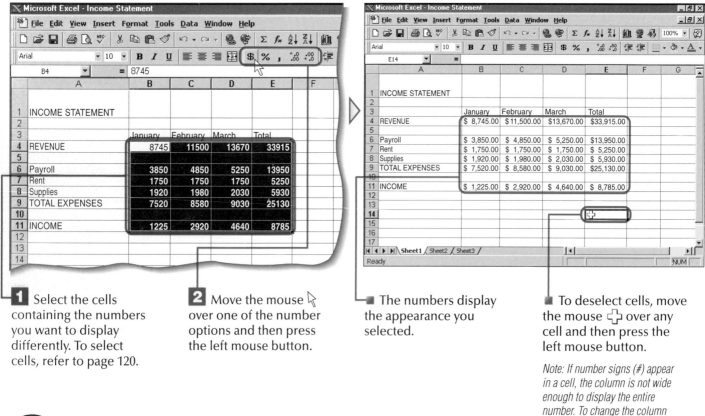

1 Select the cells containing the numbers you want to display differently. To select cells, refer to page 120.

2 Move the mouse over one of the number options and then press the left mouse button.

■ The numbers display the appearance you selected.

■ To deselect cells, move the mouse over any cell and then press the left mouse button.

Note: If number signs (#) appear in a cell, the column is not wide enough to display the entire number. To change the column width, refer to page 166.

BOLD, ITALIC AND UNDERLINE

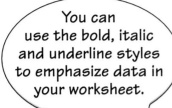

You can use the bold, italic and underline styles to emphasize data in your worksheet.

Bold *Italic* <u>Underline</u>

BOLD, ITALIC AND UNDERLINE

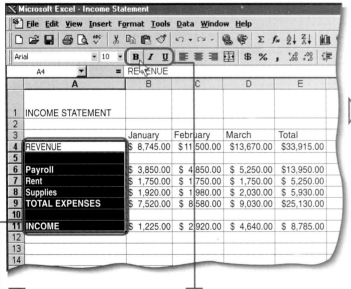

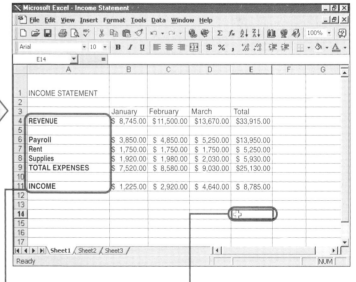

1 Select the cells containing the data you want to emphasize. To select cells, refer to page 120.

2 Move the mouse over one of the following options and then press the left mouse button.

B Bold

I Italic

<u>U</u> Underline

■ The data displays the style you selected.

■ To deselect cells, move the mouse over any cell and then press the left mouse button.

■ To remove a bold, italic or underline style, repeat steps **1** and **2**.

CHANGE FONT OF DATA

You can enhance the appearance of your worksheet by changing the font of data.

CHANGE FONT OF DATA

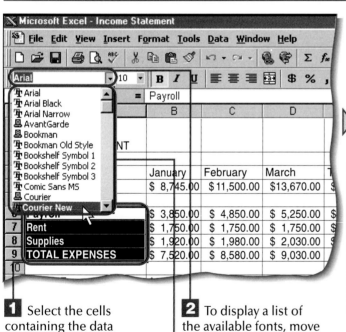

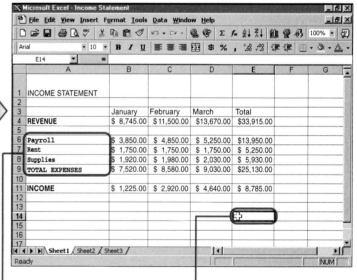

1 Select the cells containing the data you want to change to a new font. To select cells, refer to page 120.

2 To display a list of the available fonts, move the mouse ₖ over ▾ in this area and then press the left mouse button.

3 Move the mouse ₖ over the font you want to use and then press the left mouse button.

■ The data displays the font you selected.

■ To deselect cells, move the mouse ⊹ over any cell and then press the left mouse button.

CHANGE SIZE OF DATA

You can increase or decrease the size of data in your worksheet.

CHANGE SIZE OF DATA

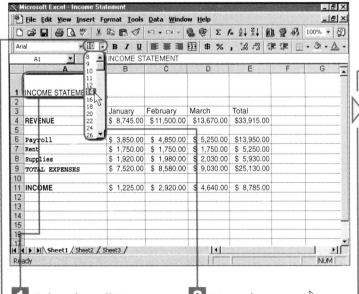

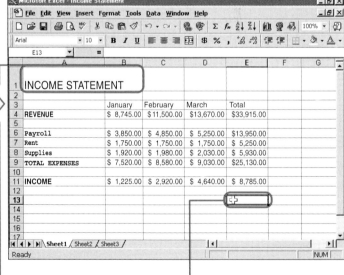

1 Select the cell(s) containing the data you want to change to a new size. To select cells, refer to page 120.

2 To display a list of the available sizes, move the mouse ⌖ over ▾ in this area and then press the left mouse button.

3 Move the mouse ⌖ over the size you want to use and then press the left mouse button.

■ The data displays the size you selected.

■ To deselect cells, move the mouse ⊕ over any cell and then press the left mouse button.

CHANGE ALIGNMENT OF DATA

You can change the position of data in each cell of your worksheet.

CHANGE ALIGNMENT OF DATA

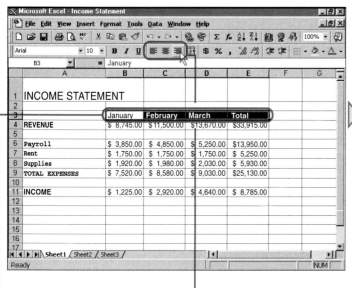

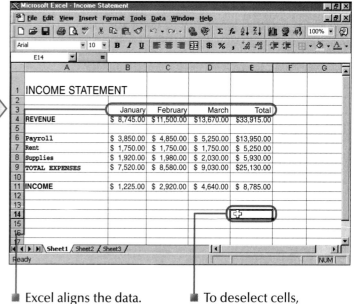

1 Select the cells containing the data you want to align differently. To select cells, refer to page 120.

2 Move the mouse ⟨ over one of the following options and then press the left mouse button.

▤ Left align

▤ Center

▤ Right align

■ Excel aligns the data.

■ To deselect cells, move the mouse ⊕ over any cell and then press the left mouse button.

You can use the Indent feature to move data away from the left edge of a cell.

INDENT DATA

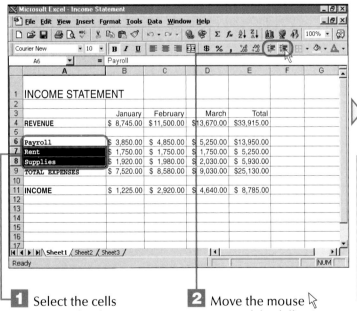

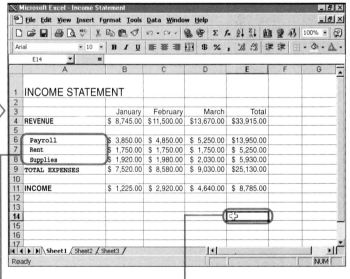

1 Select the cells containing the data you want to indent. To select cells, refer to page 120.

2 Move the mouse ⌖ over one of the following options and then press the left mouse button.

▤ Move data to the left

▤ Move data to the right

■ Excel indents the data.

■ To deselect cells, move the mouse ⊹ over any cell and then press the left mouse button.

You can add borders to enhance the appearance of your worksheet.

ADD BORDERS

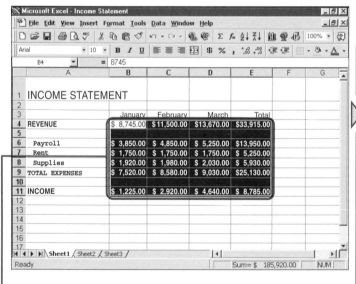

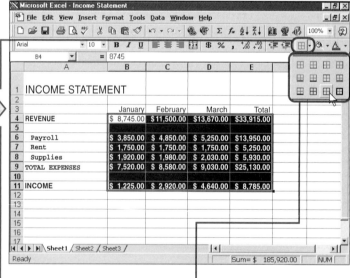

1 Select the cells you want to display borders. To select cells, refer to page 120.

2 Move the mouse ▷ over ▾ in this area and then press the left mouse button.

3 Move the mouse ▷ over the type of border you want to add and then press the left mouse button.

174

Can I print lines in my worksheet without adding borders?

Instead of adding borders to your worksheet, you can have Excel automatically print light lines, called gridlines, around each cell. To print gridlines, refer to page 190.

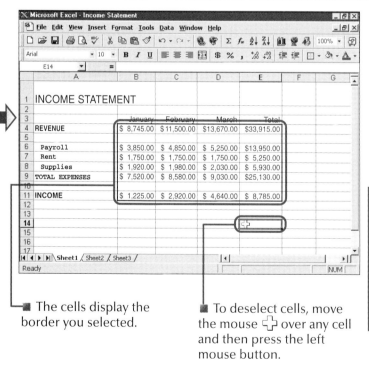

■ The cells display the border you selected.

■ To deselect cells, move the mouse ╬ over any cell and then press the left mouse button.

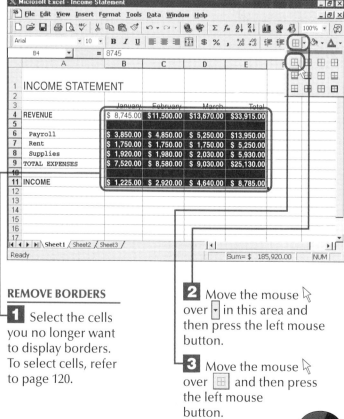

REMOVE BORDERS

1 Select the cells you no longer want to display borders. To select cells, refer to page 120.

2 Move the mouse ☞ over ▾ in this area and then press the left mouse button.

3 Move the mouse ☞ over ⊞ and then press the left mouse button.

CHANGE COLOR

You can make your worksheet more attractive by adding color.

CHANGE CELL COLOR

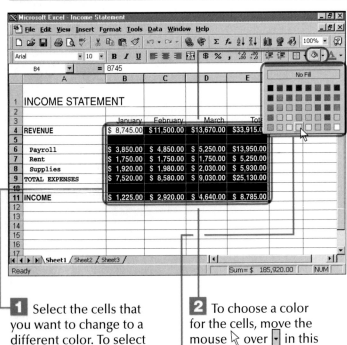

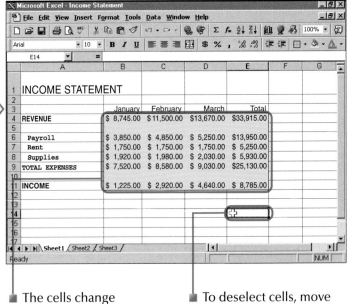

1 Select the cells that you want to change to a different color. To select cells, refer to page 120.

2 To choose a color for the cells, move the mouse ⌖ over ▾ in this area and then press the left mouse button.

3 Move the mouse ⌖ over the color you want to use and then press the left mouse button.

■ The cells change to the new color.

■ To deselect cells, move the mouse ⊕ over any cell and then press the left mouse button.

REMOVE CELL COLOR

■ Perform steps 1 to 3, selecting **No Fill** in step 3.

176

What colors should I choose?

When adding color to a worksheet, make sure you choose cell and data colors that work well together. For example, red text on a blue background is difficult to read. To choose from many ready-to-use designs offered by Excel, refer to page 180.

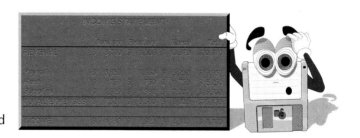

CHANGE DATA COLOR

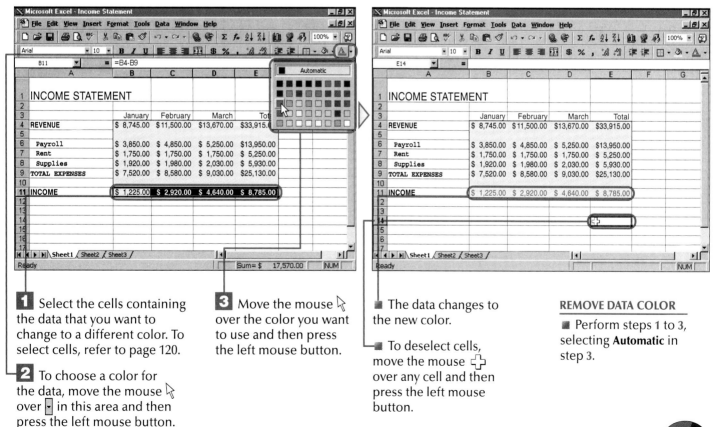

1 Select the cells containing the data that you want to change to a different color. To select cells, refer to page 120.

2 To choose a color for the data, move the mouse ⌖ over ▾ in this area and then press the left mouse button.

3 Move the mouse ⌖ over the color you want to use and then press the left mouse button.

■ The data changes to the new color.

■ To deselect cells, move the mouse ⌖ over any cell and then press the left mouse button.

REMOVE DATA COLOR

■ Perform steps 1 to 3, selecting **Automatic** in step 3.

If you like the appearance of a cell in your worksheet, you can make other cells look exactly the same.

COPY FORMATTING

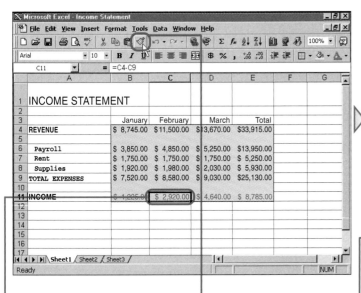

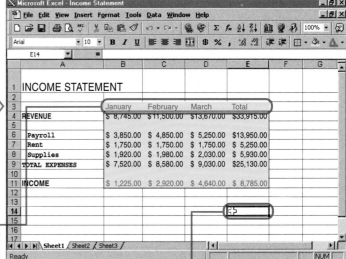

1 Move the mouse ⊕ over a cell displaying the formats you like and then press the left mouse button.

2 Move the mouse ⬚ over ✍ and then press the left mouse button (⬚ changes to ⊕🖌 when over the worksheet).

3 Select the cells you want to display the same formats. To select cells, refer to page 120.

■ When you release the mouse button, the cells display the formats.

■ To deselect cells, move the mouse ⊕ over any cell and then press the left mouse button.

Note: If number signs (#) appear in a cell, the column is too narrow to fit the data. To change the column width, refer to page 166.

CENTER DATA ACROSS COLUMNS

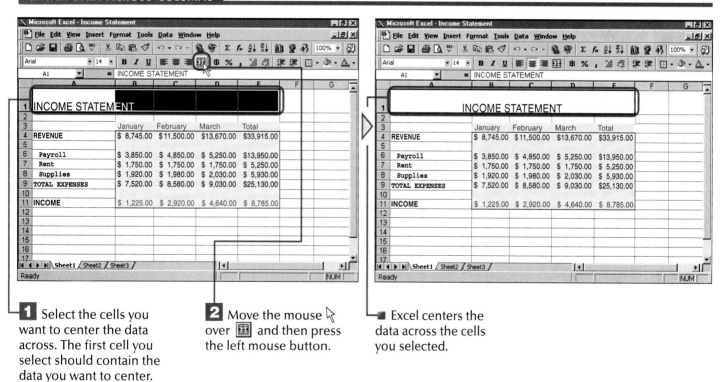

1 Select the cells you want to center the data across. The first cell you select should contain the data you want to center.

2 Move the mouse over ⊞ and then press the left mouse button.

Excel centers the data across the cells you selected.

QUICKLY APPLY A DESIGN

Excel offers many ready-to-use designs that you can choose from to give your worksheet a new appearance.

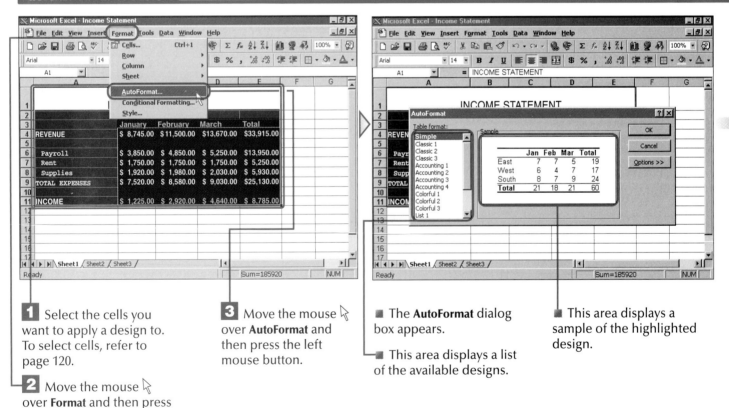

1 Select the cells you want to apply a design to. To select cells, refer to page 120.

2 Move the mouse over **Format** and then press the left mouse button.

3 Move the mouse over **AutoFormat** and then press the left mouse button.

■ The **AutoFormat** dialog box appears.

■ This area displays a list of the available designs.

■ This area displays a sample of the highlighted design.

What are some designs offered by Excel?

	Jan	Feb	Mar	Total
East	7	7	5	19
West	6	4	7	17
South	8	7	9	24
Total	21	18	21	60

List 2

	Jan	Feb	Mar	Total
East	$ 7	$ 7	$ 5	$ 19
West	6	4	7	17
South	8	7	9	24
Total	$ 21	$ 18	$ 21	$ 60

Accounting 2

	Jan	Feb	Mar	Total
East	7	7	5	19
West	6	4	7	17
South	8	7	9	24
Total	21	18	21	60

Classic 2

	Jan	Feb	Mar	Total
East	7	7	5	19
West	6	4	7	17
South	8	7	9	24
Total	21	18	21	60

3D Effects 1

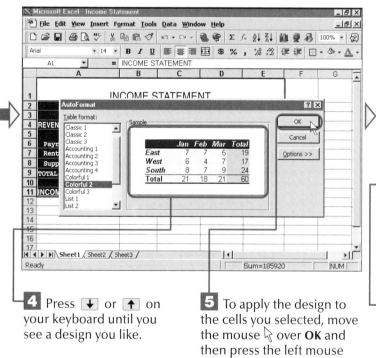

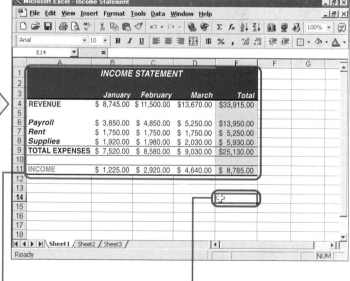

4 Press ↓ or ↑ on your keyboard until you see a design you like.

5 To apply the design to the cells you selected, move the mouse ⇖ over **OK** and then press the left mouse button.

■ The cells display the design you selected.

■ To deselect cells, move the mouse ⊹ over any cell and then press the left mouse button.

REMOVE AUTOFORMAT

■ Perform steps **1** to **5**, selecting **None** in step **4**.

You can see on the screen how your worksheet will look when printed.

PREVIEW A WORKSHEET

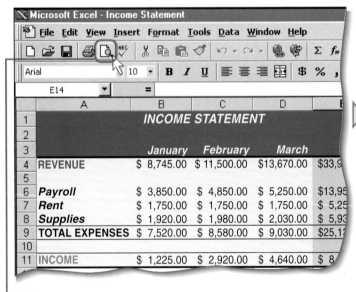

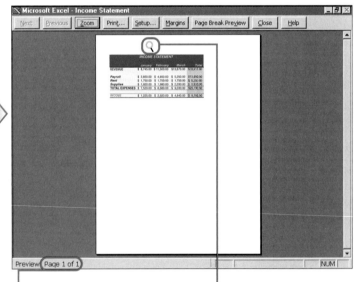

1 Move the mouse ⌐ over 🔍 and then press the left mouse button.

■ The Print Preview window appears.

■ This area tells you which page is displayed and the total number of pages in the worksheet.

Note: If you have a black-and-white printer, Excel displays the page in black and white.

2 To magnify an area of the page, move the mouse ⌐ over the area (⌐ changes to 🔍) and then press the left mouse button.

182

What should I do before printing my worksheet?

Before printing your worksheet, preview the worksheet to ensure it will print the way you want. Also make sure the printer is turned on and contains paper.

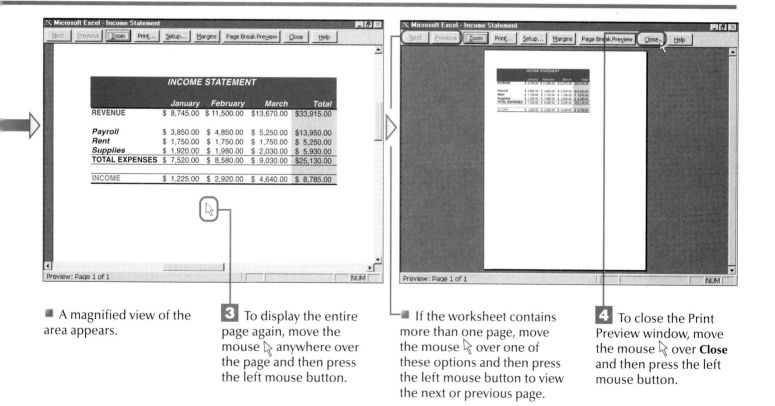

■ A magnified view of the area appears.

3 To display the entire page again, move the mouse ⬚ anywhere over the page and then press the left mouse button.

■ If the worksheet contains more than one page, move the mouse ⬚ over one of these options and then press the left mouse button to view the next or previous page.

4 To close the Print Preview window, move the mouse ⬚ over **Close** and then press the left mouse button.

CHANGE MARGINS

A margin is the amount of space between data and an edge of your paper. You can easily change the margins.

CHANGE MARGINS

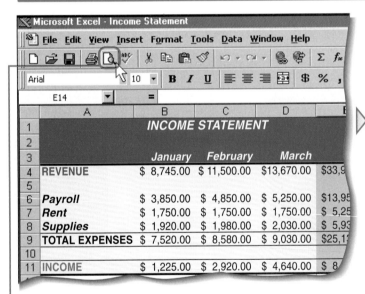

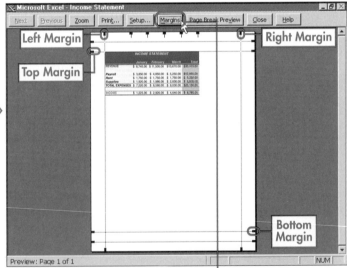

1 To display the worksheet in the Print Preview window, move the mouse ⇧ over 🔍 and then press the left mouse button.

■ The worksheet appears in the Print Preview window. For information on previewing a worksheet, refer to page 182.

2 If the margins are not displayed, move the mouse ⇧ over **Margins** and then press the left mouse button.

Why would I change the margins?

Changing margins lets you accommodate letterhead and other specialty paper.

You can also change the margins to fit more or less information on a page.

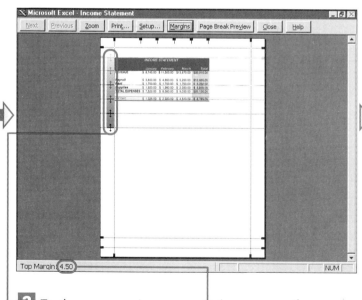

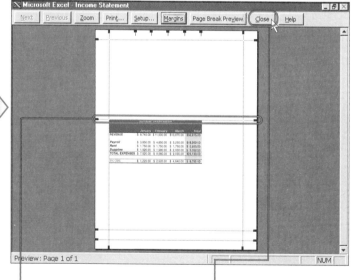

3 To change a margin, move the mouse ◯ over the margin (◯ changes to ┿ or ┿).

4 Press and hold down the left mouse button as you move the margin to a new location. A line shows the new location.

■ As you move the margin, this area displays the distance in inches between the margin and the edge of the page.

5 Release the mouse button and the margin moves to the new location.

6 Repeat steps 3 to 5 for each margin you want to change.

7 To close the Print Preview window, move the mouse ▷ over **Close** and then press the left mouse button.

PRINT A WORKSHEET

You can produce a paper copy of the worksheet displayed on your screen.

PRINT A WORKSHEET

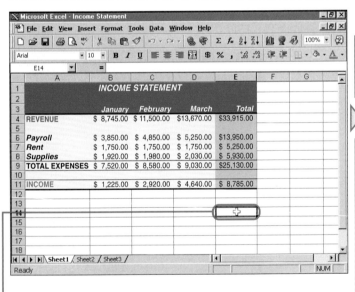

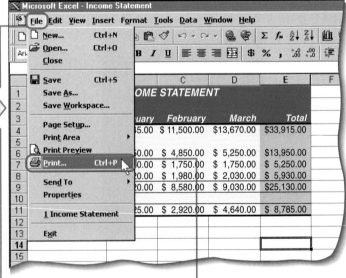

1 To print a worksheet, move the mouse ⌖ over any cell in the worksheet and then press the left mouse button.

■ To print only part of the worksheet, select the cells you want to print. To select cells, refer to page 120.

2 Move the mouse ⌖ over **File** and then press the left mouse button.

3 Move the mouse ⌖ over **Print** and then press the left mouse button.

■ The **Print** dialog box appears.

What can I print?

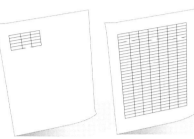

For information
on using multiple
worksheets in a
workbook, refer to
pages 194 to 199.

Selection
Print the cells
you selected.

Active sheet(s)
Print the entire
worksheet.

Entire workbook
Print every worksheet
in the workbook.

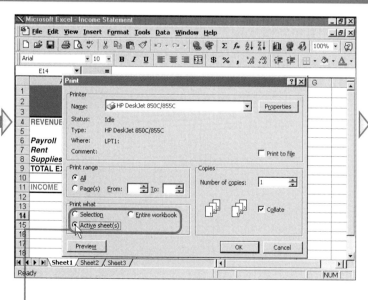

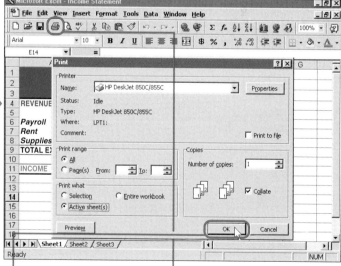

4 Move the mouse ▷
over what you want to
print and then press
the left mouse button
(○ changes to ⊙).

*Note: For information on what
you can print, refer to the top
of this page.*

5 Move the mouse ▷
over **OK** and then press
the left mouse button.

**QUICKLY PRINT ENTIRE
WORKSHEET**

■ To quickly print the
worksheet displayed on
your screen, move the
mouse ▷ over 🖨 and
then press the left
mouse button.

CENTER DATA ON A PAGE

You can center data horizontally and vertically between the margins on a page.

CENTER DATA ON A PAGE

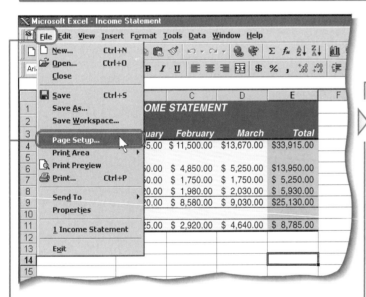

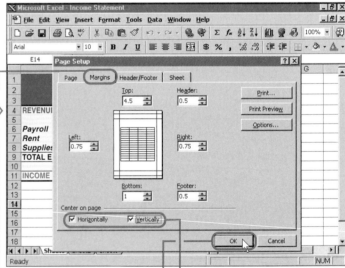

1 Move the mouse ⬈ over **File** and then press the left mouse button.

2 Move the mouse ⬈ over **Page Setup** and then press the left mouse button.

■ The **Page Setup** dialog box appears.

3 Move the mouse ⬈ over the **Margins** tab and then press the left mouse button.

4 Move the mouse ⬈ over the way you want to center the data and then press the left mouse button (☐ changes to ☑). You can select both center options if you wish.

5 Move the mouse ⬈ over **OK** and then press the left mouse button.

You can change the orientation of your printed worksheet.

Portrait

Landscape

The landscape orientation is ideal if you want a wide worksheet to fit on one page.

CHANGE PAGE ORIENTATION

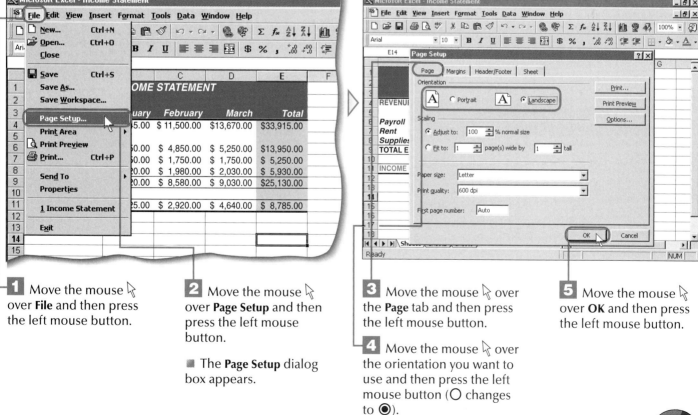

1 Move the mouse ⌖ over **File** and then press the left mouse button.

2 Move the mouse ⌖ over **Page Setup** and then press the left mouse button.

■ The **Page Setup** dialog box appears.

3 Move the mouse ⌖ over the **Page** tab and then press the left mouse button.

4 Move the mouse ⌖ over the orientation you want to use and then press the left mouse button (○ changes to ◉).

5 Move the mouse ⌖ over **OK** and then press the left mouse button.

You can change the way your worksheet appears on a printed page.

CHANGE PRINT OPTIONS

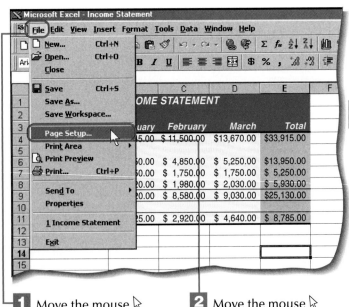

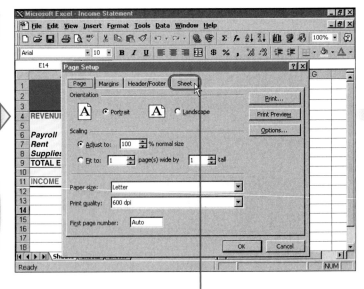

1 Move the mouse ⅄ over **File** and then press the left mouse button.

2 Move the mouse ⅄ over **Page Setup** and then press the left mouse button.

■ The **Page Setup** dialog box appears.

3 Move the mouse ⅄ over the **Sheet** tab and then press the left mouse button.

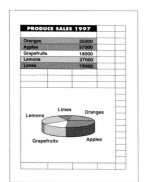

Gridlines

Prints lines around each cell in your worksheet.

Black and white

Prints the worksheet in black and white. This can make a colored worksheet printed on a black-and-white printer easier to read.

Draft quality

Does not print gridlines or most graphics to reduce printing time.

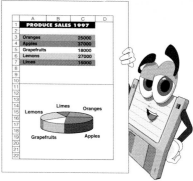

Row and column headings

Prints the row numbers and column letters.

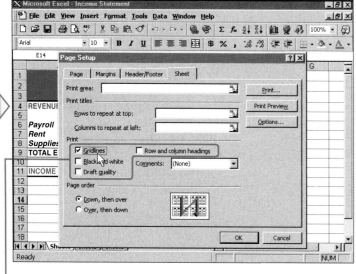

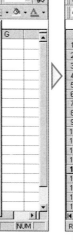

4 Move the mouse ⬡ over the print option you want to select and then press the left mouse button (☐ changes to ☑).

Note: For information on the print options, refer to the top of this page.

5 Repeat step **4** for each print option you want to select.

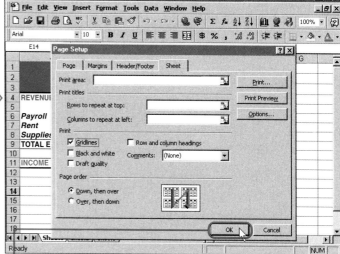

6 Move the mouse ⬡ over **OK** and then press the left mouse button.

■ The print options you selected only change the way the worksheet appears on a printed page. The print options do not affect the way the worksheet appears on your screen.

INSERT A PAGE BREAK

If you want to start a new page at a specific place in your worksheet, you can add a page break. A page break defines where one page ends and another begins.

When you fill a page with data, Excel automatically starts a new page by inserting a page break for you.

INSERT A PAGE BREAK

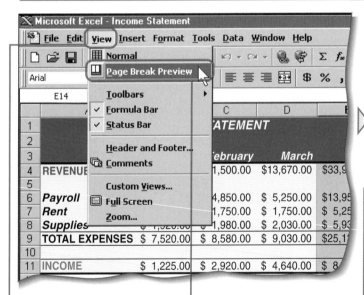

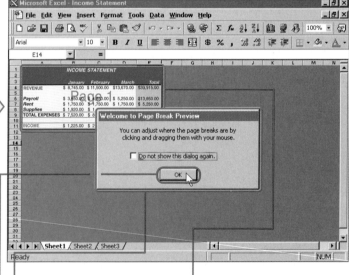

1 To display the page breaks in the worksheet, move the mouse over **View** and then press the left mouse button.

2 Move the mouse over **Page Break Preview** and then press the left mouse button.

■ A **Welcome** dialog box appears.

3 To close the dialog box, move the mouse over **OK** and then press the left mouse button.

■ Blue lines show where page breaks currently occur in the worksheet.

*Note: To return to the normal view at any time, repeat steps 1 and 2, selecting **Normal** in step 2.*

How can I move a page break?

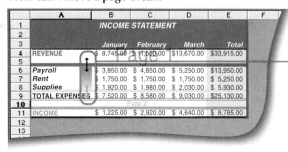

1 To move a page break, move the mouse ⊕ over the page break line (⊕ changes to ↔ or ↕).

2 Press and hold down the left mouse button as you move the page break line to a new location. Then release the mouse button.

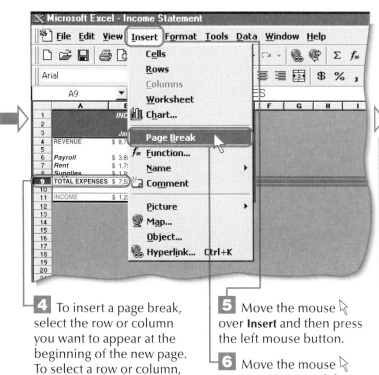

4 To insert a page break, select the row or column you want to appear at the beginning of the new page. To select a row or column, refer to page 120.

5 Move the mouse ⬧ over **Insert** and then press the left mouse button.

6 Move the mouse ⬧ over **Page Break** and then press the left mouse button.

■ A page break line appears.

■ To deselect the row or column, move the mouse ⊕ over any cell and then press the left mouse button.

DELETE A PAGE BREAK

■ Select the row directly below or the column directly to the right of the page break line. Perform steps 5 and 6, selecting **Remove Page Break** in step 6.

193

SWITCH BETWEEN WORKSHEETS

> The worksheet displayed on your screen is one of several worksheets in a workbook. You can easily switch between the worksheets.

SWITCH BETWEEN WORKSHEETS

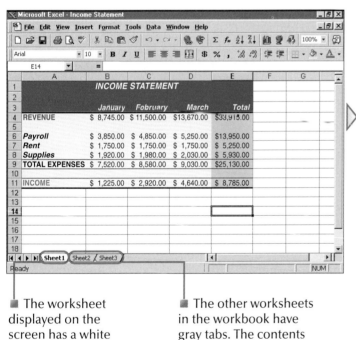

■ The worksheet displayed on the screen has a white tab.

■ The other worksheets in the workbook have gray tabs. The contents of these worksheets are hidden.

1 To display the contents of a worksheet, move the mouse ⬡ over the tab of the worksheet and then press the left mouse button.

Why would I need more than one worksheet?

Worksheets allow you to keep related information in a single file, called a workbook. For example, information for each division of a company can be stored on a separate worksheet in one workbook.

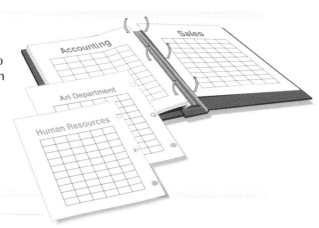

BROWSE THROUGH TABS

■ The contents of the worksheet appear. The contents of the other worksheets in the workbook are hidden.

■ The worksheet you selected now has a white tab.

BROWSE THROUGH TABS

■ If you have many worksheets in your workbook, you may not be able to see all the tabs.

Note: To insert additional worksheets, refer to page 196.

1 To browse through the tabs, move the mouse ⌖ over one of the following options and then press the left mouse button.

⏮ Display first tab

◀ Display tab to the left

▶ Display tab to the right

⏭ Display last tab

INSERT A WORKSHEET

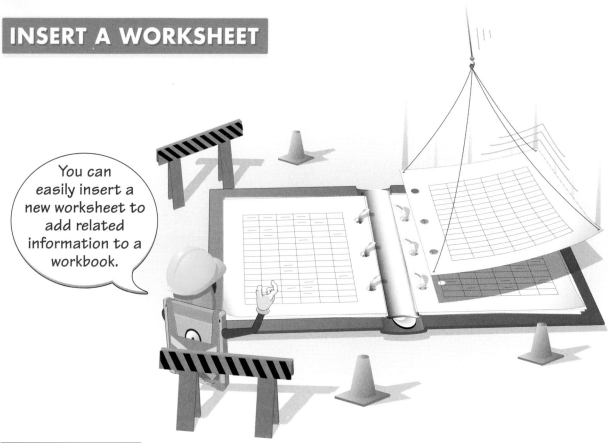

You can easily insert a new worksheet to add related information to a workbook.

INSERT A WORKSHEET

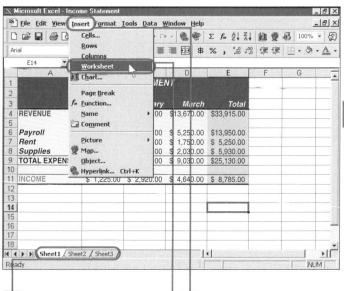

1 Move the mouse ⌖ over the tab of the worksheet you want to appear after the new worksheet and then press the left mouse button.

2 Move the mouse ⌖ over **Insert** and then press the left mouse button.

3 Move the mouse ⌖ over **Worksheet** and then press the left mouse button.

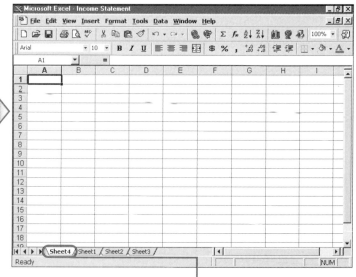

■ The new worksheet appears.

■ This area displays the tab for the new worksheet.

196

DELETE A WORKSHEET

You can permanently remove a worksheet you no longer need.

DELETE A WORKSHEET

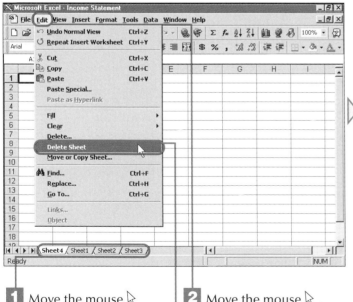

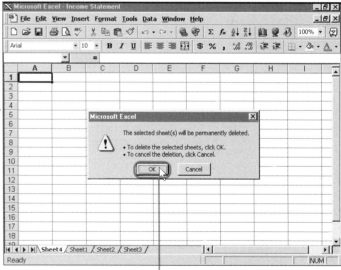

1 Move the mouse ▷ over the tab of the worksheet you want to delete and then press the left mouse button.

2 Move the mouse ▷ over **Edit** and then press the left mouse button.

3 Move the mouse ▷ over **Delete Sheet** and then press the left mouse button.

■ A warning dialog box appears.

4 To permanently delete the worksheet, move the mouse ▷ over **OK** and then press the left mouse button.

197

RENAME A WORKSHEET

You can give each worksheet in a workbook a descriptive name. This helps you remember where you stored your data.

RENAME A WORKSHEET

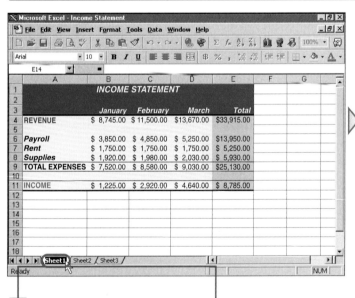

1 Move the mouse over the tab of the worksheet you want to rename and then quickly press the left mouse button twice.

■ The current name is highlighted.

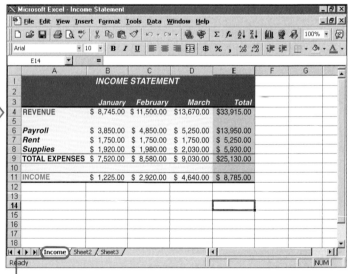

2 Type a new name and then press **Enter** on your keyboard. A worksheet name can contain up to 31 characters, including spaces.

198

You can reorganize information by moving a worksheet to a new location in a workbook.

MOVE A WORKSHEET

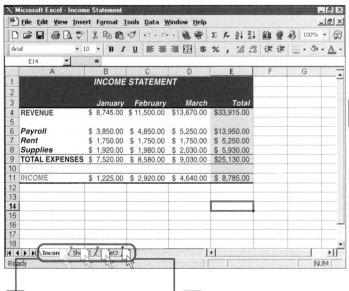

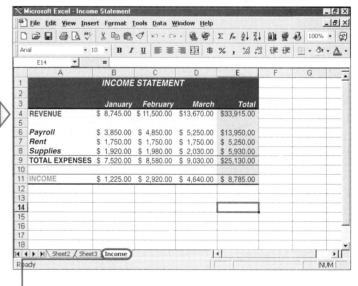

1 Move the mouse ⌖ over the tab of the worksheet you want to move.

2 Press and hold down the left mouse button as you move the worksheet to a new location.

■ An arrow (▾) shows where the worksheet will appear.

3 Release the mouse button and the worksheet appears in the new location.

You can graphically display your worksheet data in a chart.

CREATE A CHART

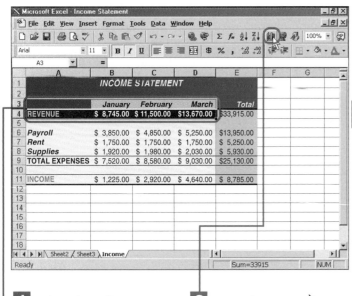

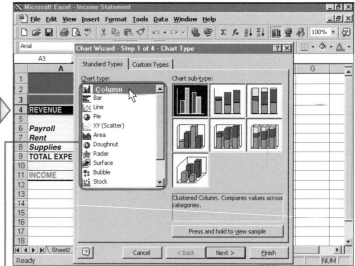

1 Select the cells containing the data you want to display in a chart, including the row and column labels. To select cells, refer to page 120.

2 Move the mouse ⌖ over 📊 and then press the left mouse button.

■ The **Chart Wizard** dialog box appears.

3 Move the mouse ⌖ over the type of chart you want to create and then press the left mouse button.

Note: You can easily change the type of chart later on. For information, refer to page 204.

Can I change my selections?

While creating a chart, you can return to a previous step at any time to change the choices you made.

■ To do so, move the mouse ⊾ over **Back** and then press the left mouse button.

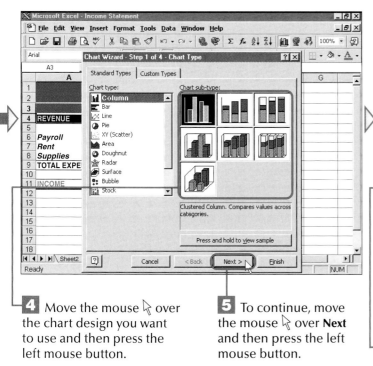

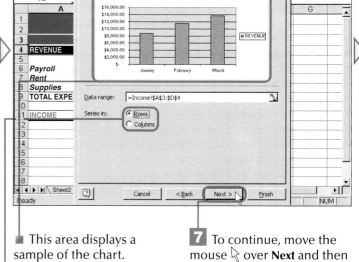

4 Move the mouse ⊾ over the chart design you want to use and then press the left mouse button.

Note: The available designs depend on the type of chart you selected in step 3.

5 To continue, move the mouse ⊾ over **Next** and then press the left mouse button.

■ This area displays a sample of the chart.

6 To select the way you want Excel to plot the data from the worksheet, move the mouse ⊾ over one of these options and then press the left mouse button (○ changes to ●).

7 To continue, move the mouse ⊾ over **Next** and then press the left mouse button.

CONTINUED

CREATE A CHART

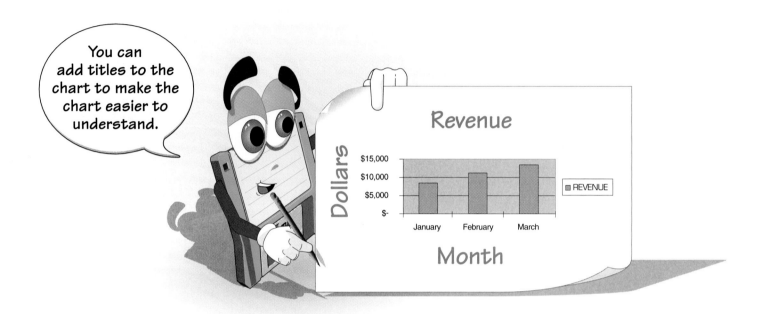

You can add titles to the chart to make the chart easier to understand.

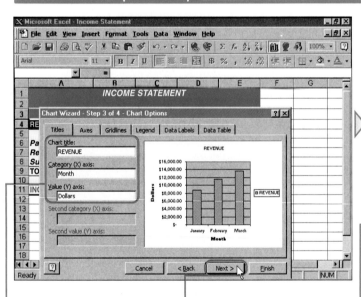

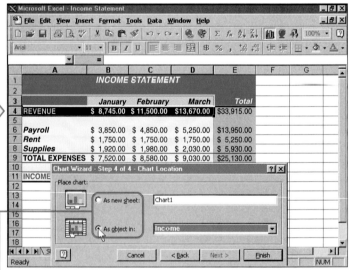

8 To add a title to the chart, move the mouse I over the box for the title you want to add and then press the left mouse button. Then type the title.

9 Repeat step **8** for each title you want to add.

10 To continue, move the mouse ⬏ over **Next** and then press the left mouse button.

11 To choose where you want to display the chart, move the mouse ⬏ over one of these options and then press the left mouse button (○ changes to ⦿).

As new sheet

Display chart on its own sheet, called a chart sheet.

As object in

Display chart on the same worksheet as the data.

What happens if I change data used in a chart?

If you change data used in a chart, Excel will automatically update the chart.

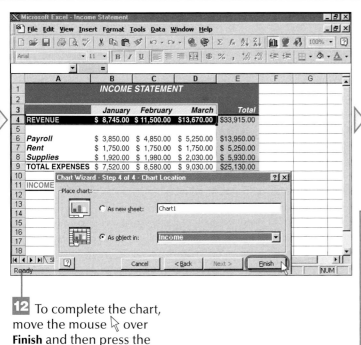

12 To complete the chart, move the mouse ⍾ over **Finish** and then press the left mouse button.

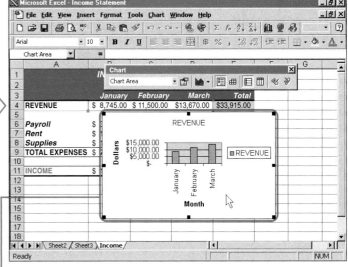

■ The chart appears.

DELETE A CHART

1 Move the mouse ⍾ over a blank area in the chart and then press the left mouse button. Handles (■) appear around the chart.

2 Press **Delete** on your keyboard.

Note: To delete a chart displayed on a chart sheet, follow the steps to delete a worksheet. To delete a worksheet, refer to page 197.

CHANGE CHART TYPE

After you create a chart, you can select a different type of chart that will better suit your data.

CHANGE CHART TYPE

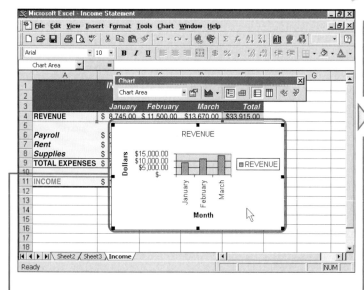

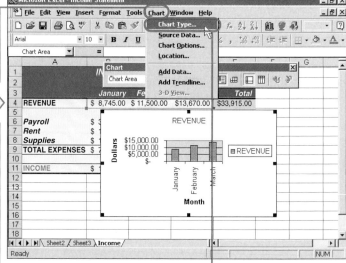

1 To change a chart on a worksheet, move the mouse ⬐ over a blank area in the chart and then press the left mouse button. Handles (■) appear around the chart.

▪ To change a chart on a chart sheet, move the mouse ⬐ over the tab for the chart sheet and then press the left mouse button.

2 Move the mouse ⬐ over **Chart** and then press the left mouse button.

3 Move the mouse ⬐ over **Chart Type** and then press the left mouse button.

▪ The **Chart Type** dialog box appears.

What type of chart should I choose?

The type of chart you should choose depends on your data. For example, area, column and line charts are ideal for showing changes to values over time, whereas pie charts are ideal for showing percentages.

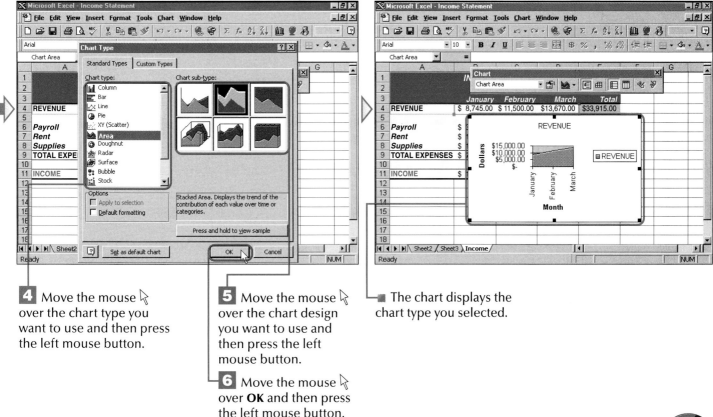

4 Move the mouse ↖ over the chart type you want to use and then press the left mouse button.

5 Move the mouse ↖ over the chart design you want to use and then press the left mouse button.

6 Move the mouse ↖ over **OK** and then press the left mouse button.

■ The chart displays the chart type you selected.

MOVE OR RESIZE A CHART

After you create a chart, you can change the location and size of the chart.

MOVE A CHART

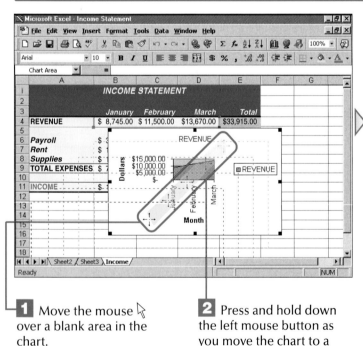

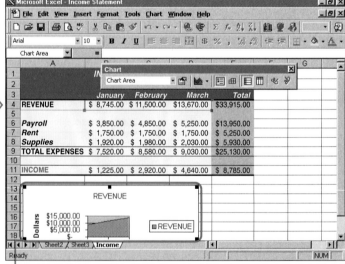

1 Move the mouse ⌖ over a blank area in the chart.

2 Press and hold down the left mouse button as you move the chart to a new location.

■ A dotted line shows the new location.

3 Release the mouse button and the chart appears in the new location.

What are the handles (■) that appear around a chart?

The handles around a chart let you change the size of the chart.

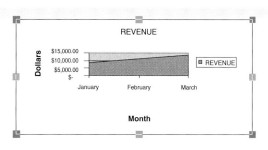

■ Change the height of a chart.

■ Change the width of a chart.

■ Change the height and width of a chart at the same time.

RESIZE A CHART

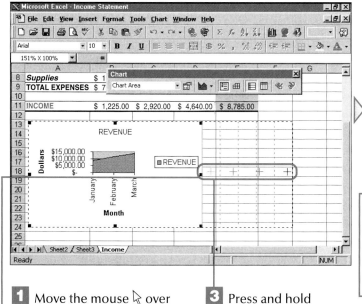

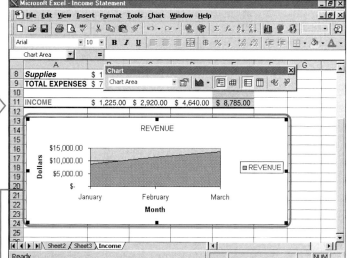

1 Move the mouse ⌖ over a blank area in the chart and then press the left mouse button. Handles (■) appear around the chart.

2 Move the mouse ⌖ over one of the handles (■) (⌖ changes to ↕ or ↔).

3 Press and hold down the left mouse button as you move the edge of the chart until the chart is the size you want.

■ A dotted line shows the new size.

4 Release the mouse button and the chart appears in the new size.

PRINT A CHART

You can print your chart with the worksheet data or on its own page.

PRINT A CHART WITH WORKSHEET DATA

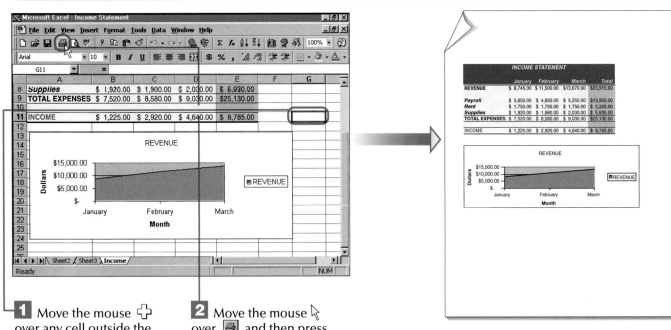

1 Move the mouse ✛ over any cell outside the chart and then press the left mouse button.

2 Move the mouse ⬚ over 🖨 and then press the left mouse button.

Note: For more information on printing, refer to pages 182 to 193.

208

Can I see what my chart will look like when printed?

You can preview your chart to see what the chart will look like when printed. To preview a chart, refer to page 182.

PRINT A CHART ON ITS OWN PAGE

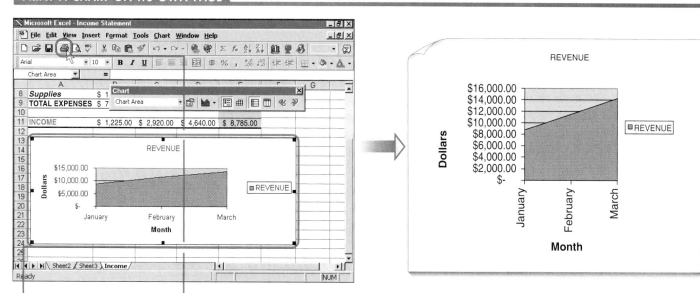

Note: When you print a chart on its own page, the chart will expand to fill the page. The printed chart may look different from the chart on the worksheet.

1 To print a chart displayed on a worksheet, move the mouse over a blank area in the chart and then press the left mouse button.

▪ To print a chart displayed on a chart sheet, move the mouse over the tab for the chart sheet and then press the left mouse button.

2 Move the mouse over 🖨 and then press the left mouse button.

Create a Presentation
Page 218

Add a Chart
Page 246

Microsoft PowerPoint helps you plan, organize and design professional presentations.

Delete Text
Page 234

Change Text Color
Page 262

Save a Presentation
Page 224

POWERPOINT

Change the Slide Layout
Page 240

Change Slide Design
Page 254

INTRODUCTION TO POWERPOINT

WAYS TO USE POWERPOINT

On-Screen Presentations

You can deliver a colorful, professional presentation on your computer screen.

35mm Slides or Overheads

You can create 35mm slides or overhead transparencies for presenting your ideas to a large audience.

Handouts

You can print handouts to help the audience follow your presentation. Handouts contain copies of your slides.

Speaker Notes

You can create speaker notes to help you deliver your presentation. Speaker notes contain copies of your slides along with all the ideas you want to discuss.

START POWERPOINT

You can start PowerPoint to create a professional presentation.

START POWERPOINT

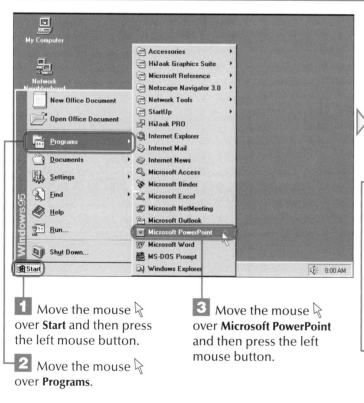

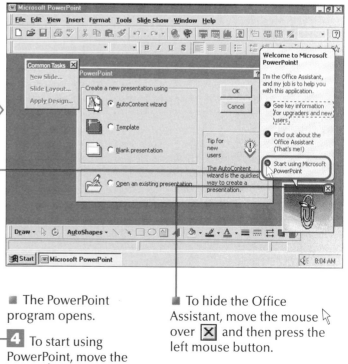

1 Move the mouse over **Start** and then press the left mouse button.

2 Move the mouse over **Programs**.

3 Move the mouse over **Microsoft PowerPoint** and then press the left mouse button.

■ The PowerPoint program opens.

4 To start using PowerPoint, move the mouse over this option and then press the left mouse button.

■ To hide the Office Assistant, move the mouse over ⊠ and then press the left mouse button.

CREATE A PRESENTATION

You can use the AutoContent wizard to quickly create a presentation.

The wizard will ask you a series of questions and then set up a presentation based on your answers.

CREATE A PRESENTATION

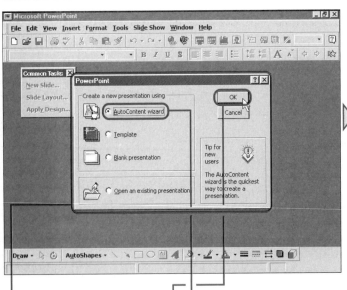

■ The **PowerPoint** dialog box appears each time you start PowerPoint.

1 To create a new presentation, move the mouse ⬚ over **AutoContent wizard** and then press the left mouse button (○ changes to ◉).

2 Move the mouse ⬚ over **OK** and then press the left mouse button.

■ The **AutoContent Wizard** dialog box appears.

3 To start creating the presentation, move the mouse ⬚ over **Next** and then press the left mouse button.

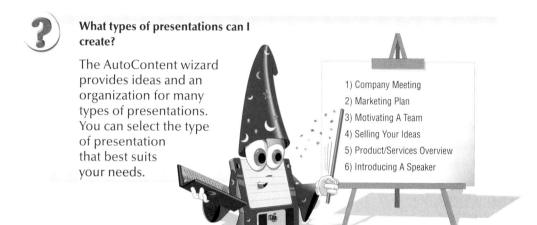

What types of presentations can I create?

The AutoContent wizard provides ideas and an organization for many types of presentations. You can select the type of presentation that best suits your needs.

1) Company Meeting
2) Marketing Plan
3) Motivating A Team
4) Selling Your Ideas
5) Product/Services Overview
6) Introducing A Speaker

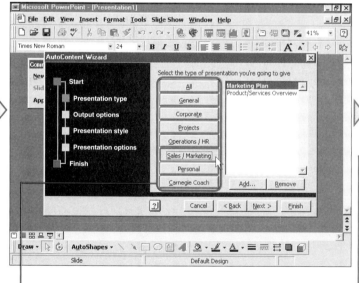

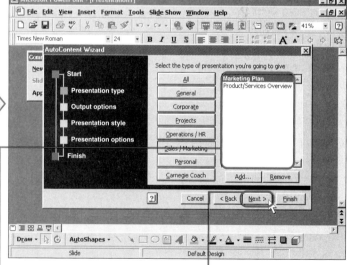

4 Move the mouse ↕ over the category that best describes the type of presentation you want to create and then press the left mouse button.

■ If you are not sure which category best describes the presentation, select **All**.

■ This area displays the types of presentations within the category you selected.

5 Move the mouse ↕ over the type of presentation that best suits your needs and then press the left mouse button.

6 To continue, move the mouse ↕ over **Next** and then press the left mouse button.

CONTINUED▶

You can choose to deliver a presentation to an audience or have people view the presentation on their own.

CREATE A PRESENTATION (CONTINUED)

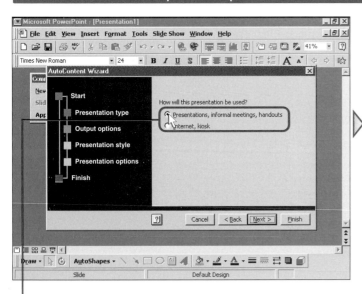

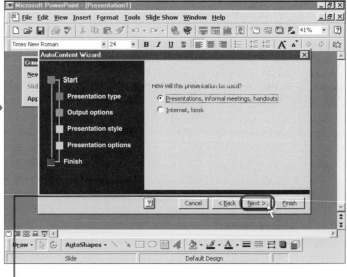

7 Move the mouse ⌖ over the way you plan to use the presentation and then press the left mouse button (○ changes to ⦿).

Presentations
You will deliver the presentation to an audience.

Internet
People will view the presentation on their own.

8 To continue, move the mouse ⌖ over **Next** and then press the left mouse button.

216

How can I output my presentation?

There are four ways you can output your presentation.

On-screen presentation   Black and white overheads   Color overheads   35mm slides

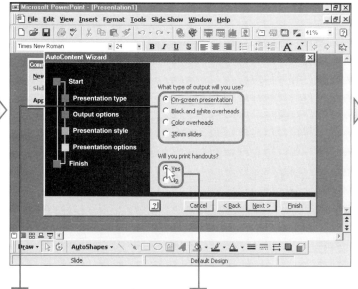

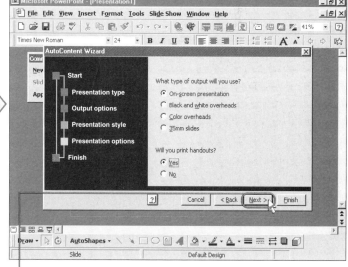

9 Move the mouse ⌖ over the type of output you want to use for the presentation and then press the left mouse button (○ changes to ◉).

10 To choose whether or not you want to print handouts for the audience, move the mouse ⌖ over **Yes** or **No** and then press the left mouse button (○ changes to ◉).

11 To continue, move the mouse ⌖ over **Next** and then press the left mouse button.

CONTINUED

The AutoContent wizard asks you what information you want to appear on your first slide.

CREATE A PRESENTATION (CONTINUED)

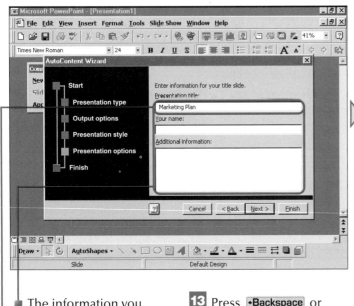

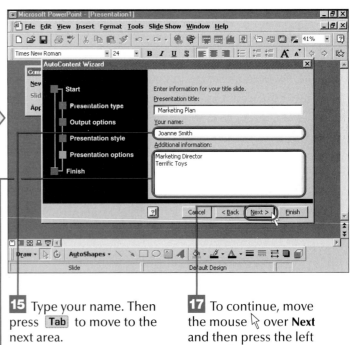

■ The information you enter in these areas will appear on the first slide in the presentation.

12 Move the mouse ⌖ over this area and then press the left mouse button.

13 Press **◆Backspace** or **Delete** on your keyboard until you have deleted all the text. Then type the title of the presentation.

14 Press **Tab** on your keyboard to move to the next area.

15 Type your name. Then press **Tab** to move to the next area.

16 Type any additional information you want to appear on the first slide.

17 To continue, move the mouse ⌖ over **Next** and then press the left mouse button.

218

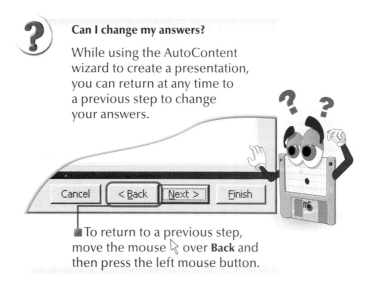

Can I change my answers?

While using the AutoContent
wizard to create a presentation,
you can return at any time to
a previous step to change
your answers.

■ To return to a previous step,
move the mouse ⍾ over **Back** and
then press the left mouse button.

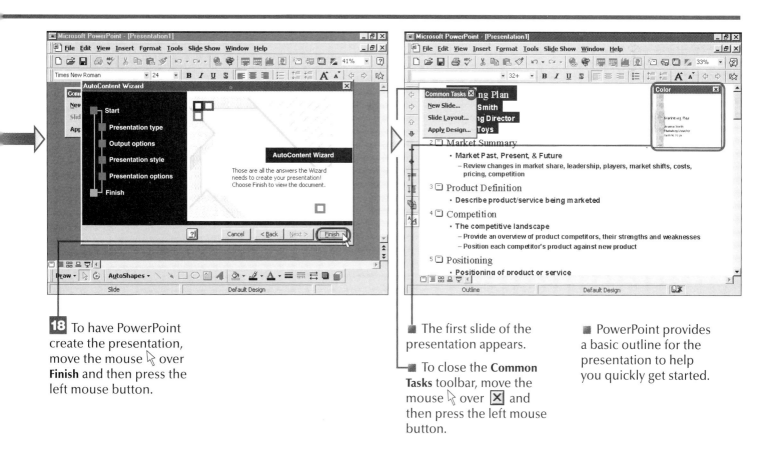

18 To have PowerPoint
create the presentation,
move the mouse ⍾ over
Finish and then press the
left mouse button.

■ The first slide of the
presentation appears.

■ To close the **Common
Tasks** toolbar, move the
mouse ⍾ over ☒ and
then press the left mouse
button.

■ PowerPoint provides
a basic outline for the
presentation to help
you quickly get started.

CHANGE THE VIEW

PowerPoint offers four different ways that you can view a presentation on your screen.

CHANGE THE VIEW

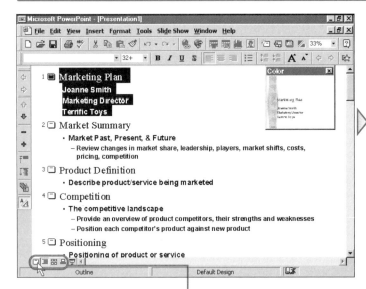

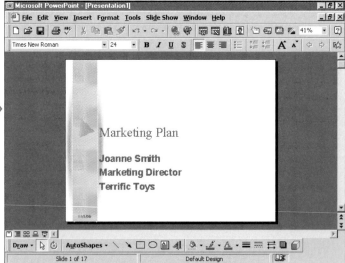

■ When you first create a presentation, PowerPoint displays the presentation in the Outline view.

1 To display the presentation in a different view, move the mouse ⌖ over one of the following options and then press the left mouse button.

▭ Slide   ▦ Slide Sorter

▤ Outline   ▣ Notes Page

■ PowerPoint displays the presentation in the new view.

■ All views display the same presentation. If you make changes to a slide in one view, the other views will also change.

THE FOUR VIEWS

Slide

The Slide view displays one slide at a time. This view is useful for changing the layout or design of your slides.

Slide Sorter

The Slide Sorter view displays a miniature version of each slide. This view lets you see a general overview of your presentation.

Outline

The Outline view displays the text on all the slides. This view lets you develop the content and organization of your presentation.

Notes Page

The Notes Page view displays one slide at a time, with space to type comments. You can use these comments as a guide when delivering your presentation.

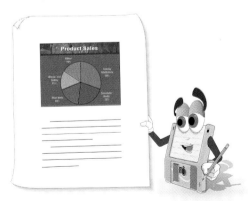

BROWSE THROUGH A PRESENTATION

Your computer screen cannot display your entire presentation at once. You must browse through the presentation to view slides or text not displayed on your screen.

SLIDE OR NOTES PAGE VIEW

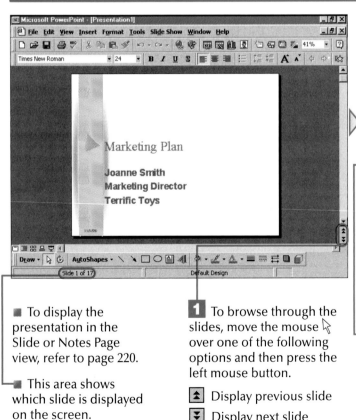

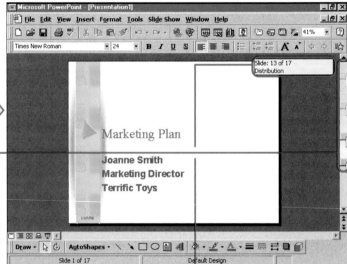

■ To display the presentation in the Slide or Notes Page view, refer to page 220.

■ This area shows which slide is displayed on the screen.

1 To browse through the slides, move the mouse ☐ over one of the following options and then press the left mouse button.

⬆ Display previous slide

⬇ Display next slide

QUICKLY BROWSE

1 Move the mouse ☐ over the scroll box. Then press and hold down the left mouse button as you move the mouse ☐ up or down the scroll bar.

2 When this box displays the number of the slide you want to view, release the mouse button.

222

Which views let me see more than one slide at a time?

These views display one slide at a time.

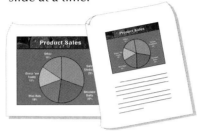

These views display more than one slide at a time.

Slide   Notes Page   Outline   Slide Sorter

OUTLINE OR SLIDE SORTER VIEW

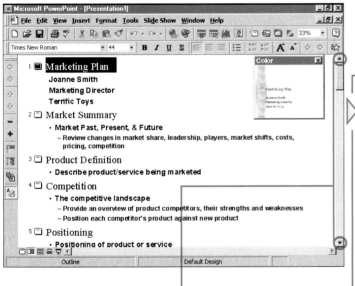

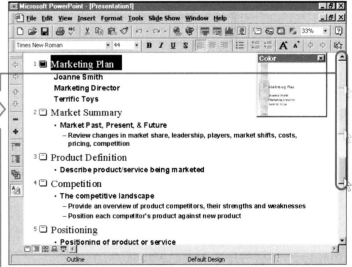

■ To display the presentation in the Outline or Slide Sorter view, refer to page 220.

1 To browse through the slides, move the mouse over one of the following options and then press the left mouse button.

▲ Scroll up

▼ Scroll down

QUICKLY BROWSE

1 Move the mouse over the scroll box. Then press and hold down the left mouse button as you move the mouse up or down the scroll bar.

2 Release the mouse button.

SAVE AND EXIT

You should save your presentation to store it for future use. This lets you later review and make changes to the presentation.

SAVE A PRESENTATION

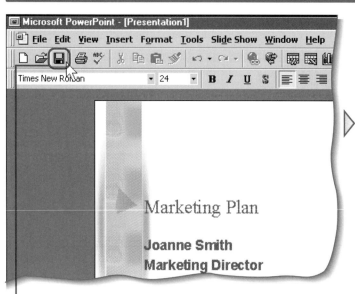

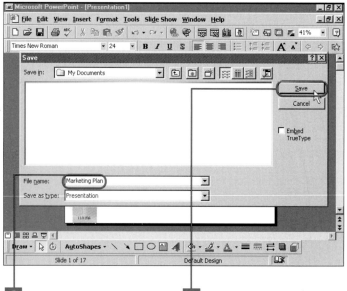

1 Move the mouse 🔖 over 💾 and then press the left mouse button.

■ The **Save** dialog box appears.

*Note: If you previously saved the presentation, the **Save** dialog box will not appear since you have already named the presentation.*

2 Type a name for your presentation.

Note: You can use up to 255 characters to name a presentation.

3 Move the mouse 🔖 over **Save** and then press the left mouse button.

When you finish using PowerPoint, you can exit the program.

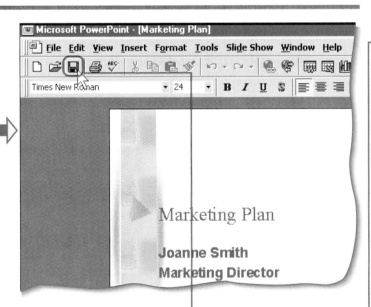

■ PowerPoint saves the presentation and displays the name at the top of the screen.

SAVE CHANGES

To avoid losing your work, you should regularly save changes to the presentation.

◼1 Move the mouse ⬚ over 🖬 and then press the left mouse button.

■ Make sure you save the presentation before exiting PowerPoint.

◼1 Move the mouse ⬚ over **File** and then press the left mouse button.

◼2 Move the mouse ⬚ over **Exit** and then press the left mouse button.

Note: To restart PowerPoint, refer to page 213.

225

You can open a saved presentation and display it on your screen. This lets you review and make changes to the presentation.

OPEN A PRESENTATION

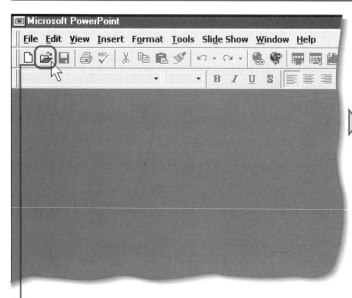

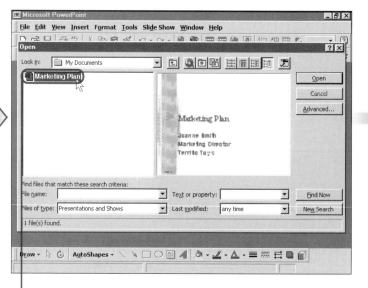

1 Move the mouse ▧ over ▧ and then press the left mouse button.

■ The **Open** dialog box appears.

2 Move the mouse ▧ over the name of the presentation you want to open and then press the left mouse button.

How can I quickly open a presentation when I first start PowerPoint?

The **PowerPoint** dialog box appears when you start PowerPoint.

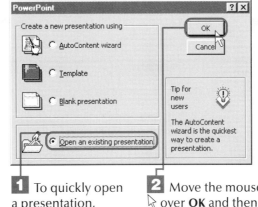

1 To quickly open a presentation, move the mouse ⬡ over this option and then press the left mouse button.

2 Move the mouse ⬡ over **OK** and then press the left mouse button. Then perform steps 2 and 3 starting on page 226.

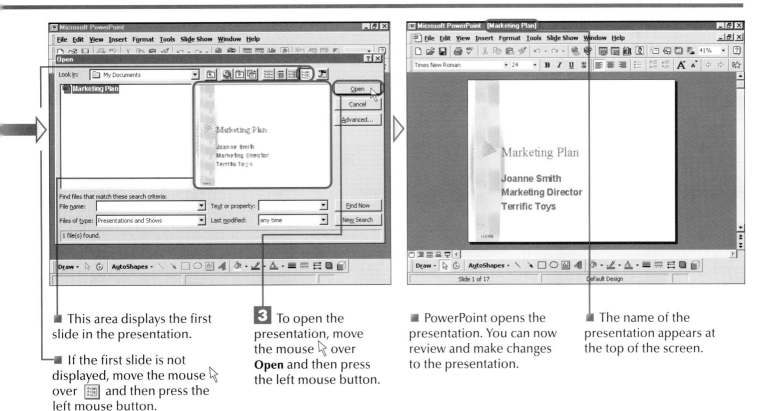

■ This area displays the first slide in the presentation.

■ If the first slide is not displayed, move the mouse ⬡ over [⊞] and then press the left mouse button.

3 To open the presentation, move the mouse ⬡ over **Open** and then press the left mouse button.

■ PowerPoint opens the presentation. You can now review and make changes to the presentation.

■ The name of the presentation appears at the top of the screen.

Before changing text in a presentation, you must select the text you want to work with. Selected text appears highlighted on your screen.

SELECT TEXT

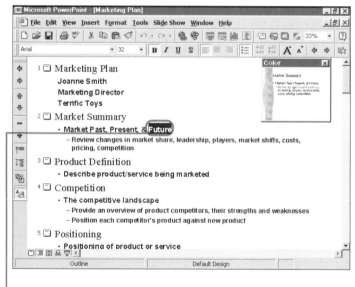

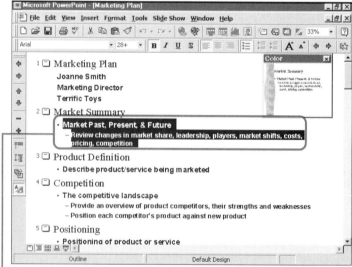

SELECT A WORD

1 Move the mouse I over the word you want to select and then quickly press the left mouse button twice.

■ To deselect text, move the mouse I outside the selected area and then press the left mouse button.

SELECT A POINT

1 Move the mouse I over the bullet (■) beside the point you want to select (I changes to ✛) and then press the left mouse button.

How do I select all the text in my presentation?

To quickly select all the text in your presentation, press and hold down `Ctrl` and then press `A` on your keyboard. Then release both keys.

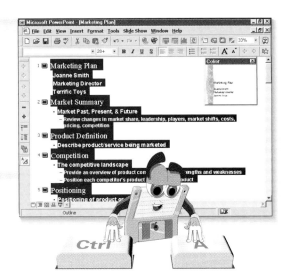

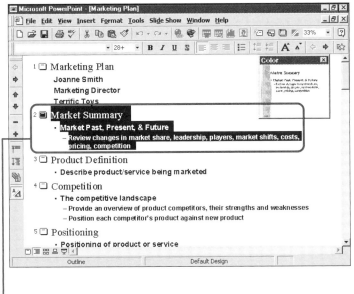

SELECT A SLIDE

1 Move the mouse I over the number of the slide you want to select (I changes to) and then press the left mouse button.

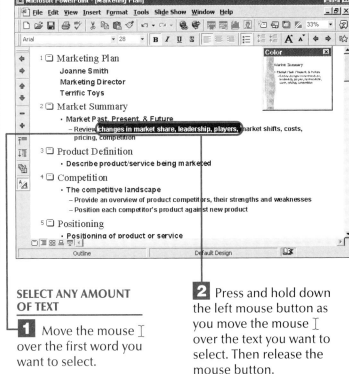

SELECT ANY AMOUNT OF TEXT

1 Move the mouse I over the first word you want to select.

2 Press and hold down the left mouse button as you move the mouse I over the text you want to select. Then release the mouse button.

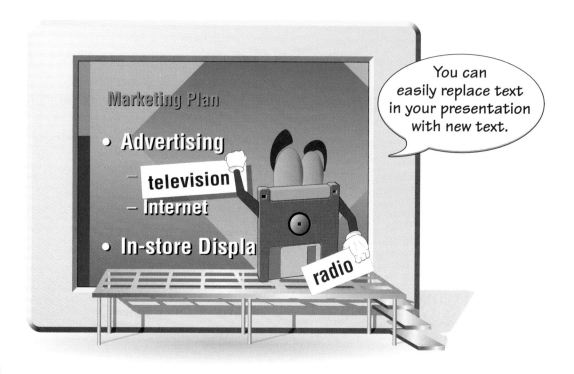

You can easily replace text in your presentation with new text.

REPLACE TEXT

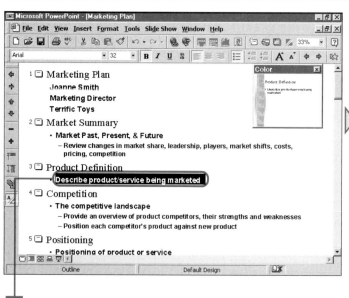

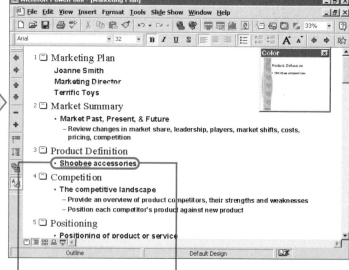

1 Select the text you want to replace with new text. To select text, refer to page 228.

2 Type the new text. The text you type will replace the selected text.

■ If a word in the presentation appears with a red underline, PowerPoint does not recognize the word and considers it misspelled. To spell check the presentation, refer to page 238.

UNDO LAST CHANGE

PowerPoint remembers the last changes you made to your presentation. If you regret these changes, you can cancel them by using the Undo feature.

UNDO LAST CHANGE

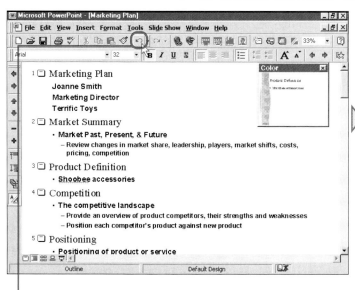

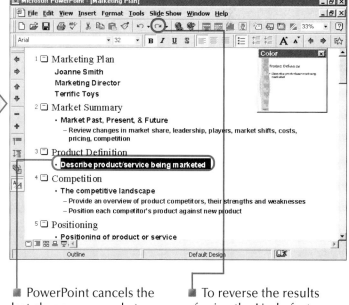

1 To undo your last change, move the mouse ⩗ over ↶ and then press the left mouse button.

■ PowerPoint cancels the last change you made to the presentation.

■ You can repeat step 1 to cancel previous changes you made.

■ To reverse the results of using the Undo feature, move the mouse ⩗ over ↷ and then press the left mouse button.

INSERT TEXT

You can easily add new text to your presentation.

INSERT CHARACTERS

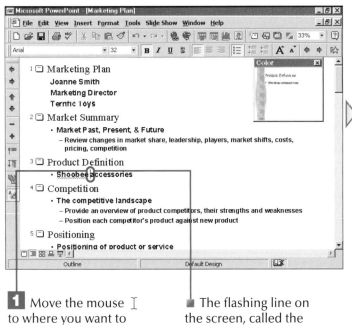

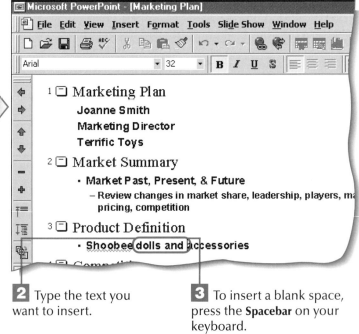

1 Move the mouse I to where you want to insert the new text and then press the left mouse button.

■ The flashing line on the screen, called the insertion point, indicates where the text you type will appear.

Note: You can also use the → , ← , ↑ and ↓ keys on your keyboard to move the insertion point on the screen.

2 Type the text you want to insert.

3 To insert a blank space, press the **Spacebar** on your keyboard.

Why are some words in my presentation underlined with a wavy, red line?

If PowerPoint does not recognize a word in your presentation and considers it misspelled, the word will display a wavy, red underline. To spell check your presentation, refer to page 238.

INSERT A NEW POINT

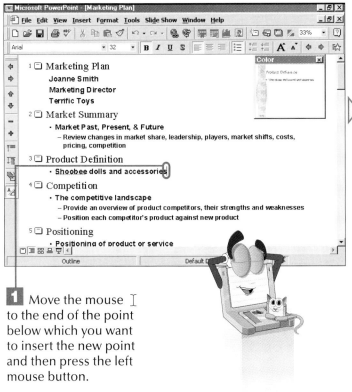

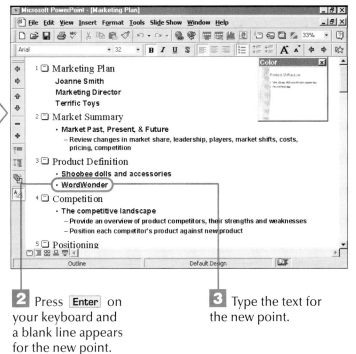

1 Move the mouse I to the end of the point below which you want to insert the new point and then press the left mouse button.

2 Press **Enter** on your keyboard and a blank line appears for the new point.

3 Type the text for the new point.

DELETE TEXT

You can easily remove text you no longer need from your presentation.

DELETE CHARACTERS

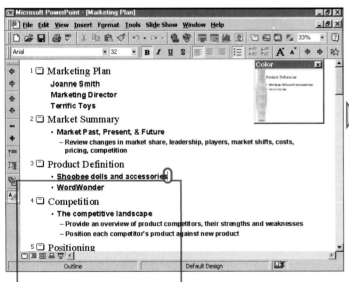

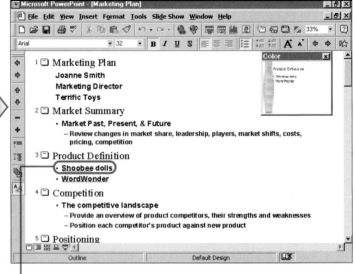

1 Move the mouse I to the right of the first character you want to delete and then press the left mouse button.

■ The flashing line on the screen, called the insertion point, moves to the location you selected.

Note: You can also use the →, ←, ↑ and ↓ keys on your keyboard to move the insertion point on the screen.

2 Press **+Backspace** on your keyboard once for each character or space you want to delete.

Can I delete text in the Slide view?

You can delete, insert and change text when viewing your slides in the Slide view. To change to the Slide view, refer to page 220.

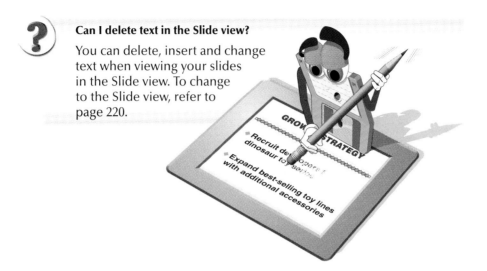

DELETE SELECTED TEXT

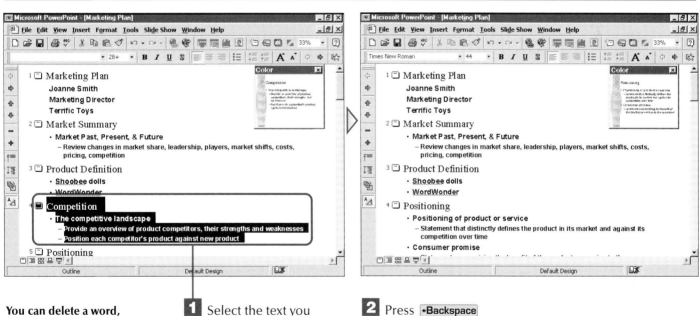

You can delete a word, point or entire slide from the outline.

1 Select the text you want to delete. To select text, refer to page 228.

2 Press +Backspace on your keyboard to remove the text.

MOVE TEXT

You can move text in your presentation to reorganize your ideas.

MOVE TEXT

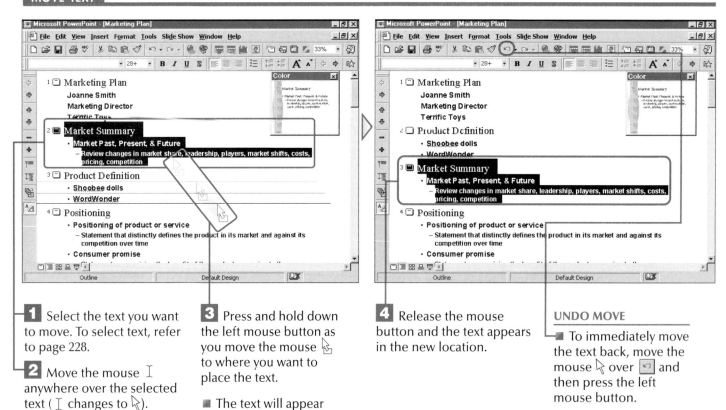

1 Select the text you want to move. To select text, refer to page 228.

2 Move the mouse I anywhere over the selected text (I changes to).

3 Press and hold down the left mouse button as you move the mouse to where you want to place the text.

■ The text will appear where you position the solid line or dotted insertion point on the screen.

4 Release the mouse button and the text appears in the new location.

UNDO MOVE

■ To immediately move the text back, move the mouse over and then press the left mouse button.

CHANGE IMPORTANCE OF TEXT

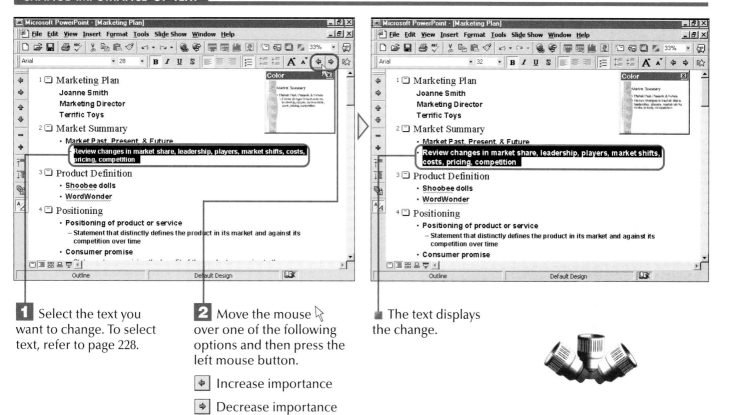

1 Select the text you want to change. To select text, refer to page 228.

2 Move the mouse over one of the following options and then press the left mouse button.

Increase importance

Decrease importance

■ The text displays the change.

You can quickly find and correct spelling errors in your presentation.

PowerPoint compares every word in your presentation to words in its dictionary. If a word does not exist in the dictionary, PowerPoint considers it misspelled.

CHECK SPELLING

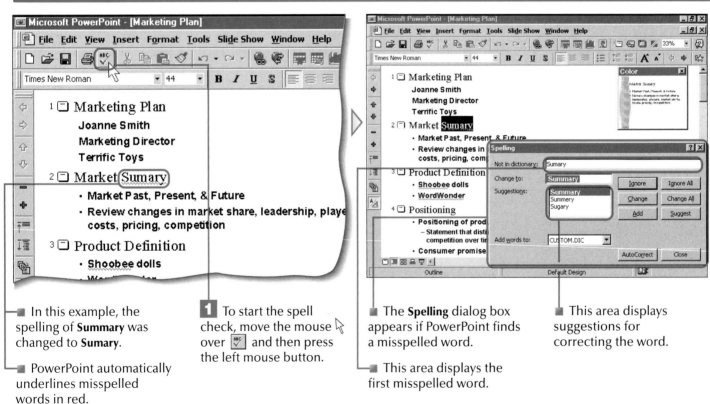

■ In this example, the spelling of **Summary** was changed to **Sumary**.

■ PowerPoint automatically underlines misspelled words in red.

1 To start the spell check, move the mouse over and then press the left mouse button.

■ The **Spelling** dialog box appears if PowerPoint finds a misspelled word.

■ This area displays the first misspelled word.

■ This area displays suggestions for correcting the word.

Can PowerPoint automatically correct my typing mistakes?

PowerPoint automatically corrects common spelling errors as you type.

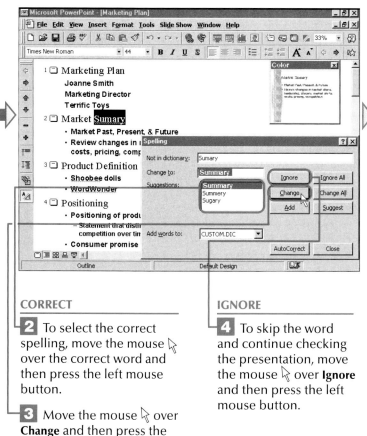

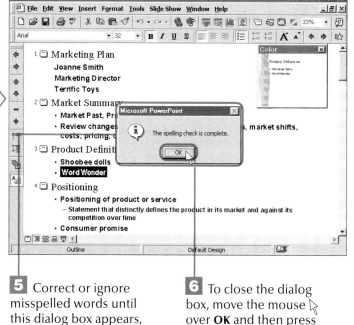

CORRECT

2 To select the correct spelling, move the mouse ⬚ over the correct word and then press the left mouse button.

3 Move the mouse ⬚ over **Change** and then press the left mouse button.

IGNORE

4 To skip the word and continue checking the presentation, move the mouse ⬚ over **Ignore** and then press the left mouse button.

5 Correct or ignore misspelled words until this dialog box appears, telling you the spell check is complete.

6 To close the dialog box, move the mouse ⬚ over **OK** and then press the left mouse button.

CHANGE THE SLIDE LAYOUT

You can have PowerPoint arrange text and objects on a slide for you.

CHANGE THE SLIDE LAYOUT

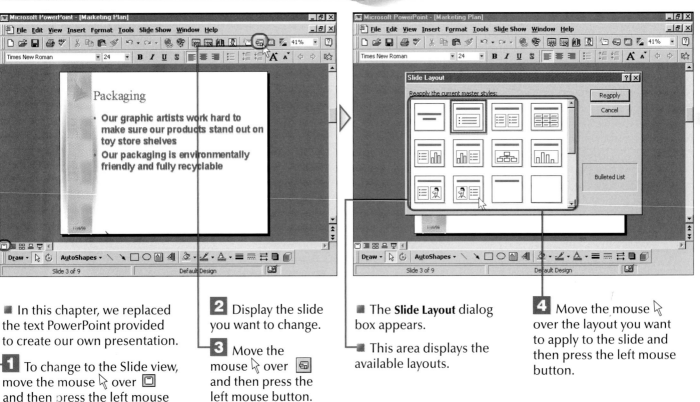

■ In this chapter, we replaced the text PowerPoint provided to create our own presentation.

1 To change to the Slide view, move the mouse ⇘ over 🔲 and then press the left mouse button.

2 Display the slide you want to change.

3 Move the mouse ⇘ over 🔲 and then press the left mouse button.

■ The **Slide Layout** dialog box appears.

■ This area displays the available layouts.

4 Move the mouse ⇘ over the layout you want to apply to the slide and then press the left mouse button.

240

 How can changing the slide layout help me add objects to my slides?

PowerPoint offers slide layouts that allow you to easily add objects such as a bulleted list, a chart or clip art to your slides.

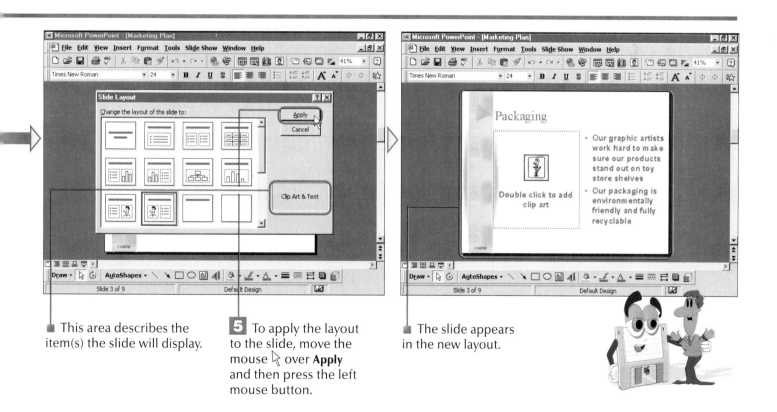

■ This area describes the item(s) the slide will display.

5 To apply the layout to the slide, move the mouse ⌖ over **Apply** and then press the left mouse button.

■ The slide appears in the new layout.

You can insert a new slide into your presentation to add a new topic you want to discuss.

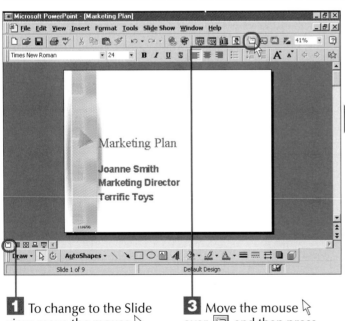

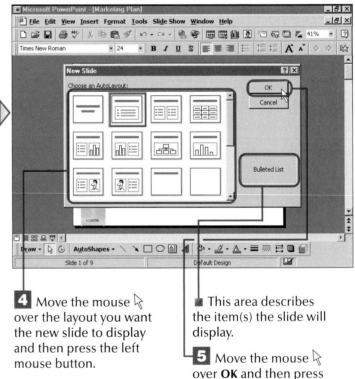

1 To change to the Slide view, move the mouse over ▢ and then press the left mouse button.

2 Display the slide you want to appear before the new slide.

3 Move the mouse over 🔲 and then press the left mouse button.

■ The **New Slide** dialog box appears.

4 Move the mouse over the layout you want the new slide to display and then press the left mouse button.

■ This area describes the item(s) the slide will display.

5 Move the mouse over **OK** and then press the left mouse button.

How much text should I display on one slide?

Too many words on a slide can minimize the impact of important ideas. If a slide contains too much text, place the text on two or three slides.

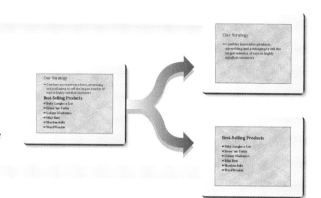

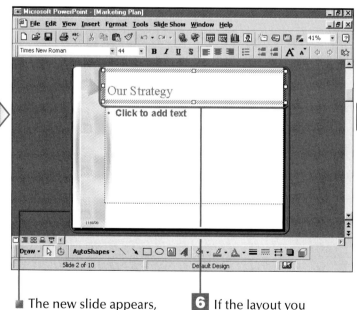

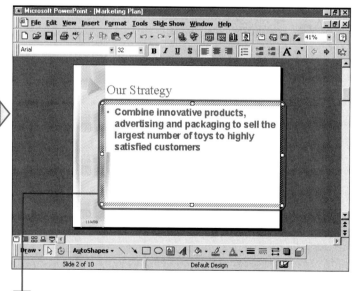

■ The new slide appears, displaying the layout you selected.

Note: You can change the layout at any time. To change the slide layout, refer to page 240.

6 If the layout you selected displays an area for a title, move the mouse I over the title area and then press the left mouse button. Then type the title.

7 If the layout you selected displays an area for text, move the mouse I over the text area and then press the left mouse button. Then type the text.

■ Press **Enter** on your keyboard each time you want to start a new point.

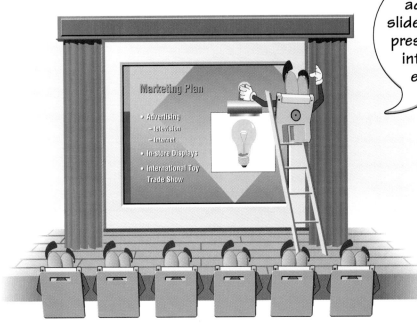

You can add images to slides to make your presentation more interesting and entertaining.

ADD CLIP ART OR PICTURES

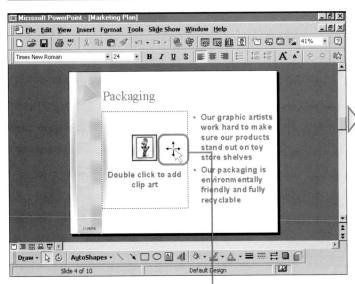

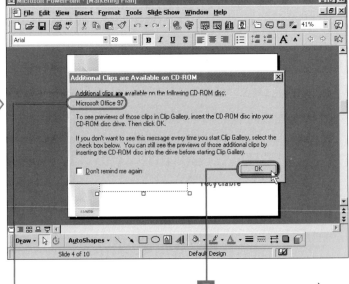

1 Display the slide you want to add an image to.

2 Change the layout of the slide to one that includes space for a clip art image. To change the slide layout, refer to page 240.

3 To add an image, move the mouse over the clip art area and then quickly press the left mouse button twice.

■ A dialog box appears if additional images are available on the CD-ROM disc identified in this area.

4 To view the additional images, insert the CD-ROM disc into your CD-ROM drive.

5 Move the mouse over **OK** and then press the left mouse button.

■ The **Microsoft Clip Gallery** dialog box appears.

How do I delete an image from a slide?

To delete an image from a slide in your presentation, move the mouse ⌖ over the image and then press the left mouse button. Then press **Delete** on your keyboard.

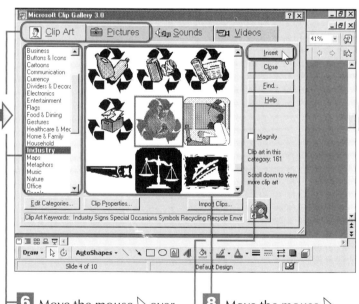

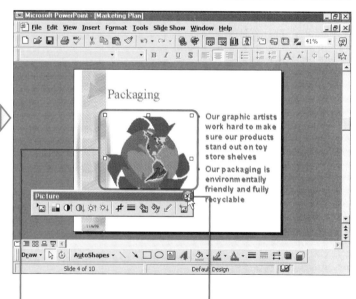

6 Move the mouse ⇖ over the **Clip Art** or **Pictures** tab and then press the left mouse button.

7 Move the mouse ⇖ over the category of images you want to display and then press the left mouse button.

8 Move the mouse ⇖ over the image you want to add to the slide and then press the left mouse button.

9 To add the image to the slide, move the mouse ⇖ over **Insert** and then press the left mouse button.

■ The image appears on the slide. The handles (☐) around the image let you change the size of the image. To resize the image, refer to page 253.

■ To close the **Picture** toolbar, move the mouse ⇖ over ☒ and then press the left mouse button.

You can add a chart to a slide to show trends and compare data.

ADD A CHART

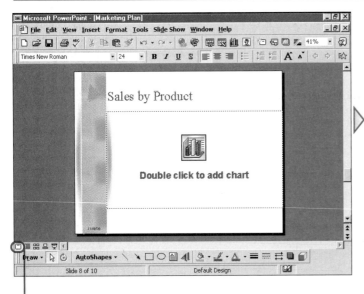

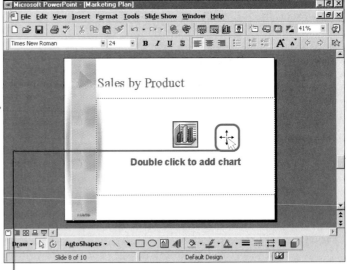

1 To change to the Slide view, move the mouse ⬐ over ▭ and then press the left mouse button.

2 Display the slide you want to add a chart to.

3 Change the layout of the slide to one that includes space for a chart. To change the slide layout, refer to page 240.

4 To add a chart, move the mouse ✛ over the chart area and then quickly press the left mouse button twice.

When should I use a chart in my presentation?

A chart is more appealing and often easier to understand than a list of numbers.

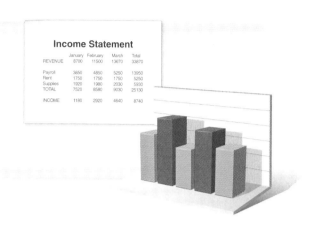

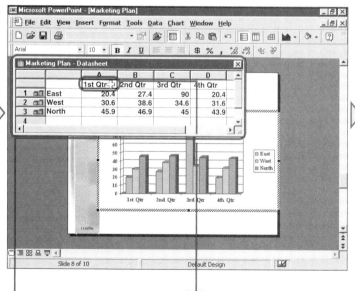

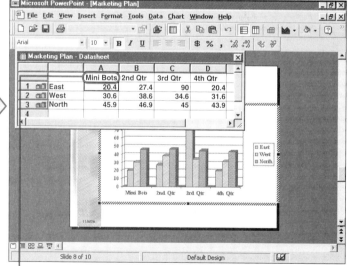

■ A datasheet appears, displaying sample data to show you where to enter your information.

5 To change the data in a cell, move the mouse ⊹ over the cell and then press the left mouse button. A thick border appears around the cell.

6 Type your data and then press **Enter** on your keyboard.

7 Repeat steps 5 and 6 until you finish entering all your data.

CONTINUED➡

ADD A CHART

You can choose the type of chart you want to create.

ADD A CHART (CONTINUED)

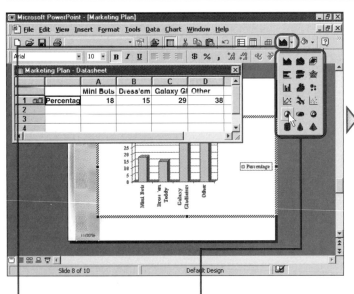

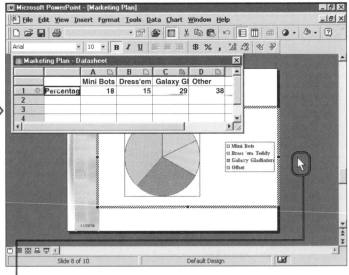

8 To select the type of chart you want to create, move the mouse ⇧ over ▼ in this area and then press the left mouse button.

9 Move the mouse ⇧ over the type of chart you want to use and then press the left mouse button.

10 To hide the datasheet, move the mouse ⇧ over a blank area on the screen and then press the left mouse button.

What type of chart should I choose?

The type of chart you should choose depends on your data. For example, area, column and line charts are ideal for showing changes to values over time, whereas pie charts are ideal for showing percentages.

EDIT A CHART

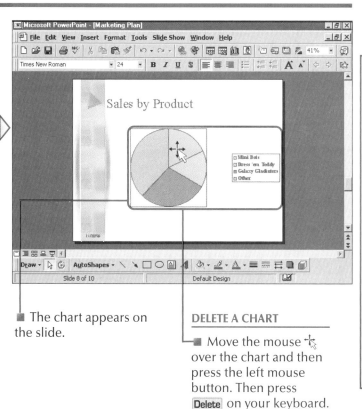

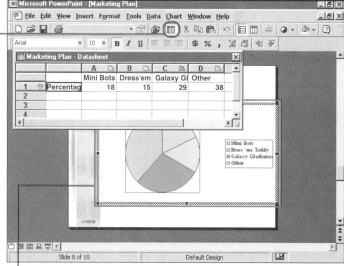

■ The chart appears on the slide.

DELETE A CHART

■ Move the mouse ⌖ over the chart and then press the left mouse button. Then press Delete on your keyboard.

1 Move the mouse ⌖ over the chart and then quickly press the left mouse button twice.

■ If the datasheet does not appear, move the mouse ⌖ over ▦ and then press the left mouse button to display the datasheet.

2 To make changes to the chart, perform steps 5 to 10 starting on page 247.

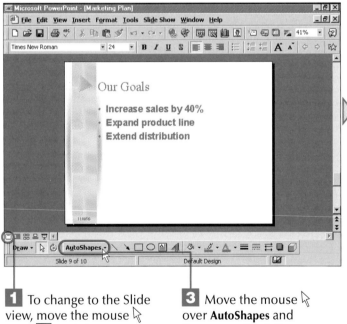

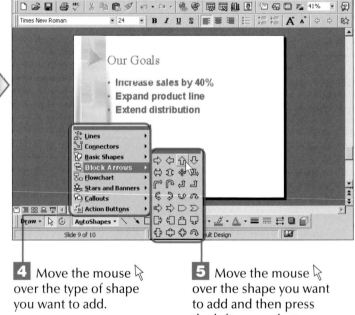

1 To change to the Slide view, move the mouse over 🔲 and then press the left mouse button.

2 Display the slide you want to add a shape to.

3 Move the mouse over **AutoShapes** and then press the left mouse button.

4 Move the mouse over the type of shape you want to add.

5 Move the mouse over the shape you want to add and then press the left mouse button.

Why should I use an AutoShape?

You can use AutoShapes to emphasize important information on your slides.

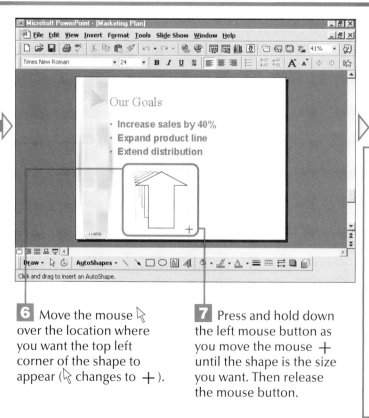

6 Move the mouse ⬚ over the location where you want the top left corner of the shape to appear (⬚ changes to ✛).

7 Press and hold down the left mouse button as you move the mouse ✛ until the shape is the size you want. Then release the mouse button.

■ The shape appears on the slide. The handles (□) around the shape let you change the size of the shape. To resize the shape, refer to page 253.

8 To hide the handles, move the mouse ⬚ outside the shape area and then press the left mouse button.

DELETE AN AUTOSHAPE

■ Move the mouse ✛ over the shape and then press the left mouse button. Then press Delete on your keyboard.

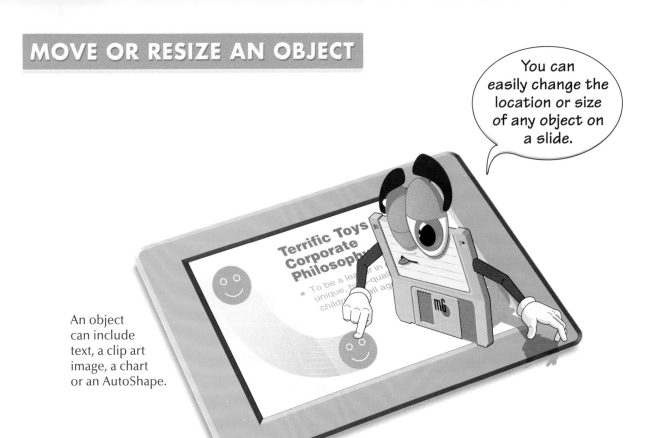

You can easily change the location or size of any object on a slide.

An object can include text, a clip art image, a chart or an AutoShape.

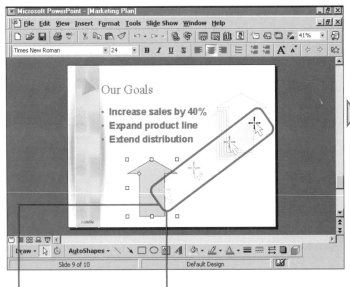

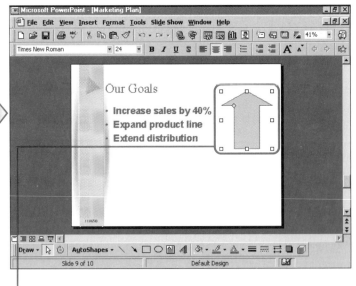

1 Move the mouse over the object you want to move and then press the left mouse button.

2 Move the mouse over an edge of the object (changes to).

3 Press and hold down the left mouse button as you move the object to a new location. Then release the mouse button.

■ The object appears in the new location.

How can I use the handles (□) that appear around a selected object?

The handles around an object let you change the size of the object.

■ Changes the height of an object.

■ Changes the width of an object.

■ Changes the height and width of an object at the same time.

RESIZE AN OBJECT

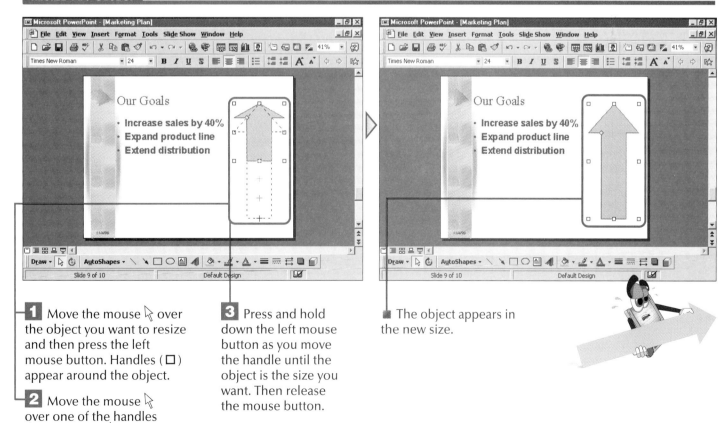

1 Move the mouse ⍨ over the object you want to resize and then press the left mouse button. Handles (□) appear around the object.

2 Move the mouse ⍨ over one of the handles (⍨ changes to ↕ or ↔).

3 Press and hold down the left mouse button as you move the handle until the object is the size you want. Then release the mouse button.

■ The object appears in the new size.

PowerPoint offers many ready-to-use designs that you can choose from to give the slides in your presentation a new appearance.

CHANGE SLIDE DESIGN

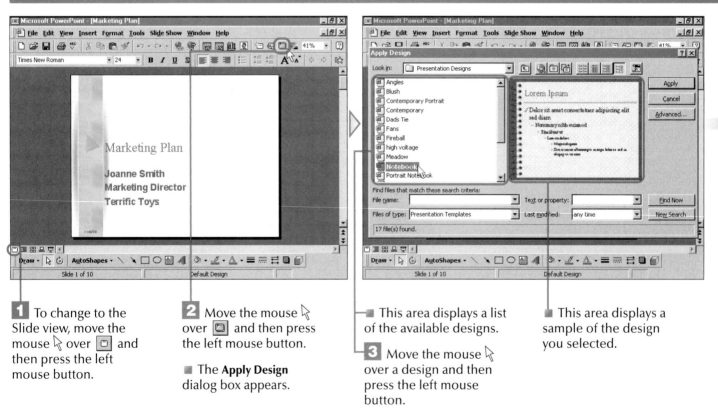

1 To change to the Slide view, move the mouse ↖ over ⬜ and then press the left mouse button.

2 Move the mouse ↖ over 🖼 and then press the left mouse button.

■ The **Apply Design** dialog box appears.

■ This area displays a list of the available designs.

3 Move the mouse ↖ over a design and then press the left mouse button.

■ This area displays a sample of the design you selected.

What slide designs does PowerPoint offer?

Here are some of the designs that PowerPoint offers.

Contemporary

Fans

Professional

Whirlpool

4 Repeat step 3 until the design you want to use appears.

5 To apply the design to all the slides in the presentation, move the mouse ⬁ over **Apply** and then press the left mouse button.

■ The slides in the presentation display the new design.

■ The design you selected only changes the appearance of the slides. The content of the slides does not change.

CHANGE COLOR SCHEME

You can select a different color scheme for your entire presentation.

CHANGE COLOR SCHEME

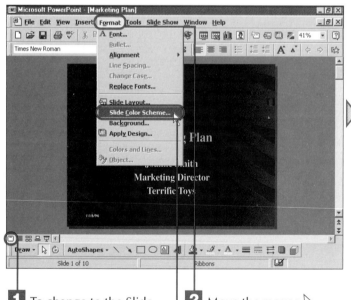

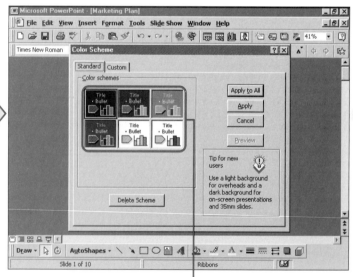

1 To change to the Slide view, move the mouse ⬡ over 🔲 and then press the left mouse button.

2 Move the mouse ⬡ over **Format** and then press the left mouse button.

3 Move the mouse ⬡ over **Slide Color Scheme** and then press the left mouse button.

■ The **Color Scheme** dialog box appears.

■ This area displays samples of the color schemes that PowerPoint offers for a presentation.

Note: The color schemes offered depend on the slide design. To change the slide design, refer to page 254.

How can I emphasize one slide in my presentation?

You can make an important slide stand out from the rest of your presentation by changing the color scheme for only that slide.

To change the color scheme for only one slide, display the slide you want to change. Then perform steps 1 to 5 starting on page 256, selecting **Apply** in step 5.

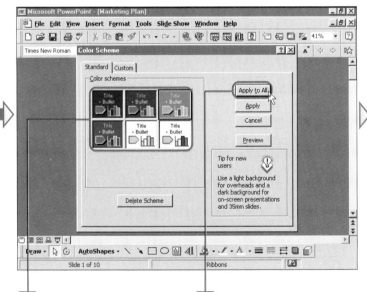

4 Move the mouse ⊳ over the color scheme you want to use and then press the left mouse button.

5 To apply the color scheme to all the slides in the presentation, move the mouse ⊳ over **Apply to All** and then press the left mouse button.

■ All the slides in the presentation display the new color scheme.

PowerPoint offers several styles that you can use to emphasize information on your slides.

Bold
Italic
<u>Underline</u>
Shadow

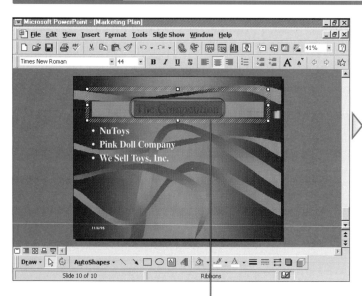

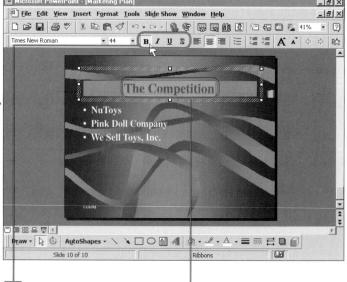

1 Display the slide containing the text you want to change.

2 Select the text you want to change. To select text, refer to page 228.

3 Move the mouse ▷ over one of the following options and then press the left mouse button.

B Bold   <u>U</u> Underline

I Italic   **S** Shadow

■ The text you selected appears in the new style. To remove the style, repeat steps 2 and 3.

CHANGE ALIGNMENT OF TEXT

You can enhance the appearance of your slides by aligning text in different ways.

LEFT

CENTER

RIGHT

CHANGE ALIGNMENT OF TEXT

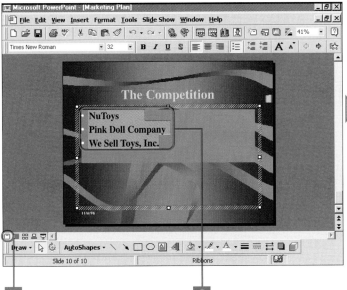

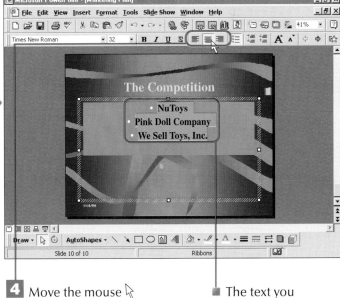

1 To change to the Slide view, move the mouse ⌖ over 🔲 and then press the left mouse button.

2 Display the slide containing the text you want to align differently.

3 Select the text you want to align differently. To select text, refer to page 228.

4 Move the mouse ⌖ over one of the following options and then press the left mouse button.

☰ Left align

☰ Center

☰ Right align

■ The text you selected displays the new alignment.

CHANGE FONT OF TEXT

You can enhance the appearance of slides in your presentation by changing the design of the text.

Arial
Courier
Times New Roman

CHANGE FONT OF TEXT

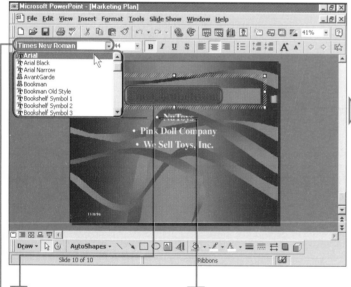

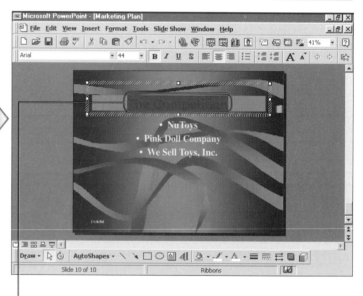

1 Select the text you want to change. To select text, refer to page 228.

2 To display a list of the available fonts, move the mouse ⫞ over ▾ in this area and then press the left mouse button.

3 Move the mouse ⫞ over the font you want to use and then press the left mouse button.

■ The text you selected changes to the new font.

CHANGE SIZE OF TEXT

You can increase or decrease the size of text in your presentation.

CHANGE SIZE OF TEXT

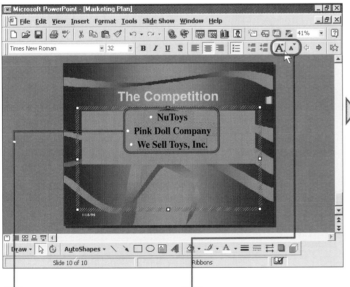

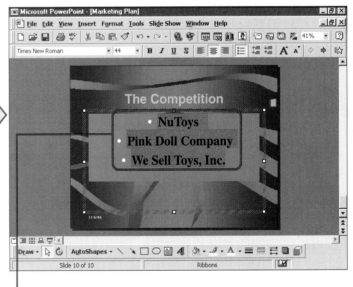

1 Select the text you want to change. To select text, refer to page 228.

2 Move the mouse ⊳ over one of the following options and then press the left mouse button until the text is the size you want.

A Increase size of text

A Decrease size of text

■ The text you selected changes to the new size.

CHANGE TEXT COLOR

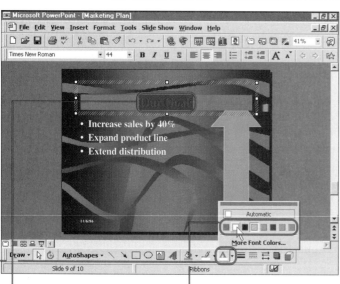

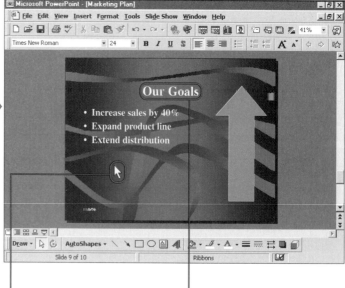

1 Select the text you want to change. To select text, refer to page 228.

2 Move the mouse ⬚ over ▾ in this area and then press the left mouse button.

3 Move the mouse ⬚ over the color you want to use and then press the left mouse button.

■ To deselect text, move the mouse ⬚ outside the text area and then press the left mouse button.

■ The text you selected appears in the new color.

You can change the color of an object on a slide.

CHANGE OBJECT COLOR

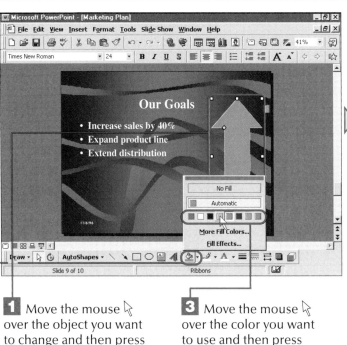

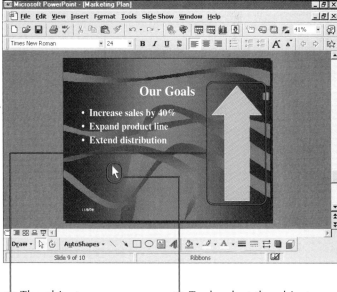

1 Move the mouse ⌖ over the object you want to change and then press the left mouse button.

2 Move the mouse ⌖ over ▾ in this area and then press the left mouse button.

3 Move the mouse ⌖ over the color you want to use and then press the left mouse button.

■ The object you selected appears in the new color.

■ To deselect the object, move the mouse ⌖ outside the object area and then press the left mouse button.

You can add information to every slide or page in your presentation.

ADD HEADER AND FOOTER

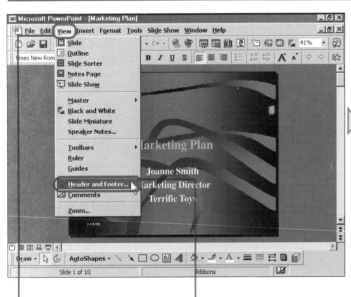

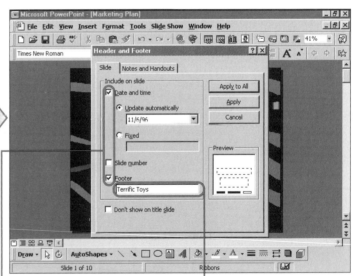

1 Move the mouse ⬉ over **View** and then press the left mouse button.

2 Move the mouse ⬉ over **Header and Footer** and then press the left mouse button.

■ The **Header and Footer** dialog box appears.

■ Each option that displays a check mark (✔) will appear on all the slides in the presentation.

3 To add or remove a check mark (✔) for an option, move the mouse ⬉ over the check box beside the option and then press the left mouse button.

4 To type the footer text you want to appear at the bottom of each slide, move the mouse ⌶ over this area and then press the left mouse button. Then type the footer text.

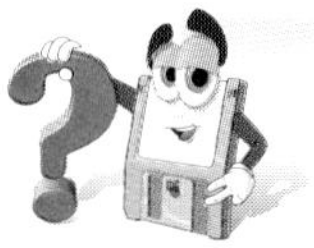

What information can I add to my presentation?

Slides can include a date, footer and slide number.

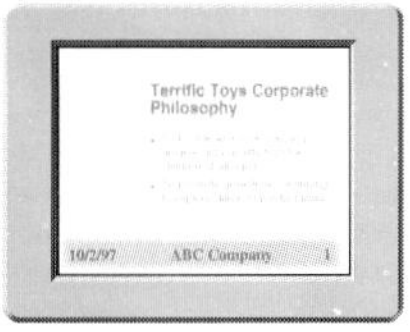

Notes and handouts can include a header, date, footer and page number.

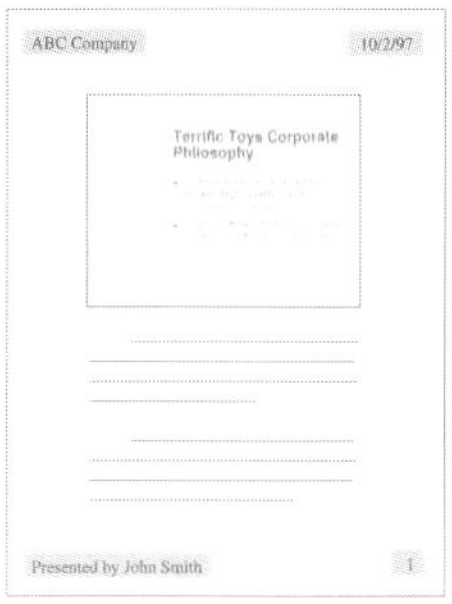

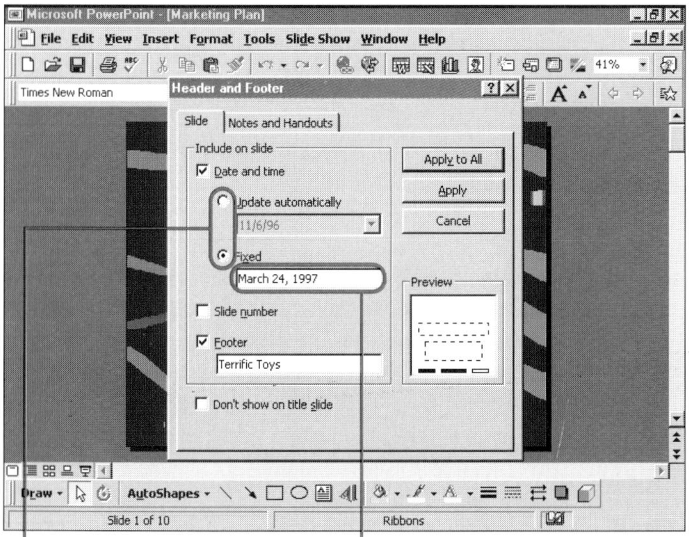

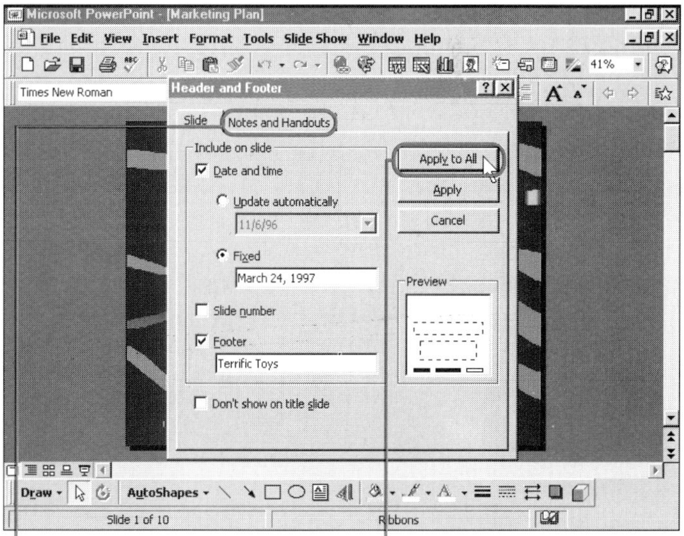

5 To select the date you want each slide to display, move the mouse over one of these options and then press the left mouse button (○ changes to ◉).

Update automatically - Display the current date.

Fixed - Display the date you specify.

6 If you selected **Fixed** in step 5, type the date.

■ To specify the information you want to appear on the notes and handout pages, move the mouse over this tab and then press the left mouse button. Then repeat steps 3 to 6 to specify the information.

7 To apply the changes to all the slides and pages, move the mouse over **Apply to All** and then press the left mouse button.

You can add movement and sound effects to the objects on your slides.

1 To change to the Slide view, move the mouse ➤ over ▢ and then press the left mouse button.

2 Move the mouse I over the object you want to animate and then press the left mouse button.

3 To display the **Animation Effects** toolbar, move the mouse ➤ over ⭐ and then press the left mouse button.

◼ The **Animation Effects** toolbar appears.

4 Move the mouse ➤ over the type of animation you want to use and then press the left mouse button.

Note: The animation effects available depend on the type of object you selected in step 2.

What animation effects can I add to my presentation?

 Drive-In

 Laser Text

 Flying

 Typewriter Text

Camera

 Reverse Text Order

Flash Once

Drop In

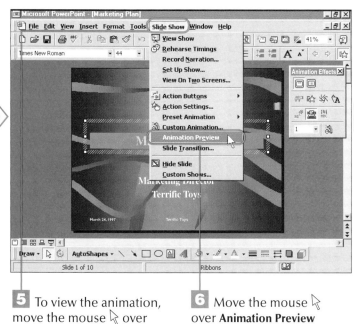

5 To view the animation, move the mouse ⌖ over **Slide Show** and then press the left mouse button.

6 Move the mouse ⌖ over **Animation Preview** and then press the left mouse button.

■ A preview window appears, displaying the animation.

Note: To view the animation again, move the mouse ⌖ over the preview window and then press the left mouse button.

■ To close the preview window, move the mouse ⌖ over ⊠ and then press the left mouse button.

■ To close the **Animation Effects** toolbar, repeat step 3.

REORDER SLIDES

You can easily change the order of the slides in your presentation.

REORDER SLIDES

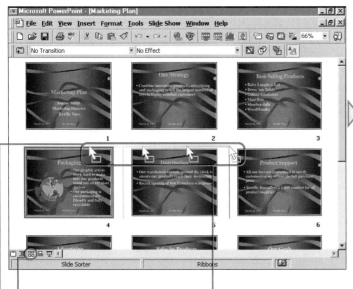

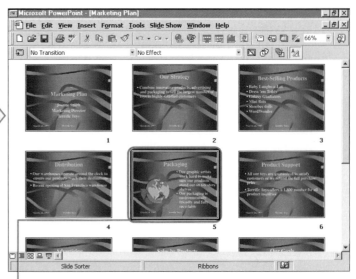

1 To change to the Slide Sorter view, move the mouse ⌖ over 🔠 and then press the left mouse button.

2 Move the mouse ⌖ over the slide you want to move.

3 Press and hold down the left mouse button as you move the slide to a new location.

▪ A line shows the new location. The slide will appear to the left of the line.

4 Release the left mouse button and the slide appears in the new location.

DELETE A SLIDE

You can remove a slide you no longer need.

DELETE A SLIDE

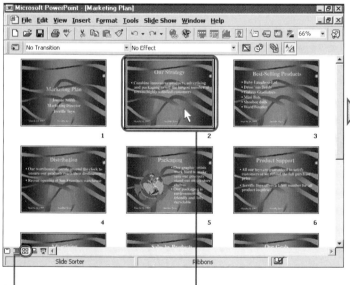

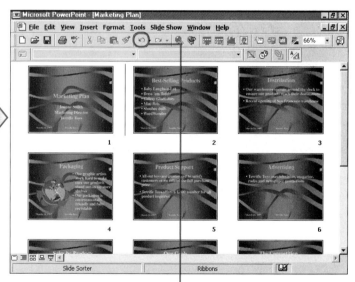

1 To change to the Slide Sorter view, move the mouse ⌖ over ⊞ and then press the left mouse button.

2 Move the mouse ⌖ over the slide you want to delete and then press the left mouse button.

3 Press **Delete** on your keyboard.

■ The slide disappears.

■ To immediately return the slide to the presentation, move the mouse ⌖ over ↺ and then press the left mouse button.

CREATE SPEAKER NOTES

You can create speaker notes that contain copies of your slides with all the ideas you want to discuss. These notes will help you deliver your presentation.

CREATE SPEAKER NOTES

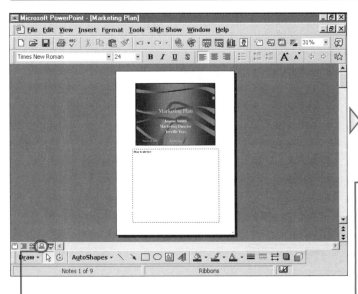

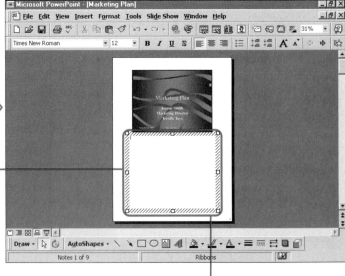

1 To change to the Notes Page view, move the mouse ⬚ over 🖳 and then press the left mouse button.

2 Display the slide you want to create speaker notes for.

Note: You can add speaker notes to each slide in the presentation.

■ The notes page displays an area where you can add text.

3 Move the mouse I over the text area and then press the left mouse button.

■ A thick border appears around the text area.

270

What should I include in my speaker notes?

When creating speaker notes, include the key points you want to discuss during your presentation.

Speaker notes can also include statistics or additional information that will support your ideas and help you answer questions from the audience.

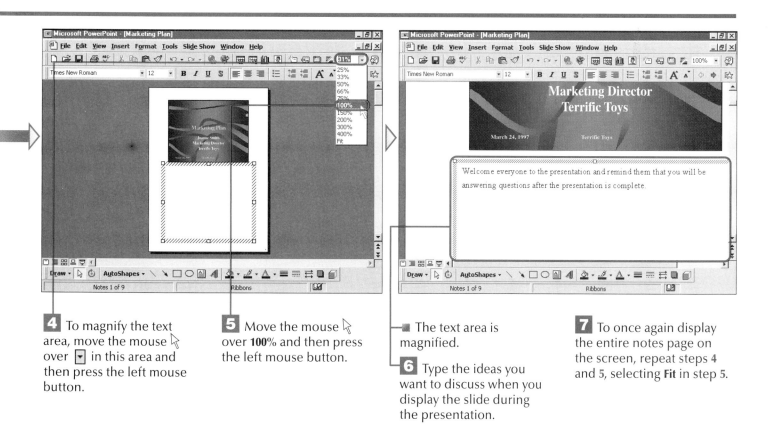

4 To magnify the text area, move the mouse ▷ over ▼ in this area and then press the left mouse button.

5 Move the mouse ▷ over **100%** and then press the left mouse button.

■ The text area is magnified.

6 Type the ideas you want to discuss when you display the slide during the presentation.

7 To once again display the entire notes page on the screen, repeat steps **4** and **5**, selecting **Fit** in step **5**.

You can view a slide show of your presentation on a computer screen.

VIEW A SLIDE SHOW

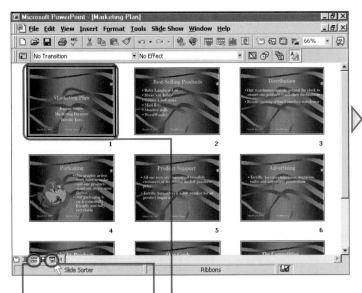

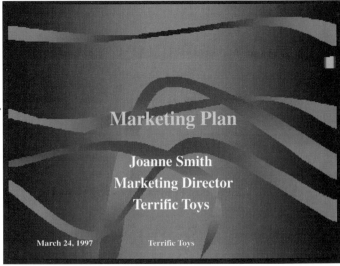

1 To change to the Slide Sorter view, move the mouse ⟲ over ⊞ and then press the left mouse button.

2 Move the mouse ⟲ over the first slide in the presentation and then press the left mouse button.

3 To start the slide show, move the mouse ⟲ over ⬚ and then press the left mouse button.

■ The first slide fills the screen.

4 To display the next slide, press the **Spacebar** on your keyboard or press the left mouse button.

Is the speed at which I deliver a presentation important?

Make sure you rehearse the pace of your presentation before delivering it to an audience. A fast pace can overwhelm an audience whereas a slow pace may put the audience to sleep.

■ The next slide appears.

5 Repeat step 4 until you finish viewing all the slides in the presentation.

QUICK REFERENCE

You can use the keyboard to help you move through your presentation.

 Display the next slide — Press the **Spacebar**.

 Display the previous slide — Press `+Backspace`.

 Display any slide — Press the number of the slide on your keyboard and then press `Enter`.

 End the presentation — Press `Esc`.

ADD SLIDE TRANSITIONS

You can use special effects, called transitions, to help you move from one slide to the next. Transitions help to introduce each slide during an on-screen slide show.

ADD SLIDE TRANSITIONS

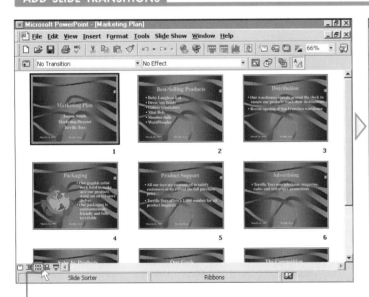

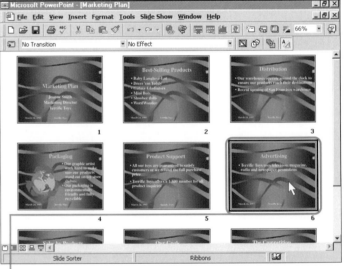

1 To change to the Slide Sorter view, move the mouse ᐳ over ⊞ and then press the left mouse button.

Note: PowerPoint automatically adds transitions to slides for some types of presentations. A symbol (⊡) appears below every slide with a transition.

2 To add or change a transition for a slide, move the mouse ᐳ over the slide and then press the left mouse button.

What slide transitions does PowerPoint offer?

These are a few of the slide transitions PowerPoint offers.

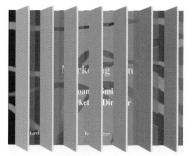

Blinds Vertical

Dissolve

Checkerboard Across

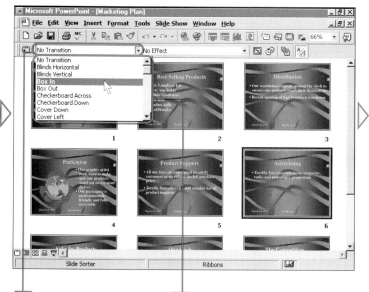

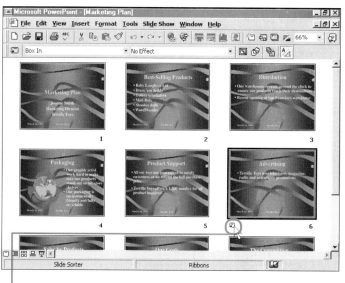

3 To display the available transitions, move the mouse ⍺ over this area and then press the left mouse button.

4 Move the mouse ⍺ over the transition you want to use and then press the left mouse button.

5 To view the transition for the slide, move the mouse ⍺ over the symbol (⌨) below the slide and then press the left mouse button.

PRINT A PRESENTATION

You can produce a paper copy of a presentation for your own use or to hand out to an audience.

PRINT A PRESENTATION

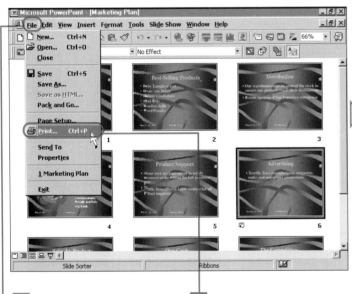

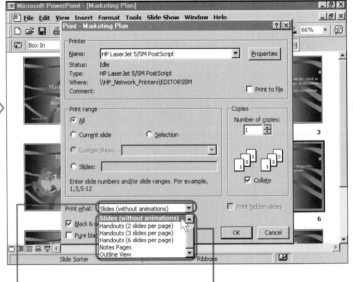

1 Move the mouse over **File** and then press the left mouse button.

2 Move the mouse over **Print** and then press the left mouse button.

■ The **Print** dialog box appears.

3 To select what you want to print, move the mouse over this area and then press the left mouse button.

4 Move the mouse over what you want to print and then press the left mouse button.

276

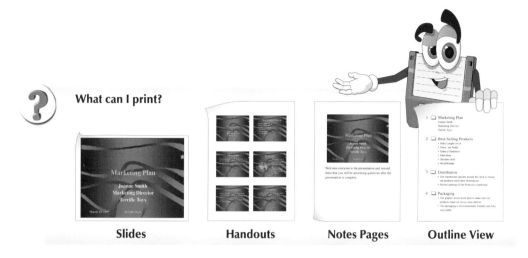

What can I print?

Slides   Handouts   Notes Pages   Outline View

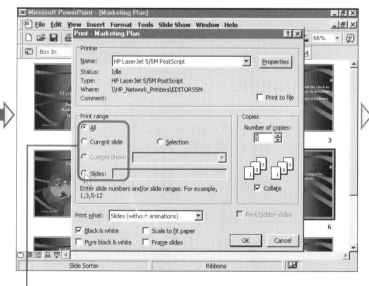

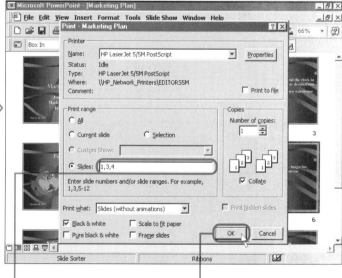

5 Move the mouse ⬚ over one of these options and then press the left mouse button (○ changes to ◉).

All - Prints every slide in the presentation.

Current slide - Prints the selected slide or the slide displayed on the screen.

Slides - Prints the slides you specify.

6 If you selected **Slides** in step **5**, type the slide numbers you want to print (examples: 1,3,4 or 2-4).

7 Move the mouse ⬚ over **OK** and then press the left mouse button.

Update a Contact
Page 308

Microsoft Outlook is a program that helps you keep track of your business and personal activities, including your appointments, contacts, tasks and e-mail messages.

Create a Note
Page 292

Open a Message
Page 284

Delete a Message
Page 285

Mark a Task as Complete
Page 298

OUTLOOK

View Calendar
Page 300

Start Outlook
Page 280

Outlook can help you manage your messages, appointments, contacts, tasks and activities.

START OUTLOOK

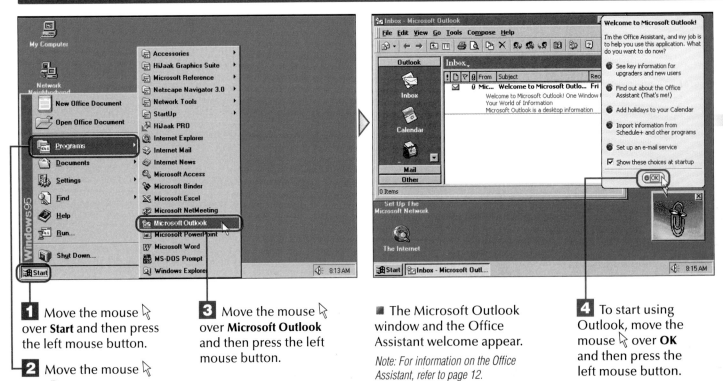

1 Move the mouse ⌖ over **Start** and then press the left mouse button.

2 Move the mouse ⌖ over **Programs**.

3 Move the mouse ⌖ over **Microsoft Outlook** and then press the left mouse button.

■ The Microsoft Outlook window and the Office Assistant welcome appear.

Note: For information on the Office Assistant, refer to page 12.

4 To start using Outlook, move the mouse ⌖ over **OK** and then press the left mouse button.

Outlook is groupware

What can I do with Outlook?

 Inbox
Send and receive messages.

 Calendar
Schedule appointments.

 Contacts
Maintain an address book.

 Tasks
Create a list of things to do.

 Journal
Keep track of activities.

 Notes
Create brief reminder notes.

 Deleted Items
Store items you delete.

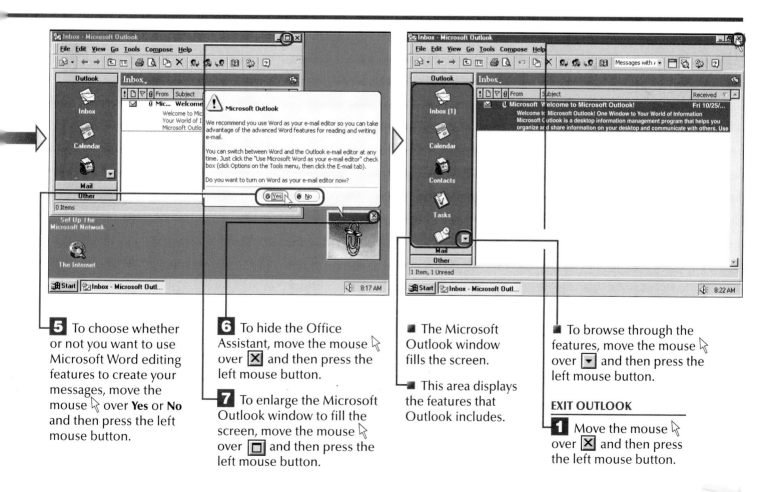

5 To choose whether or not you want to use Microsoft Word editing features to create your messages, move the mouse ⇖ over **Yes** or **No** and then press the left mouse button.

6 To hide the Office Assistant, move the mouse ⇖ over ✕ and then press the left mouse button.

7 To enlarge the Microsoft Outlook window to fill the screen, move the mouse ⇖ over □ and then press the left mouse button.

■ The Microsoft Outlook window fills the screen.

■ This area displays the features that Outlook includes.

■ To browse through the features, move the mouse ⇖ over ▼ and then press the left mouse button.

EXIT OUTLOOK

1 Move the mouse ⇖ over ✕ and then press the left mouse button.

The Inbox lets you exchange electronic mail (e-mail) messages with friends, family members, colleagues and clients.

VIEW INBOX

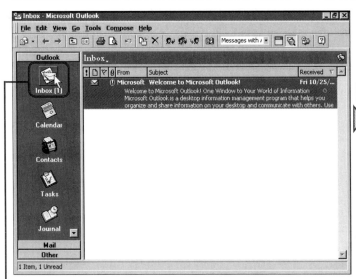

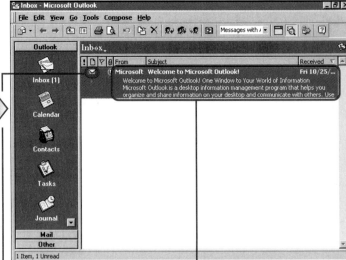

1 To view your messages, move the mouse ⬚ over **Inbox** and then press the left mouse button.

■ If there are messages you have not read, the number of unread messages will appear in brackets beside **Inbox**.

■ This area shows you whether or not you have read each message.

✉ Unread message

✉ Read message

■ This area displays the author, subject and date of each message along with a few lines of text from each unread message.

Note: To view all the text in a message, refer to page 284 to open the message.

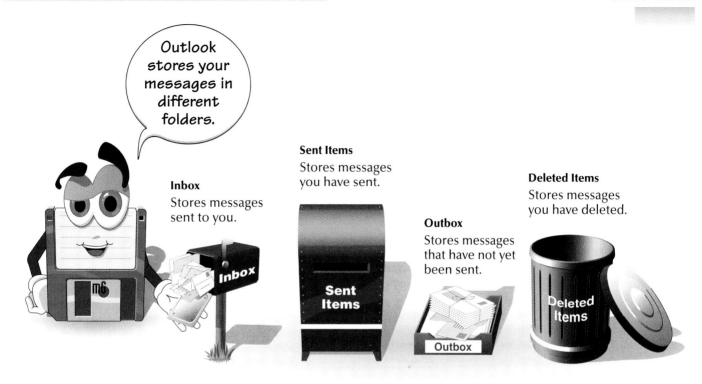

Outlook stores your messages in different folders.

Inbox
Stores messages sent to you.

Sent Items
Stores messages you have sent.

Outbox
Stores messages that have not yet been sent.

Deleted Items
Stores messages you have deleted.

DISPLAY THE MAIL FOLDERS

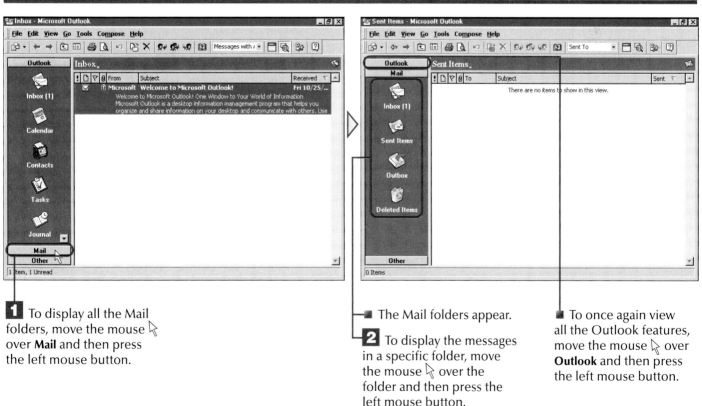

1 To display all the Mail folders, move the mouse over **Mail** and then press the left mouse button.

■ The Mail folders appear.

2 To display the messages in a specific folder, move the mouse over the folder and then press the left mouse button.

■ To once again view all the Outlook features, move the mouse over **Outlook** and then press the left mouse button.

You can easily open a message to view its contents.

OPEN A MESSAGE

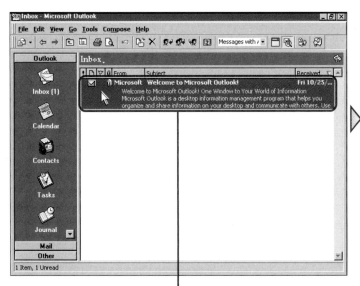

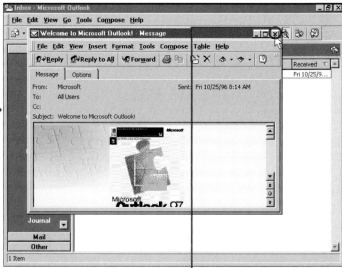

Note: To display the messages in a specific folder, refer to page 283.

1 Move the mouse ⬚ over the message you want to open and then quickly press the left mouse button twice.

■ The contents of the message appear on the screen.

2 To close the message, move the mouse ⬚ over ✕ and then press the left mouse button.

DELETE A MESSAGE

You can delete a message you no longer need. This prevents your folders from becoming cluttered with messages.

DELETE A MESSAGE

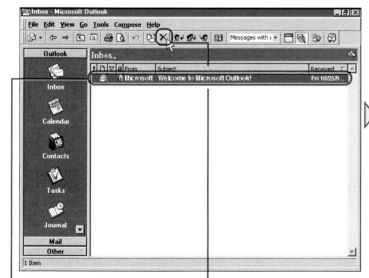

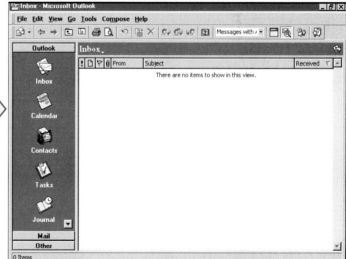

1 Move the mouse ⌖ over the message you want to delete and then press the left mouse button.

2 Move the mouse ⌖ over ⊠ and then press the left mouse button.

■ The message disappears.

■ Outlook places the deleted message in the **Deleted Items** folder.

Note: To display the messages in the Deleted Items folder, refer to page 283.

SEND A MESSAGE

You can send a message to exchange ideas or request information.

SEND A MESSAGE

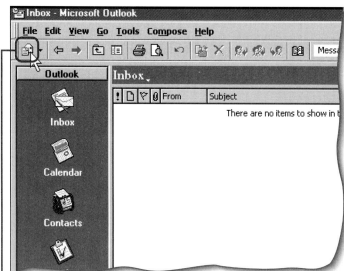

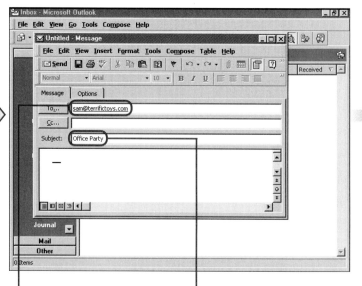

1 To create a message, move the mouse ![cursor] over ![icon] and then press the left mouse button.

■ A window appears.

2 Type the e-mail address of the person you want to receive the message.

Note: You can practice sending a message by sending a message to yourself.

3 To enter a subject, press **Tab** twice on your keyboard. Then type the subject.

Why can't I send or receive messages?

Before you can send and receive messages, you must be connected to a service that allows you to exchange messages. These services include an office network, a commercial online service or an Internet service provider.

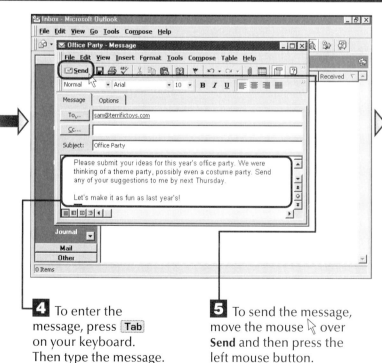

4 To enter the message, press **Tab** on your keyboard. Then type the message.

5 To send the message, move the mouse ⤏ over **Send** and then press the left mouse button.

■ Outlook sends the message and stores a copy of the message in the **Sent Items** folder.

*Note: To display the messages in the **Sent Items** folder, refer to page 283.*

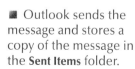

REPLY TO A MESSAGE

You can reply to a message to answer a question, express an opinion or supply additional information.

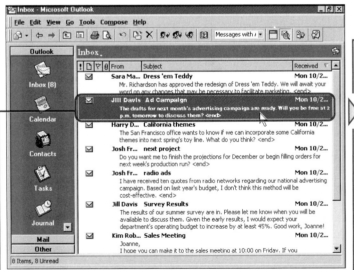

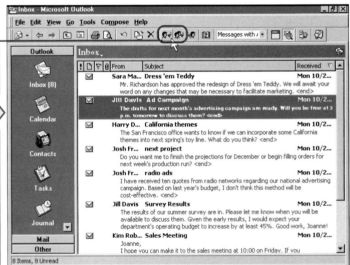

1 Move the mouse ⟍ over the message you want to reply to and then press the left mouse button.

2 Move the mouse ⟍ over one of the following reply options and then press the left mouse button.

⬛ Reply to sender

⬛ Reply to sender and everyone who received the original message

---

Why haven't I received a response to my message?

When you send a message, do not assume the person receiving the message will read it right away. Some people may not regularly check their e-mail.

You have e-mail!

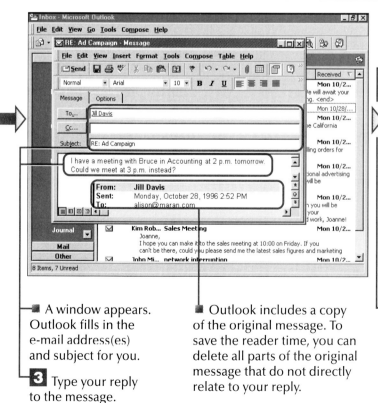

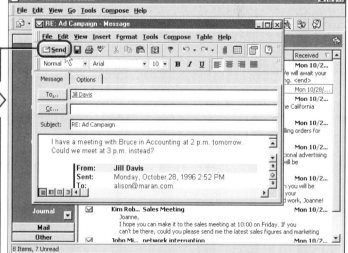

■ A window appears. Outlook fills in the e-mail address(es) and subject for you.

3 Type your reply to the message.

■ Outlook includes a copy of the original message. To save the reader time, you can delete all parts of the original message that do not directly relate to your reply.

4 To send the reply, move the mouse ⟨ over **Send** and then press the left mouse button.

■ Outlook sends the reply and stores a copy of the reply in the **Sent Items** folder.

*Note: To display the messages in the **Sent Items** folder, refer to page 283.*

FORWARD A MESSAGE

After reading a message, you can add comments and then send the message to a friend or colleague.

There is a 10th anniversary High School Reunion on August 8, 9 and 10 at Woodblock High School. We all hope to see you there. Contact Susan Hughes for more information.

Rick, I thought you might be interested in the reunion. Unfortunately, I will be out of town.

FORWARD A MESSAGE

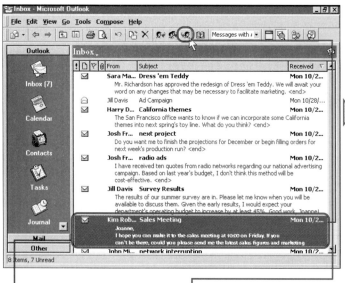

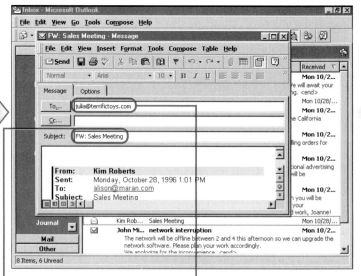

1 Move the mouse ⇖ over the message you want to forward and then press the left mouse button.

2 Move the mouse ⇖ over 🐾 and then press the left mouse button.

■ A window appears. Outlook fills in the subject for you.

3 Type the e-mail address of the person you want to forward the message to.

Can exchanging e-mail save me money?

Using e-mail can save you money on long distance calls to colleagues, friends and family. The next time you are about to use the telephone, consider sending an e-mail message instead.

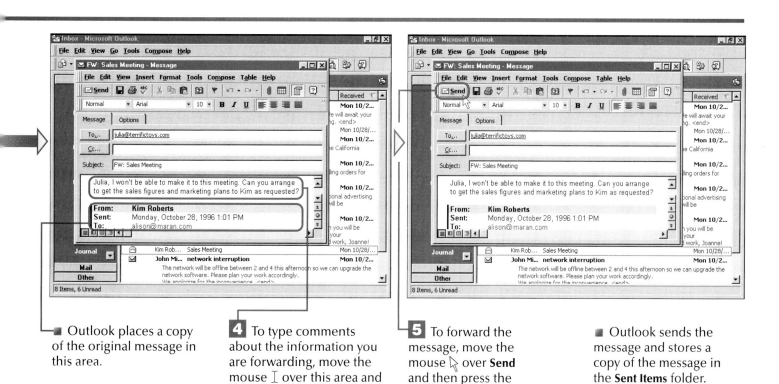

■ Outlook places a copy of the original message in this area.

4 To type comments about the information you are forwarding, move the mouse I over this area and then press the left mouse button. Then type your comments.

5 To forward the message, move the mouse ♦ over **Send** and then press the left mouse button.

■ Outlook sends the message and stores a copy of the message in the **Sent Items** folder.

*Note: To display the messages in the **Sent Items** folder, refer to page 283.*

CREATE A NOTE

You can create electronic notes that are similar to paper sticky notes.

CREATE A NOTE

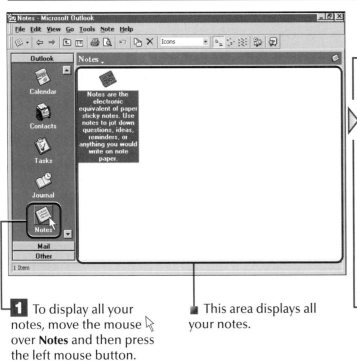

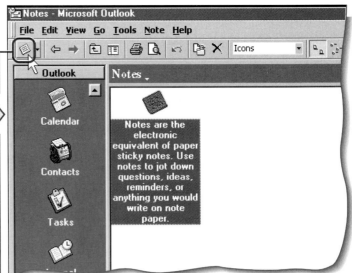

1 To display all your notes, move the mouse ⏳ over **Notes** and then press the left mouse button.

■ This area displays all your notes.

2 To create a new note, move the mouse ⏳ over 🔲 and then press the left mouse button.

What can I use notes for?

Notes are ideal for storing bits of information such as reminders, questions, ideas and anything else you would record on note paper.

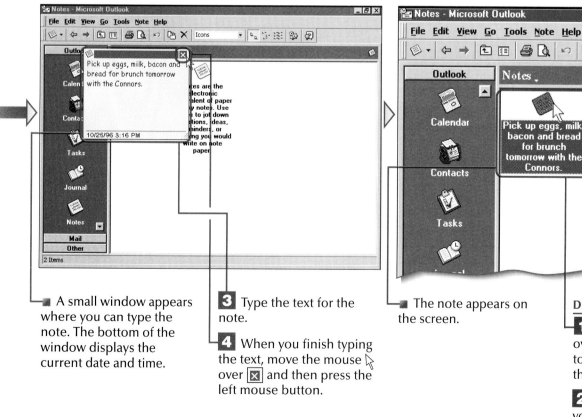

■ A small window appears where you can type the note. The bottom of the window displays the current date and time.

3 Type the text for the note.

4 When you finish typing the text, move the mouse ⟲ over 🗙 and then press the left mouse button.

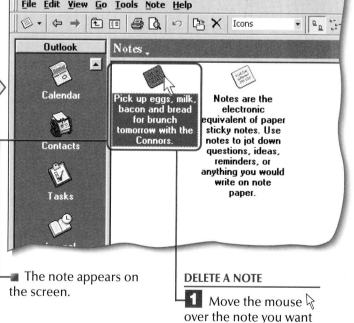

■ The note appears on the screen.

DELETE A NOTE

1 Move the mouse ⟲ over the note you want to delete and then press the left mouse button.

2 Press Delete on your keyboard.

You can easily open a note to view its contents.

OPEN A NOTE

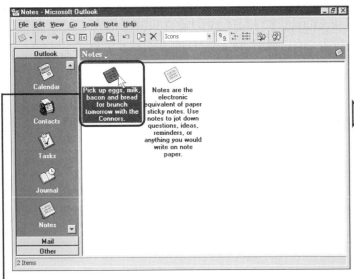

1 Move the mouse ⌖ over the note you want to open and then quickly press the left mouse button twice.

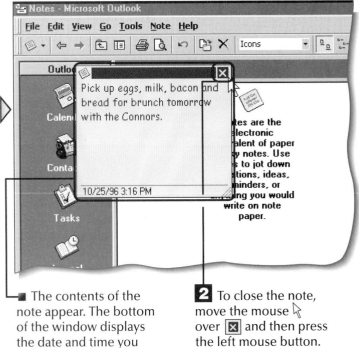

■ The contents of the note appear. The bottom of the window displays the date and time you created the note.

2 To close the note, move the mouse ⌖ over ☒ and then press the left mouse button.

RESIZE A NOTE

QUICK CHEESE MELT
For a quick and easy lunchtime
snack, try this delicious melt:
You will need white or whole wheat
bread, cheese, onions, bacon and
chives.
1. Microwave the bacon until crisp.
2. Lay thin slices of cheese, diced onion, bacon and chives
3. Cook this in the oven for 5-7 minutes, or until cheese is

You can change the size of a note. This is useful when the window is too small to display all the text.

RESIZE A NOTE

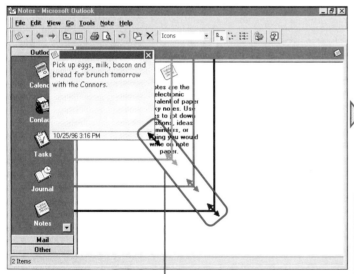

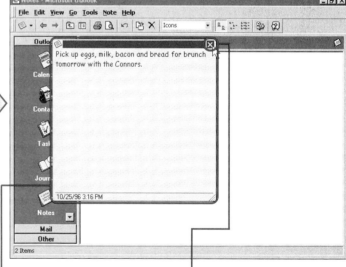

1 Open the note you want to resize. To open a note, perform step 1 on page 294.

2 Move the mouse ⟋ over the bottom right corner of the note (⟋ changes to ⟍).

3 Press and hold down the left mouse button as you move the mouse ⟍ until the outline of the note displays the size you want.

4 Release the mouse button and the note changes to the new size.

5 To close the note, move the mouse ⟋ over ⊠ and then press the left mouse button.

295

You can create a list of personal and work-related tasks that you want to accomplish.

CREATE A TASK

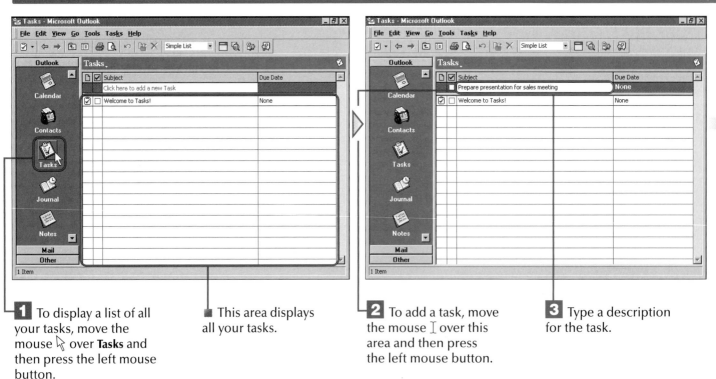

1 To display a list of all your tasks, move the mouse ▷ over **Tasks** and then press the left mouse button.

■ This area displays all your tasks.

2 To add a task, move the mouse I over this area and then press the left mouse button.

3 Type a description for the task.

Where else can I see a list of my tasks?

There is a small area in the Calendar that displays a list of your tasks.

Note: For information on the Calendar, refer to page 300.

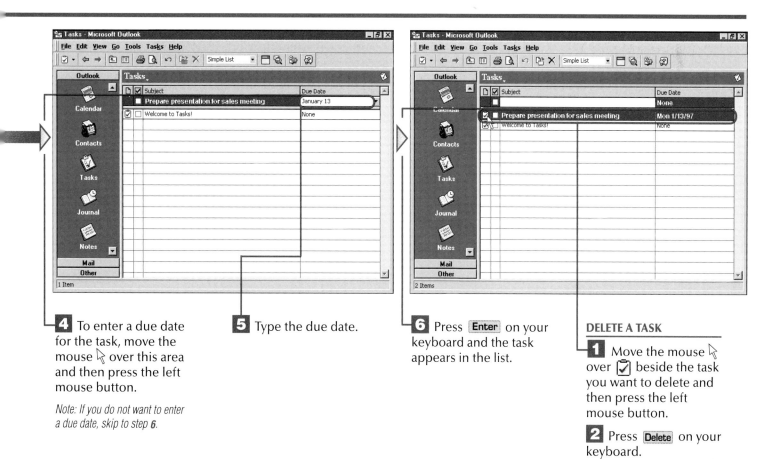

4 To enter a due date for the task, move the mouse ⬡ over this area and then press the left mouse button.

Note: If you do not want to enter a due date, skip to step 6.

5 Type the due date.

6 Press `Enter` on your keyboard and the task appears in the list.

DELETE A TASK

1 Move the mouse ⬡ over ☑ beside the task you want to delete and then press the left mouse button.

2 Press `Delete` on your keyboard.

MARK A TASK AS COMPLETE

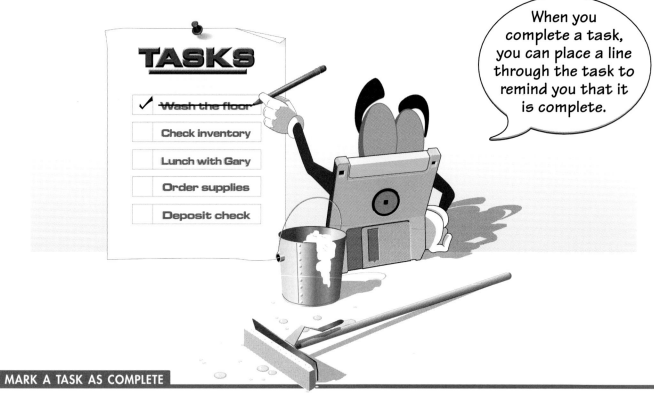

When you complete a task, you can place a line through the task to remind you that it is complete.

MARK A TASK AS COMPLETE

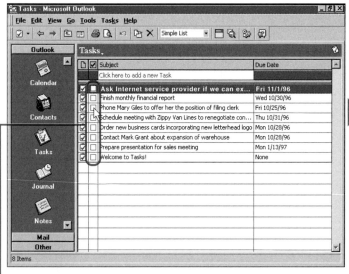

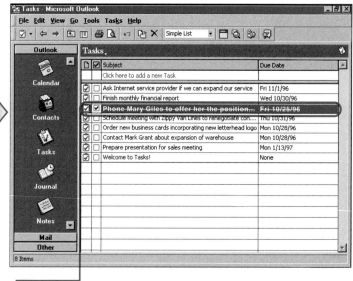

1 To mark a task as complete, move the mouse ⍔ over ☐ beside the task and then press the left mouse button (☐ changes to ☑).

■ A line appears through the task to show that the task is complete.

■ To remove the line through a task, repeat step 1.

298

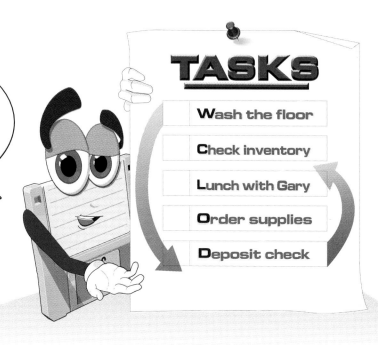

You can sort your tasks alphabetically by subject or by due date to help you quickly find tasks of interest.

SORT TASKS

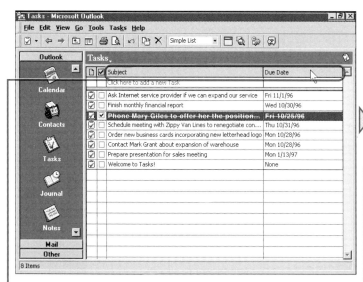

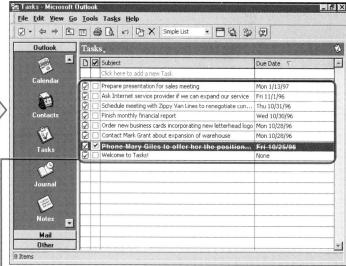

1 Move the mouse over the heading of the column you want to sort by and then press the left mouse button.

■ The tasks are sorted.

■ To sort the tasks in the opposite order, repeat step 1.

The Calendar helps you keep track of your appointments.

VIEW CALENDAR

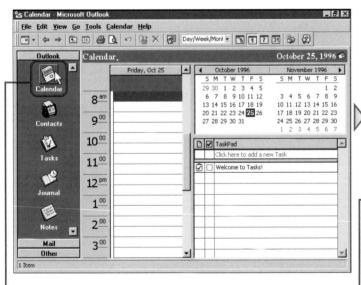

1 To display the Calendar, move the mouse ⌖ over **Calendar** and then press the left mouse button.

■ This area displays the appointments for the current day.

■ This area displays the days in the current month and the next month. Days with appointments are shown in **bold**.

Note: To add an appointment, refer to page 302.

300

How does Outlook know what day it is?

Outlook uses the date and time set in your computer to determine today's date. To change the date and time set in your computer, refer to your Windows manual.

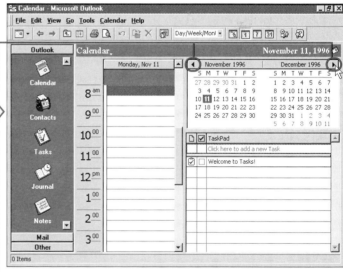

CHANGE DAYS

1 To display the appointments for another day, move the mouse ℝ over the day and then press the left mouse button.

■ The day you selected is highlighted. The current day displays a red outline.

■ This area now displays the appointments for the day you selected.

CHANGE MONTHS

1 To display the days in another month, move the mouse ℝ over one of the following options and then press the left mouse button.

◀ Display previous month

▶ Display next month

2 Repeat step 1 until the month you want to display appears.

> You can add appointments to the Calendar to remind you of activities such as meetings, lunch dates and doctor's appointments.

ADD AN APPOINTMENT

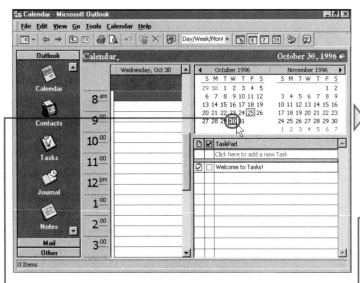

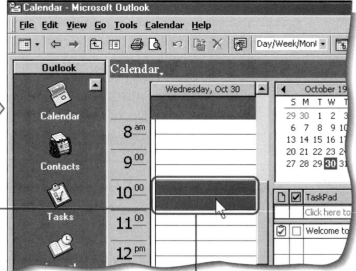

1 Move the mouse ⌖ over the day when you want to add an appointment and then press the left mouse button.

Note: To view the days in other months, refer to page 301.

2 Move the mouse ⌖ over the starting time for the appointment.

3 Press and hold down the left mouse button as you move the mouse ⌖ to select the time you want to set aside for the appointment. Then release the mouse button.

Outlook will play a brief sound and display a dialog box 15 minutes before a scheduled appointment.

APPOINTMENT REMINDER

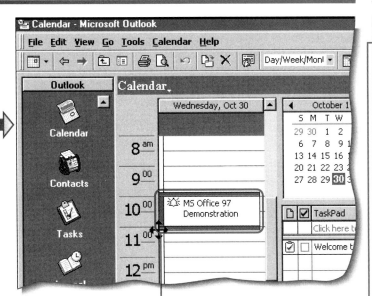

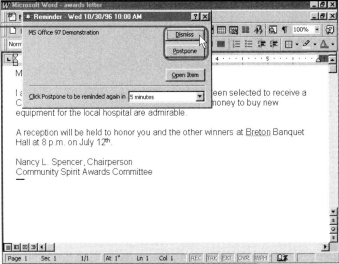

4 Type text to describe the appointment and then press **Enter** on your keyboard.

DELETE AN APPOINTMENT

1 To select the appointment you want to delete, move the mouse ▷ over the left edge of the appointment (▷ changes to ✥) and then press the left mouse button.

2 Press **Delete** on your keyboard.

1 To close the **Reminder** dialog box, move the mouse ▷ over one of the following options and then press the left mouse button.

Dismiss - Close the reminder

Postpone - Remind again in 5 minutes

DAY, WEEK AND MONTH VIEWS

You can view your appointments by day, week or month.

DAY, WEEK AND MONTH VIEWS

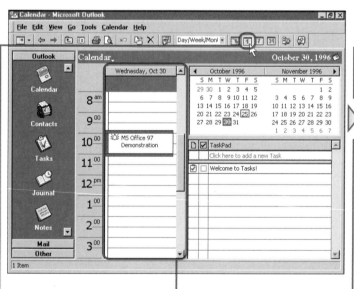

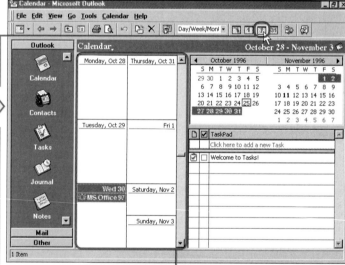

VIEW ONE DAY

1 To display the appointments for one day, move the mouse over ▥ and then press the left mouse button.

■ This area displays the appointments for one day. You can use the scroll bar to browse through the day.

VIEW ONE WEEK

1 To display the appointments for one week, move the mouse over ▥ and then press the left mouse button.

■ This area displays the appointments for one week. You can use the scroll bar to browse through other weeks.

Can I schedule appointments months in advance?

You can schedule appointments months or even years in advance. Outlook will keep track of all your appointments no matter how far in advance you schedule them.

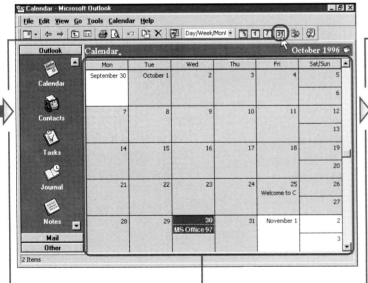

VIEW ONE MONTH

1 To display the appointments for one month, move the mouse ⬡ over 🗓 and then press the left mouse button.

■ This area displays the appointments for one month. You can use the scroll bar to browse through other months.

VIEW TODAY

1 To display the appointments for today in any view, move the mouse ⬡ over 🗓 and then press the left mouse button.

Outlook supplies an address book where you can keep detailed information about your friends, family members, colleagues and clients.

ADD A CONTACT

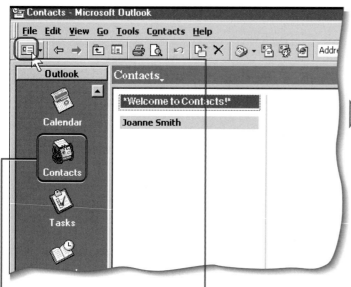

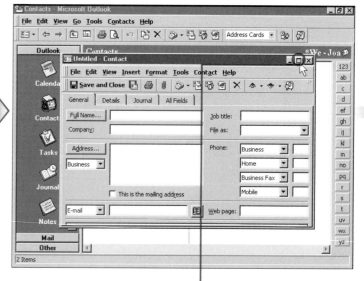

1 To display a list of all your contacts, move the mouse ▷ over **Contacts** and then press the left mouse button.

2 To add a new contact, move the mouse ▷ over 📧 and then press the left mouse button.

■ A window appears with areas where you can enter information about the contact.

3 To enlarge the window to fill the screen, move the mouse ▷ over ☐ and then press the left mouse button.

**Do I need to fill in all the
information for a contact?**

When entering information
about a contact, you do not
have to fill in all the areas. You
can always add information
later on. To update a contact,
refer to page 308.

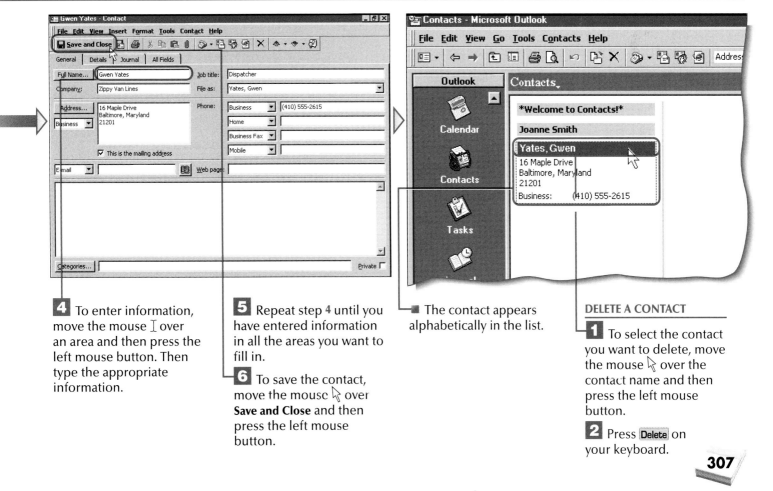

4 To enter information,
move the mouse I over
an area and then press the
left mouse button. Then
type the appropriate
information.

5 Repeat step 4 until you
have entered information
in all the areas you want to
fill in.

6 To save the contact,
move the mouse ⬆ over
Save and Close and then
press the left mouse
button.

■ The contact appears
alphabetically in the list.

DELETE A CONTACT

1 To select the contact
you want to delete, move
the mouse ⬆ over the
contact name and then
press the left mouse
button.

2 Press Delete on
your keyboard.

UPDATE A CONTACT

You can easily update or add additional information to a contact in your list.

UPDATE A CONTACT

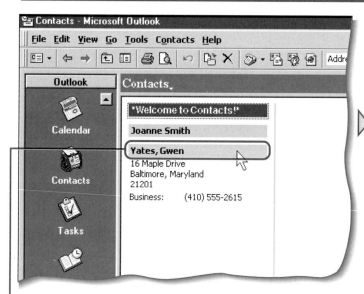

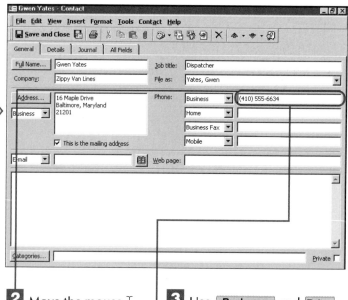

1 Move the mouse ⟍ over the name of the contact you want to update and then quickly press the left mouse button twice.

■ Information about the contact appears.

2 Move the mouse I over the information you want to change and then press the left mouse button.

3 Use `+Backspace` and `Delete` on your keyboard to remove the existing text.

4 Type the new information.

When would I need to update my contacts?

Over time, friends and colleagues may move and you will need to record their new addresses.

Also, as you learn more about your contacts, you can add information such as directions to their house or the names of their children.

We've Moved !

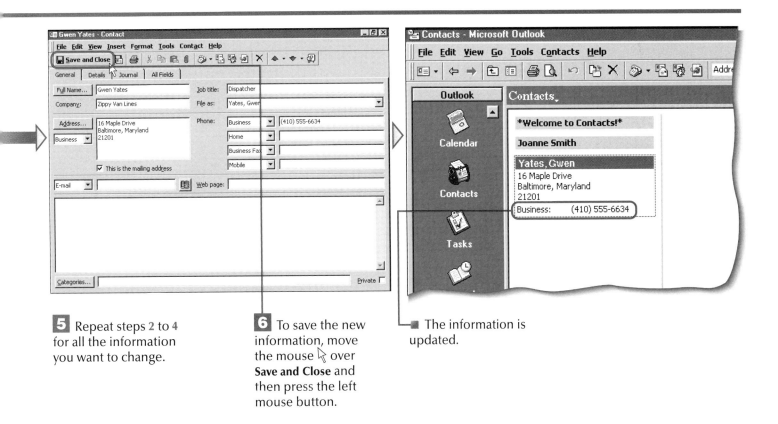

5 Repeat steps 2 to 4 for all the information you want to change.

6 To save the new information, move the mouse ↕ over **Save and Close** and then press the left mouse button.

■ The information is updated.

BROWSE THROUGH CONTACTS

You can easily browse through your contacts to find information of interest.

BROWSE THROUGH CONTACTS

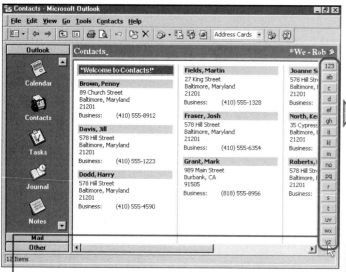

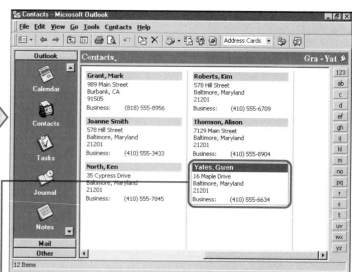

1 Move the mouse over the first letter of the contact you want to view and then press the left mouse button.

■ Contacts beginning with the letter you selected appear.

You can change the way you view your contacts.

Address Cards   Detailed Address Cards   Phone List

CHANGE VIEWS

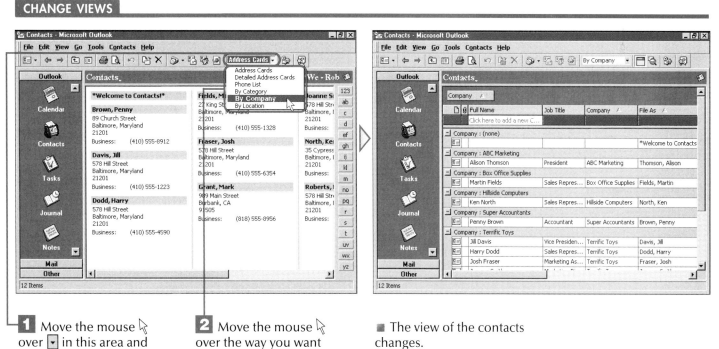

1 Move the mouse ▷ over ▾ in this area and then press the left mouse button.

2 Move the mouse ▷ over the way you want to view the contacts and then press the left mouse button.

■ The view of the contacts changes.

VIEW JOURNAL ENTRIES

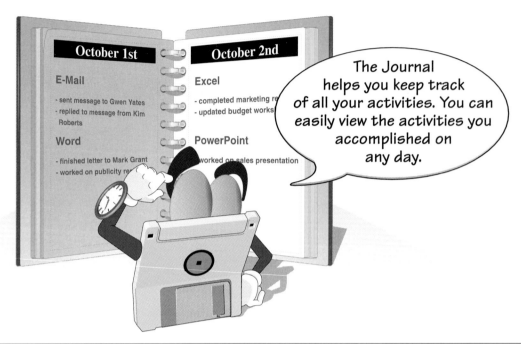

The Journal helps you keep track of all your activities. You can easily view the activities you accomplished on any day.

VIEW JOURNAL ENTRIES

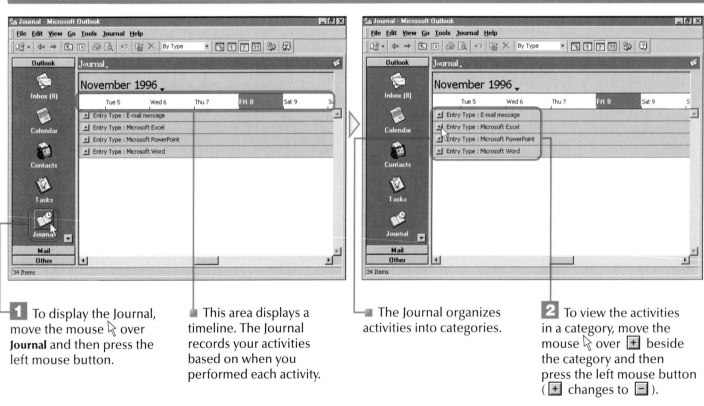

1 To display the Journal, move the mouse ⬚ over **Journal** and then press the left mouse button.

■ This area displays a timeline. The Journal records your activities based on when you performed each activity.

■ The Journal organizes activities into categories.

2 To view the activities in a category, move the mouse ⬚ over ⊞ beside the category and then press the left mouse button (⊞ changes to ⊟).

312

Can the Journal help me locate documents?

The Journal keeps track of the documents you work with each day. If you cannot remember where you stored a document, you can locate the document by looking in the Journal.

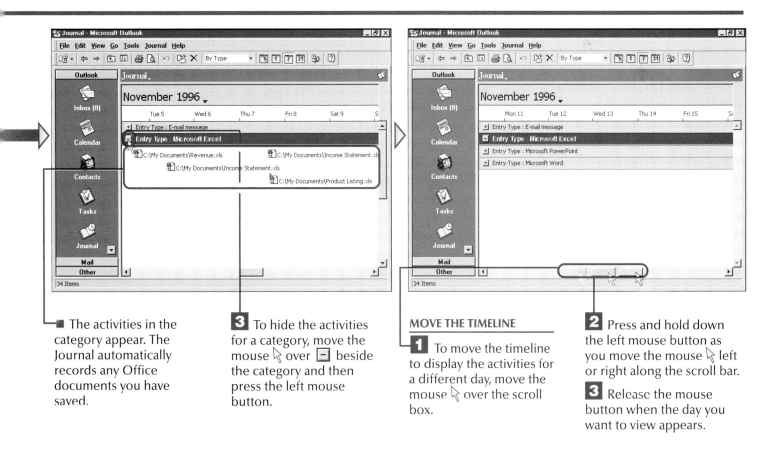

■ The activities in the category appear. The Journal automatically records any Office documents you have saved.

3 To hide the activities for a category, move the mouse ⬚ over ⊟ beside the category and then press the left mouse button.

MOVE THE TIMELINE

1 To move the timeline to display the activities for a different day, move the mouse ⬚ over the scroll box.

2 Press and hold down the left mouse button as you move the mouse ⬚ left or right along the scroll bar.

3 Release the mouse button when the day you want to view appears.

You can open a journal entry to view details about the activity or to open the document or item the entry refers to.

OPEN A JOURNAL ENTRY

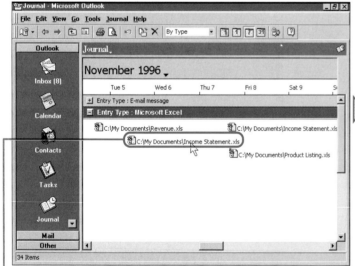

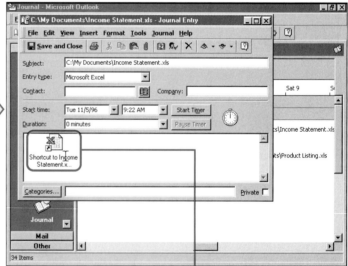

1 Move the mouse ⟍ over the journal entry you want to open and then quickly press the left mouse button twice.

■ A window appears, displaying information about the journal entry.

2 To open the document or item, move the mouse I over the shortcut and then quickly press the left mouse button twice.

What is removed from my computer when I delete a journal entry?

When you delete a journal entry, you do not delete the item or document the journal entry refers to. Only the entry itself is deleted.

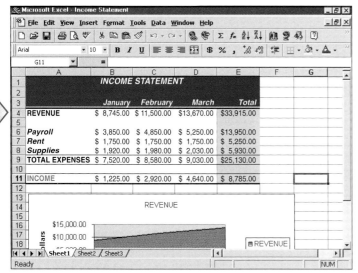

■ The document or item appears on the screen.

DELETE A JOURNAL ENTRY

You can delete a journal entry to make the Journal less cluttered.

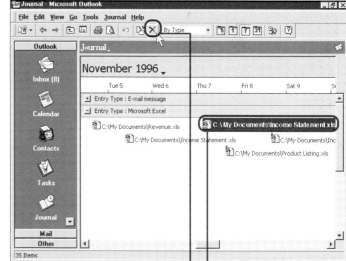

1 Move the mouse over the journal entry you want to delete and then press the left mouse button.

2 Move the mouse over ☒ and then press the left mouse button.

You can choose which activities you want the Journal to record.

SELECT ACTIVITIES TO RECORD

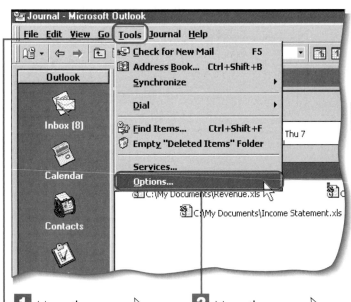

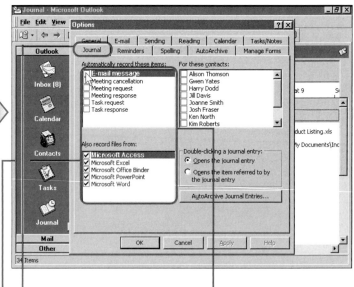

1 Move the mouse over **Tools** and then press the left mouse button.

2 Move the mouse over **Options** and then press the left mouse button.

■ The **Options** dialog box appears.

3 Move the mouse over the **Journal** tab and then press the left mouse button.

■ The Journal keeps track of each activity that displays a check mark (✔).

4 To add or remove a check mark (✔), move the mouse over the check box (☐) beside an activity and then press the left mouse button.

What activities can the Journal record?

The Journal can record communication with important contacts and work done in programs such as Word or Excel.

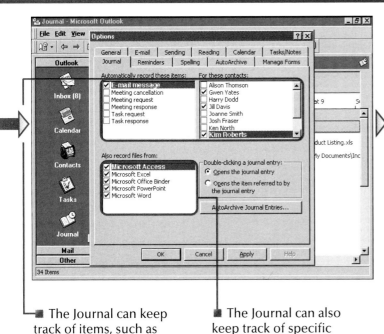

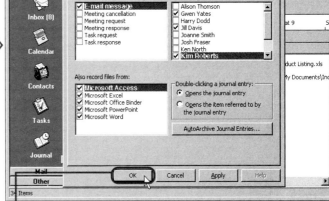

■ The Journal can keep track of items, such as e-mail messages, for the contacts you select.

Note: The list of contacts is the same list of contacts you entered into the Contacts feature. To add a contact, refer to page 306.

■ The Journal can also keep track of specific types of documents.

5 When all the activities you want the Journal to keep track of display a check mark (✔), move the mouse ⬉ over **OK** and then press the left mouse button.

You can produce a paper copy of your e-mail messages, contacts, tasks, notes, journal and calendar.

PRINT

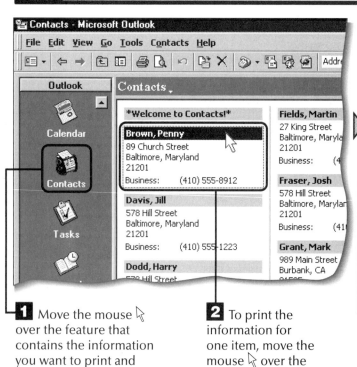

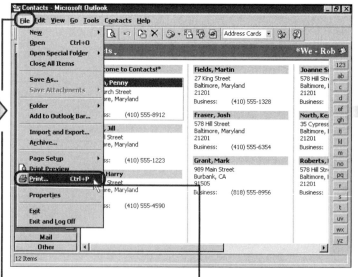

1 Move the mouse over the feature that contains the information you want to print and then press the left mouse button.

2 To print the information for one item, move the mouse over the item and then press the left mouse button.

3 Move the mouse over **File** and then press the left mouse button.

4 Move the mouse over **Print** and then press the left mouse button.

■ The **Print** dialog box appears.

What are print styles?

Outlook lets you select the way you want to print information.

For example, you can print your calendar for one day, week or month.

Daily Style

Weekly Style

Monthly Style

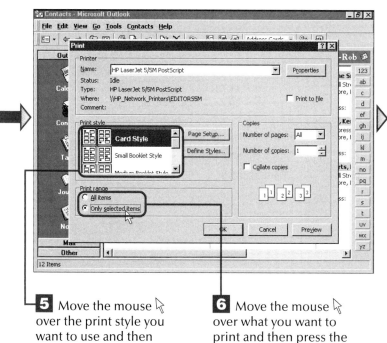

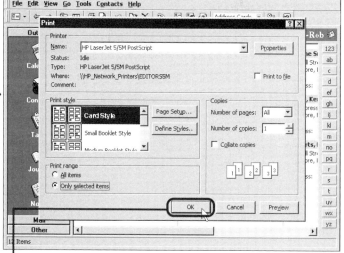

5 Move the mouse ↖ over the print style you want to use and then press the left mouse button.

Note: For information on print styles, refer to the top of this page.

6 Move the mouse ↖ over what you want to print and then press the left mouse button.

7 To print the information, move the mouse ↖ over **OK** and then press the left mouse button.

The Deleted Items folder stores all the items you have deleted in Outlook. You can easily recover any of these items.

RECOVER A DELETED ITEM

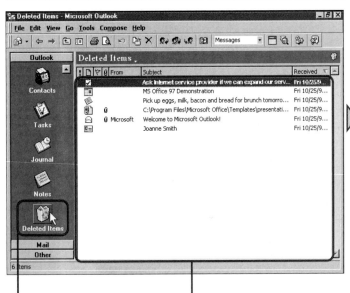

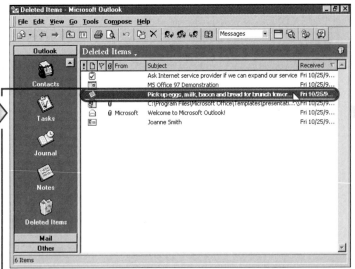

1 Move the mouse ⇖ over **Deleted Items** and then press the left mouse button.

■ This area displays a list of all the items you have deleted.

2 To select the item you want to recover, move the mouse ⇖ over the item and then press the left mouse button.

How can I identify the items in the Deleted Items folder?

Outlook places a symbol beside each deleted item.

 Calendar appointment

 Message

 Contact

 Note

 Journal activity

 Task

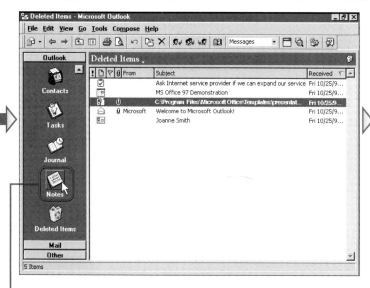

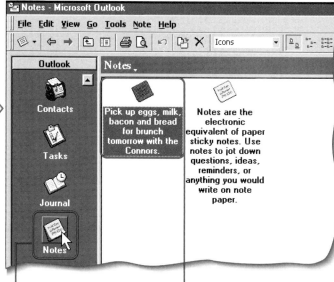

3 With the mouse still over the item, press and hold down the left mouse button as you move the item to the appropriate Outlook feature. Then release the mouse button.

■ The item disappears from the list. Outlook places the item in the feature you selected.

4 To display the item you recovered, move the mouse ▷ over the feature you selected in step 3 and then press the left mouse button.

■ The item appears in the Outlook feature.

You should regularly empty the Deleted Items folder to save space on your computer.

EMPTY DELETED ITEMS FOLDER

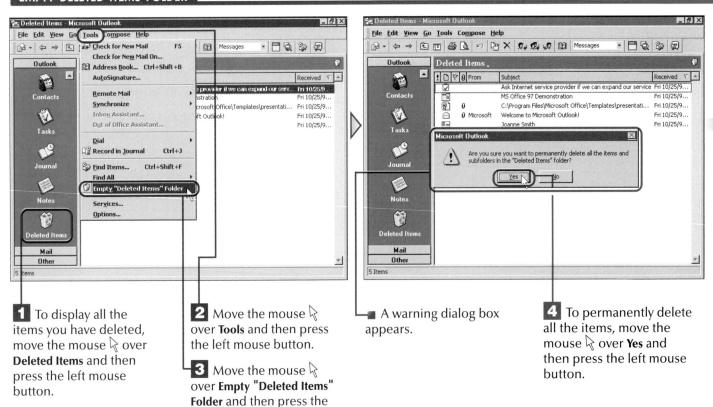

1 To display all the items you have deleted, move the mouse � over **Deleted Items** and then press the left mouse button.

2 Move the mouse � over **Tools** and then press the left mouse button.

3 Move the mouse � over **Empty "Deleted Items" Folder** and then press the left mouse button.

■ A warning dialog box appears.

4 To permanently delete all the items, move the mouse � over **Yes** and then press the left mouse button.

322

What if I may need an item in the future?

Deleting an item from the Deleted Items folder will permanently remove the item from your computer. Do not delete an item you may need in the future.

DELETE ONE ITEM

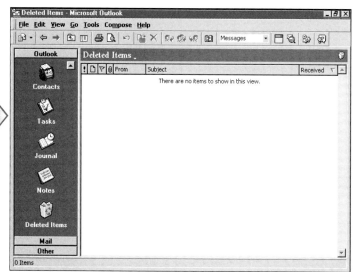

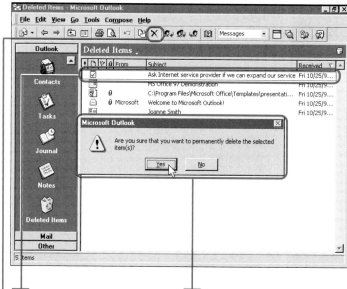

■ The items are permanently deleted.

1 To permanently delete one item, move the mouse ⌖ over the item and then press the left mouse button.

2 Move the mouse ⌖ over ☒ and then press the left mouse button.

3 A warning dialog box appears. To permanently delete the item, move the mouse ⌖ over **Yes** and then press the left mouse button.

Display the Search Page
Page 337

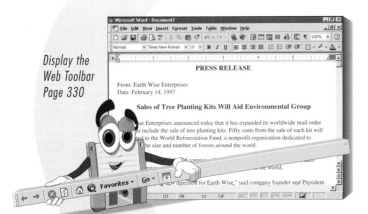
Display the Web Toolbar
Page 330

Microsoft Office has many features that make it easy for you to take advantage of the Internet.

Open a Document
Page 332

Move Between Documents
Page 331

*Stop the Connection
Page 334*

Great Web Sites
You Can Visit!
1 BMW of Germany
2 Bank of America
3 IDG Books
4 maranGraphics
5 McDonald's
6 NFL Football
7 NBC News
8 WebWeather

*Create a Hyperlink
Page 326*

> You can create a hyperlink to connect a word or phrase in one document to another document or Web page. When you select the word or phrase, the other document appears.

Great Web Sites You Can Visit!

1 BMW of Germany
2 Bank of America
3 IDG Books
4 maranGraphics
5 McDonald's
6 NFL Football
7 NBC News
8 WebWeather

CREATE A HYPERLINK

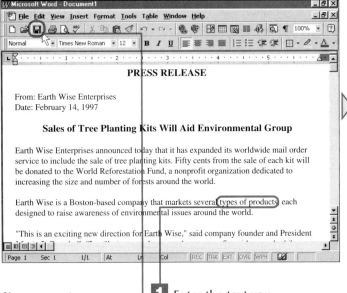

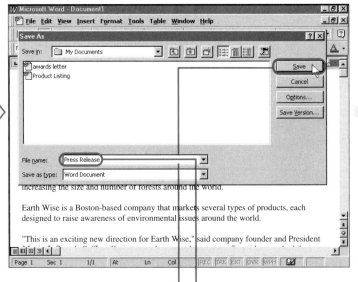

You can create a hyperlink in Word, Excel or PowerPoint.

1 Enter the text you want to link to another document.

2 To save the document, move the mouse ⌖ over 🖫 and then press the left mouse button.

■ The **Save As** dialog box appears.

*Note: If you previously saved the document, the **Save As** dialog box will not appear since you have already named the document.*

3 Type a name for the document.

4 Move the mouse ⌖ over **Save** and then press the left mouse button.

Where can a hyperlink take me?

You can create a hyperlink that takes you to another document on your computer, network, corporate intranet or the Internet.

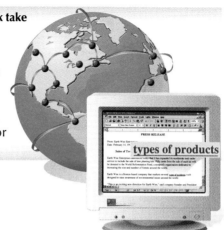

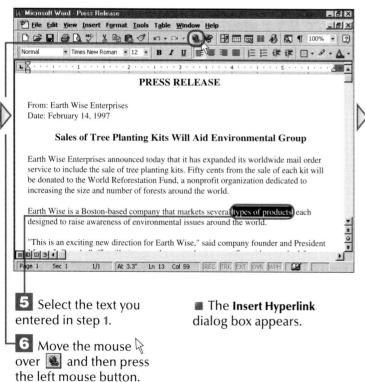

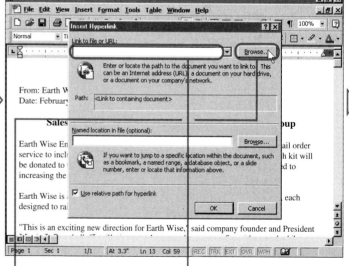

5 Select the text you entered in step 1.

6 Move the mouse ⌖ over 🖼 and then press the left mouse button.

■ The **Insert Hyperlink** dialog box appears.

7 To link the text to a document on your computer or network, move the mouse ⌖ over **Browse** and then press the left mouse button.

■ To link the text to a Web page, type the address of the Web page (example: http://www.maran.com). Then skip to step **10** on page 328.

CONTINUED

CREATE A HYPERLINK

EARTH WISE ENTERPRISES

We care about the environment.

All products created and marketed by Earth Wise Enterprises are designed to increase awareness of environmental issues around the world.

A list of our main types of products is presented below. To find out more about the products in any category, select the category name.

Tree planting kits

Recycle bins

Compost kits

> You can easily see hyperlinks in a document. Hyperlinks appear underlined and in color.

CREATE A HYPERLINK (CONTINUED)

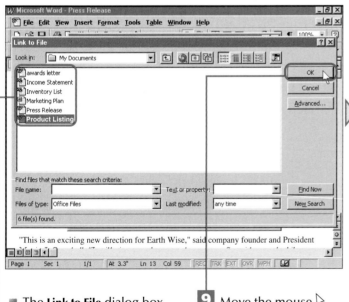

■ The **Link to File** dialog box appears.

8 Move the mouse ⬚ over the document you want to link to and then press the left mouse button.

9 Move the mouse ⬚ over **OK** and then press the left mouse button.

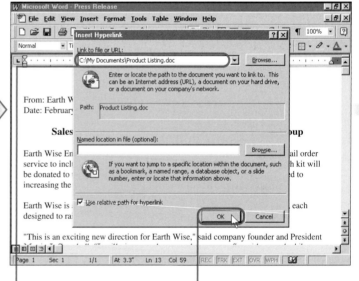

■ The address of the document appears in this area.

10 Move the mouse ⬚ over **OK** and then press the left mouse button.

Can Word automatically create hyperlinks for me?

When you type the address of a document located on a network or on the Internet, Word automatically changes the address to a hyperlink.

http://www.maran.com

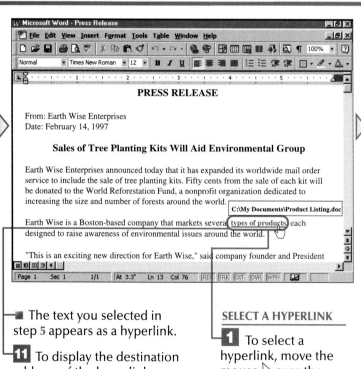

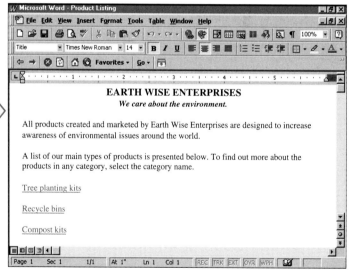

■ The text you selected in step 5 appears as a hyperlink.

11 To display the destination address of the hyperlink, move the mouse ⟍ over the hyperlink (⟍ changes to 👆). After a few seconds, the address appears.

SELECT A HYPERLINK

1 To select a hyperlink, move the mouse ⟍ over the hyperlink (⟍ changes to 👆) and then press the left mouse button.

■ The document connected to the hyperlink appears.

■ If the hyperlink is connected to a Web page, your Web browser opens and displays the Web page.

DISPLAY THE WEB TOOLBAR

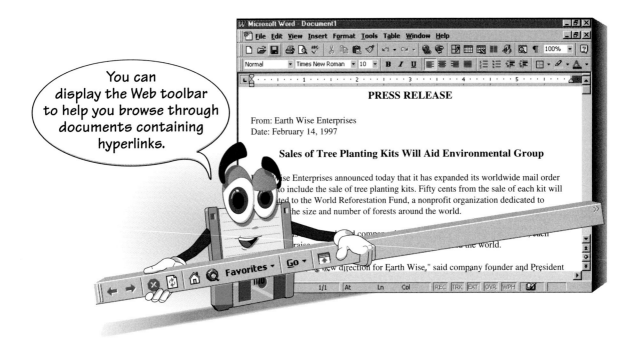

You can display the Web toolbar to help you browse through documents containing hyperlinks.

DISPLAY THE WEB TOOLBAR

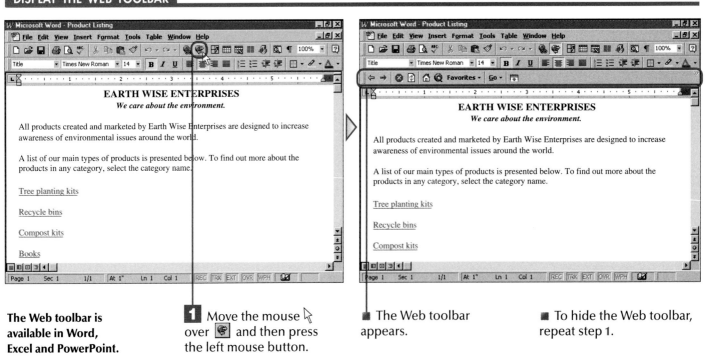

The Web toolbar is available in Word, Excel and PowerPoint.

1 Move the mouse over the icon and then press the left mouse button.

■ The Web toolbar appears.

■ To hide the Web toolbar, repeat step **1**.

MOVE BETWEEN DOCUMENTS

After selecting hyperlinks in documents, you can easily move back and forth between these documents.

MOVE BETWEEN DOCUMENTS

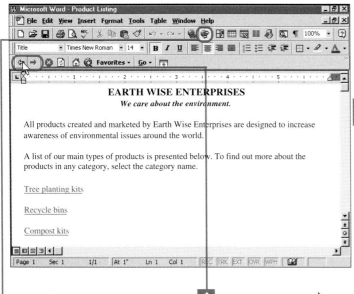

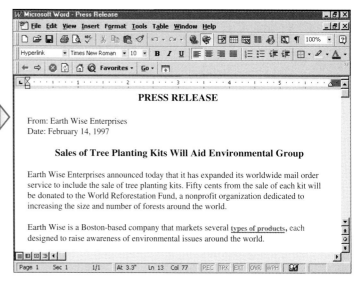

■ To display the Web toolbar, move the mouse ⌖ over 🌐 and then press the left mouse button.

1 Move the mouse ⌖ over one of the following options and then press the left mouse button.

⬅ Move back

➡ Move forward

■ The document you selected appears.

OPEN A DOCUMENT

You can quickly open a document that is on your computer, network, corporate intranet or the Internet.

OPEN A DOCUMENT

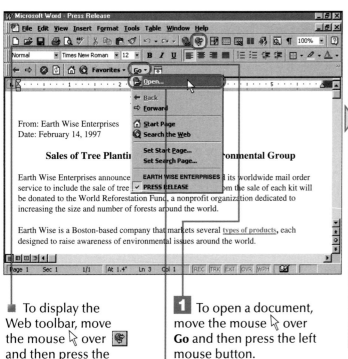

■ To display the Web toolbar, move the mouse ⤢ over 🌐 and then press the left mouse button.

1 To open a document, move the mouse ⤢ over **Go** and then press the left mouse button.

2 Move the mouse ⤢ over **Open** and then press the left mouse button.

■ The **Open Internet Address** dialog box appears.

3 Type the address of the document you want to open.

4 Move the mouse ⤢ over **OK** and then press the left mouse button.

Microsoft Office remembers the last documents you visited. You can instantly return to any of these documents.

RETURN TO A DOCUMENT

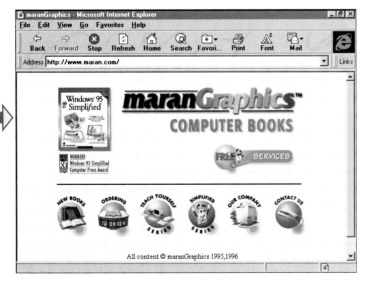

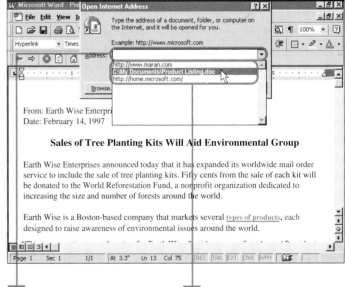

■ The document appears.

■ If the document you opened was a Web page, your Web browser opens and displays the Web page.

1 In the **Open Internet Address** dialog box, move the mouse ⓖ over ▾ in this area and then press the left mouse button.

2 Move the mouse ⓖ over the document you want to open and then press the left mouse button.

3 Press **Enter** on your keyboard to open the document.

STOP THE CONNECTION

If a Web page is taking a long time to appear, you can stop the transfer of information.

STOP THE CONNECTION

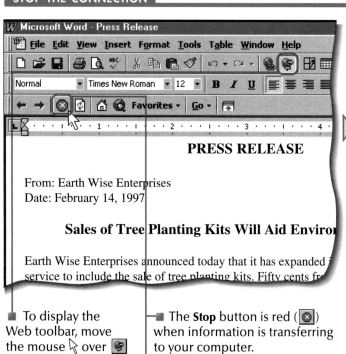

■ To display the Web toolbar, move the mouse ⇘ over 🌐 and then press the left mouse button.

■ The **Stop** button is red (⊗) when information is transferring to your computer.

1 To stop the transfer of information, move the mouse ⇘ over ⊗ and then press the left mouse button.

■ The **Stop** button turns gray (⊗). Information is no longer transferring to your computer.

334

REFRESH A DOCUMENT

While you are viewing a document, the author may make changes to the document. You can easily transfer a fresh copy of the document to your computer.

REFRESH A DOCUMENT

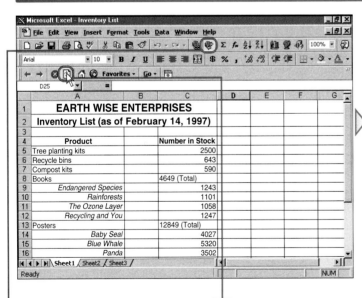

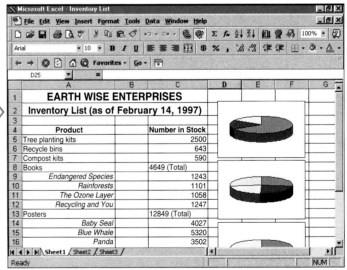

■ To display the Web toolbar, move the mouse ⌖ over 🌐 and then press the left mouse button.

1 To refresh the document, move the mouse ⌖ over 🔄 and then press the left mouse button.

■ An up-to-date copy of the document appears.

DISPLAY THE START PAGE

The start page is the first page that appears when you start a Web browser.

The start page includes instructions and hyperlinks that let you quickly connect to interesting documents.

DISPLAY THE START PAGE

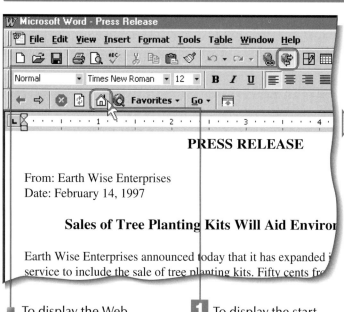

■ To display the Web toolbar, move the mouse ⬚ over 🌐 and then press the left mouse button.

1 To display the start page, move the mouse ⬚ over 🏠 and then press the left mouse button.

■ The Web browser opens and displays the start page.

DISPLAY THE SEARCH PAGE

The search page helps you find information of interest.

DISPLAY THE SEARCH PAGE

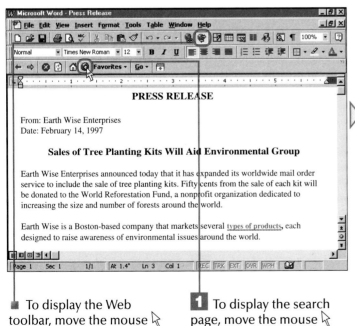

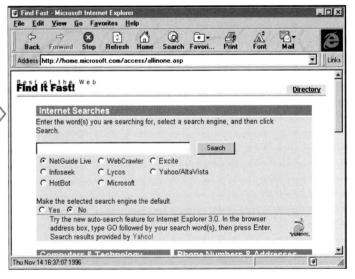

■ To display the Web toolbar, move the mouse over ■ and then press the left mouse button.

1 To display the search page, move the mouse over Q and then press the left mouse button.

■ The Web browser opens and displays the search page.

337

ADD DOCUMENT TO FAVORITES

You can add documents you frequently use to the Favorites folder. This lets you quickly open these documents at any time.

ADD DOCUMENT TO FAVORITES

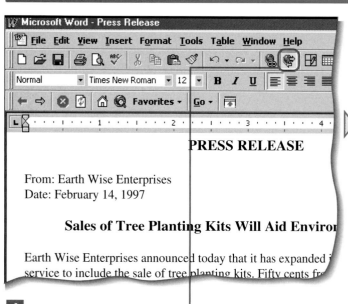

1 Open the document you want to add to the Favorites folder.

■ To display the Web toolbar, move the mouse over and then press the left mouse button.

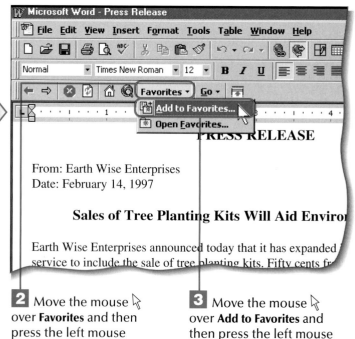

2 Move the mouse over **Favorites** and then press the left mouse button.

3 Move the mouse over **Add to Favorites** and then press the left mouse button.

When I add a document to the Favorites folder, does the document change locations?

When you add a document to the Favorites folder, you create a shortcut to the original document. The original document does not change its location on your computer.

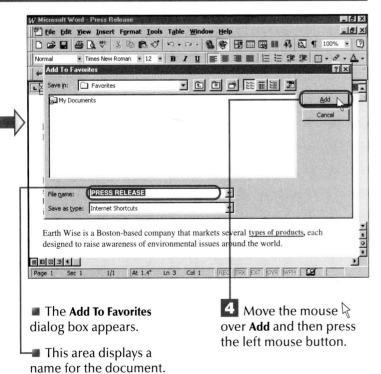

OPEN DOCUMENT IN FAVORITES

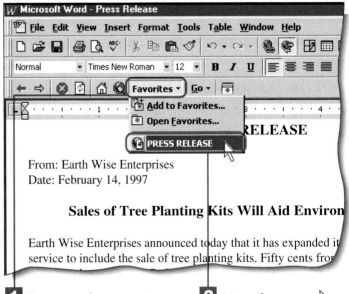

■ The **Add To Favorites** dialog box appears.

■ This area displays a name for the document. To change the name, type a new name.

4 Move the mouse ⓚ over **Add** and then press the left mouse button.

1 To open a document in the Favorites folder, move the mouse ⓚ over **Favorites** and then press the left mouse button.

2 Move the mouse ⓚ over the document you want to open and then press the left mouse button.

SAVE DOCUMENT AS A WEB PAGE

You can save a document as a Web page. This lets you place the document on your company's intranet or on the Web.

SAVE DOCUMENT AS A WEB PAGE

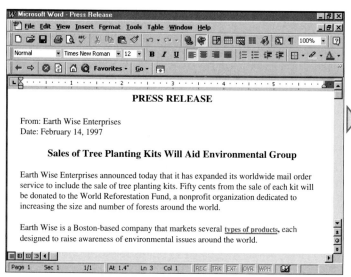

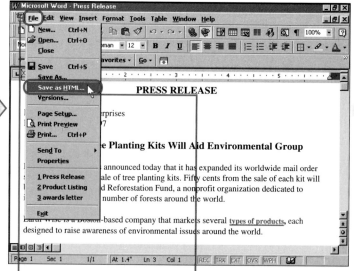

You can save a Word, Excel or PowerPoint document as a Web page.

1 Open the document you want to save as a Web page.

2 Move the mouse ⌖ over **File** and then press the left mouse button.

3 Move the mouse ⌖ over **Save as HTML** and then press the left mouse button.

*Note: If the **Save as HTML** command is not available, you need to add the Web Page Authoring (HTML) component of Microsoft Office to your computer.*

Why do Excel and PowerPoint ask me a series of questions?

When you save an Excel or PowerPoint document as a Web page, you will be asked a series of questions. Your answers help customize the resulting Web page to suit your needs.

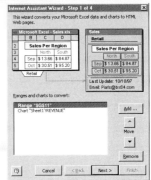

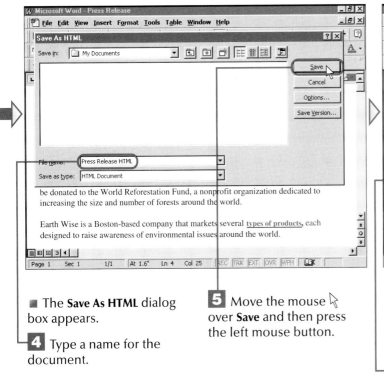

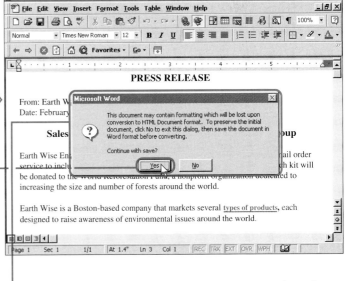

■ The **Save As HTML** dialog box appears.

4 Type a name for the document.

5 Move the mouse over **Save** and then press the left mouse button.

■ This dialog box may appear to warn that the document contains formatting that will be lost.

6 To save the document as a Web page, move the mouse over **Yes** and then press the left mouse button.

■ You can now place the document on a corporate intranet or the Web for others to view.

INDEX

INDEX

move
    charts, 206
    data, 138-139
    mouse, 6
    objects in slides, 252
    tabs, 80
    text, 48-49, 236
    through documents, 22-23
    timeline, 313
    toolbars, 99
    worksheets, 199
multiplication. *See* formulas; functions

N

#NAME? (error message), 161
Normal view, 37
notes
    close, 294
    create, 292-293
    delete, 293
    open, 294
    print, 318-319
    resize, 295
Notes Page view, 220, 221
notes pages
    display, 222
    print, 276-277
number keys, 117
number series, complete, 118-119
number signs (#) as error messages, 117, 159, 160
numbers. *See also* charts; data; formulas; functions; text
    add list of, 158-159
    appearance, 168
    in lists, 72-73
    pages, 82-83, 265
    scientific form, 117
    slides, 264-265

O

object, color, 263
Office. *See* Microsoft Office
Office Assistant, 9, 12-13, 17, 113, 213, 280-281
Online Layout view, 37
on-screen presentations, as PowerPoint feature, 212
open
    documents, 34-35, 332-333
    Excel, 113
    Favorites documents, 339
    journal entries, 314-315
    messages, 284
    notes, 294
    Outlook, 280-281
    PowerPoint, 213
    presentations, 226-227
    programs, 8-9
    Word, 17
    workbooks, 132-133

operators in calculations, 146
orientation, pages, 189
outline, print, 276-277
Outline view, 37, 220, 221, 223
Outlook. *See also* specific subject or feature
    exit, 281
    features, 281
    overview, 5
    start, 280-281
overheads, as PowerPoint feature, 212

P

Page Layout view, 37
pages. *See also* documents; paragraphs; text; worksheets
    breaks, 88-89, 192-193
    center data, 188
    center text vertically, 92-93
    columns, 96-97
    display
      search, 337
      start, 336
    footers, 86-87, 264-265
    footnotes, 84-85
    headers, 86-87, 264-265
    magnify, 38
    margins, 94-95, 184-185
    numbers, 82-83, 265
    orientation, 189
    Print Preview feature, 26-27, 182-183
    sections, 90-91
    Web, save documents, 340-341
paragraphs. *See also* pages; text
    indent, 76-77
    join, 45
    select, 21
    split, 43
    tabs, 78-81
parentheses ( )
    in formulas, 146
    in functions, 150
pictures in slides, 244-245
plus sign (+) in formulas, 146
point sizes, 63. *See also* fonts
pointers, mouse, 6
points
    insert, 233
    select, 228
portrait orientation, 189
PowerPoint. *See also* specific subject or feature
    exit, 225
    overview, 5, 212
    start, 213
presentations
    browse through, 222-223
    categories, 215
    create, 214-219
    footers, 264-265

Glencoe's Visual Series

- Microsoft Office 97
- Word 7 for Windows 95
- Excel 7 for Windows 95
- Windows 95

1-800-334-7344

GLENCOE VISUAL SERIES

Glencoe and IDG/maranGraphics have teamed to create an exciting visual learning experience that gives your students the tools they need for computer competence and confidence. Each text's full-color, 3-D graphics are enhanced by extended captions. The format is particularly useful for today's visually oriented students. Each page contains only one computer concept; a warm and inviting cartoon-like character introduces each of these concepts.

Each text is packaged with a Student Exercise and Applications Workbook, complete with numerous student activities, including cross-curricular exercises. A template disk that accompanies each text offers practice in "doing" word processing, spreadsheets, slide shows, online schedule planning, and exploring the internet. An Instructor's Manual and Key comes with each program and contains solutions for all student activities.

MICROSOFT® OFFICE 97

maranGraphics, © 1998

Includes: WORD: Getting Started; Save, Print, and Open a Document; Change Document Display; Edit a Document; Format Text; Format Pages; Working With Tables. EXCEL: Getting Started; Save and Open a Workbook; Edit a Worksheet; Using Formulas and Functions; Format a Worksheet; Print a Worksheet; Using Multiple Worksheets; Working With Charts. POWERPOINT: Getting Started; Edit Slides; Add Objects to Slides; Enhance a Presentation; Fine-Tune a Presentation. OUTLOOK: Start Outlook; Using Inbox; Using Notes; Using Tasks; Using Calendar; Using Contacts; Using Journal; Print; Using Deleted Items. OFFICE AND THE INTERNET.

Text and Workbook Package
with 3.5" IBM Disks 0-02-813944-0
Text 0-02-803963-7
Applications Workbook 0-02-803945-9
Instructor's Manual and Key
with 3.5" IBM Disk 0-02-803946-7

WORD 7 for Windows 95

maranGraphics, © 1997

Includes: Getting Started, Edit Your Documents, Smart Editing, Save and Open Your Documents, Using Multiple Documents, Print Your Documents, Format Characters, Format Paragraphs, Format Pages, Working with Tables.

Text and Workbook Package
with 3.5" IBM Disks 0-02-803947-5
Text 0-02-803966-1
Applications Workbook 0-02-803948-3
Instructor's Manual and Key
with 3.5" IBM Disk 0-02-803949-1

EXCEL 7 for Windows 95

maranGraphics, © 1997

Includes: Getting Started, Save and Open Your Workbooks, Edit Your Workbooks, Edit Your Worksheets, Using Formulas and Functions, Working with Rows and Columns, Format Your Worksheets, Smart Formatting, Print Your Worksheets, Change Your Screen Display, Using Multiple Worksheets, Using Multiple Workbooks, Charting Data, Enhance a Chart, Drawing Objects, Manage Data in a List.

Text and Workbook Package
with 3.5" IBM Disks 0-02-813951-3
Text 0-02-803965-3
Applications Workbook 0-02-803952-1
Instructor's Manual and Key
with 3.5" IBM Disk 0-02-803953-X

WINDOWS 95

maranGraphics, © 1997

Includes: Getting Started, Windows Basics, Wordpad, Paint, View Contents of Computer, Work with Files and Folders, Using Windows Explorer, Change Windows Settings, Faxing, The Microsoft Network, Electronic Mail, Maintain Your Computer, Back Up Your Files.

Text and Workbook Package
with 3.5" IBM Disks 0-02-803960-2
Text 0-02-803964-5
Applications Workbook 0-02-803961-0
Instructor's Manual and Key
with 3.5" IBM Disk 0-02-803962-9

You can also order these 3-D visual books directly from Glencoe:

Windows 3.1 Simplified

ISBN: 1-56884-654-1

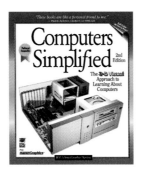

Computers Simplified 2nd Edition

ISBN: 1-56884-676-2

Word 6 For Windows Simplified

ISBN: 1-56884-660-6

Excel 5 For Windows Simplified

ISBN: 1-56884-664-9

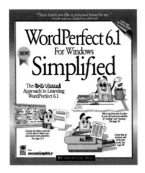

WordPerfect 6.1 For Windows Simplified

ISBN: 1-56884-665-7

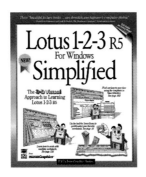

Lotus 1-2-3 R5 For Windows Simplified

ISBN: 1-56884-670-3

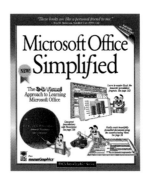

Microsoft Office 4.2 For Windows Simplified

ISBN: 1-56884-673-8

Internet and World Wide Web Simplified

ISBN: 1-56884-658-4

1-800-334-7344

Glencoe/McGraw-Hill Order Form

Detach and mail this form for your ordering convenience.

- -

Bill To:

School Name

Attention

School Address

City   State

County   Zip

Ship To: (if different from "Bill To")

School Name

Attention

School Address

City   State

County   Zip

Purchase Order #_____

Preferred Method of Shipment

UPS _____ Other _____

Account Number or S.A.N. #_____

Phone _____

Date _____

_____
Authorized Signature

_____
Title

ISBN	Title	Quantity	Price	Total

NOTE: Shipping and handling charges are additional and figured at current rates from our shipping point. Charges are prepaid and added to your invoice as a separate item. State and local taxes will be added where they apply. PRICES ARE SUBJECT TO CHANGE WITHOUT NOTICE.

TOTAL

Regional Offices

For More Information Contact Your Nearest Regional Office or Call **1-800-334-7344.**

Western Region

Glencoe/McGraw-Hill
15319 Chatsworth St.
Mission Hills, CA 91345
Phone: 800-423-9534
Fax: 818-365-5489

Mid-Continent Region

Glencoe/McGraw-Hill
1415 Elbridge Payne Rd.
Suite 180
Chesterfield, MO
63017-8522
Phone: 314-530-9942
Fax: 314-530-9034

Great Lakes Region

Glencoe/McGraw-Hill
936 Eastwind Drive
Westerville, OH 43081
Phone: 800-848-1567
Ext. 4251
Fax: 614-899-4999

Southeast Region

Glencoe/McGraw-Hill
3100 Breckinridge Blvd.
Bldg. 700, Suite 705
Duluth, GA 30136
Phone: 770-717-7007
Fax: 770-717-7422

Eastern Region

Glencoe/McGraw-Hill
936 Eastwind Drive
Westerville, OH 43081
Phone: 800-848-1567
Ext. 4990
Fax: 614-899-4999

All Business and Government Customers

Glencoe/McGraw-Hill Business & Government Training Group
936 Eastwind Drive, Westerville, Ohio 43081 • 800-848-1567, Ext. 4983